The Slow Death of American Democracy: Fifty Reasons the United States is Not a True Democracy and How We Can Fix It

Resistance Books, New York

Table of Contents

Introduction
Is the US Truly a Democracy?

Lady Liberty, don't leave us now.

If you're sick and tired of politics in America right now – if you're angry, fed-up, and you want things to change – you're reading the right book. This book is all about change. It's also about truth and about destroying myths and illusions. It's about giving you, the reader, the ammunition you need to disprove false arguments, correct misconceptions, and fight for what you believe in.

The major myth that we as a country are suffering from right now is that the United States is a democracy. Sadly, it's not. Pretty far from it, in fact. We're a quasi-democracy, perhaps, or semi-republic, if you prefer, but certainly not a full, healthy democracy. One might say that US democracy is ailing – that it's sick and getting worse – in danger, even. If we want to recover, we'll have to take our medicine – or perhaps go in for surgery at this point.

We need help, and we need it fast.

In its "Democracy Index" of 2016, *The Economist* lowered the US from a "full democracy" to a "flawed democracy." In the latest version, 2017, we ranked 21st in the world, behind nations such as Norway (#1), Canada (tied for 6th), Germany (#13), the UK (#14), and Mauritius (#16) (and, yes, that's a real country and not something from *Game of Thrones*). We tied the great republic of Italy, who had their own Trump-like figure in Silvio Berlusconi long before we did.

But *The Economist*'s estimates may be conservative: the Electoral Integrity Project ranked the US worst of all western democracies when it comes to elections, which is only the most important thing democracies do. We're seeing the deterioration of our institutions, the erosion of our rights, and the explosion of concentrated wealth.

We're in trouble, is the point, and we're going to need some drastic changes in order to address that trouble. This book will spell out for you fifty major problems with American democracy, present you with some rather shocking details that you'll likely find very illuminating, and propose some practical solutions. While discussing these overarching themes, we'll dive into many other issues progressives find important, such as guns, the environment, and job security.

The following pages are filled with a great deal of facts and statistics, because, as John Adams said, “Facts are stubborn things.” They’re also valuable things. The information you receive from this book will be like your armor as you go into battle.

Wear it well.

A Quick Note on Corrections

If you find any errors in this book, or if you feel there’s something I have left out or overlooked, please contact me at rosenfeldross@gmail.com.

1. The Electoral College

Gulliver in the Land of the Democratic Lilliputians" - Victor Gillam, *Judge*, 1890s

Let's start with perhaps the most obvious anti-democratic institution within the United States. Somehow we've convinced ourselves that a system that allows the person who received fewer votes to become president is democratic. This doesn't even make sense on the surface, and all of the nonsensical arguments that seek to support such a position can easily be disproved.

Despite popular misconceptions, the Founders did not intend for the Electoral College to work in the way that it currently does. The first five presidents were chosen without any popular vote, and it wasn't until 1824 that the popular vote mattered at all. That election year would prove to be the first time that the popular will was upended by the College. We've just witnessed the fifth time. At what point will we come to our senses and demand its abolishment?

Originally, the Electoral College was intended to be a group of "wise men" who would choose the chief executive after a fair amount of discussion. It was not instituted for democratic purposes, but out of fear that uninformed voters might choose a demagogic figure for president (which, ironically, the Electoral College has now done for us). In fact, the Founders' fears about the common people led them to curb enfranchisement, not just excluding blacks and Native Americans, but all non-whites, women, non-landholders, and anyone under twenty-one.

The Electoral College was conceived with the notion that members would not reveal their preferences, but instead would meet, consult with one another, debate, and reach a determination. Of course, it didn't take long for this system to be upended. The Electors began announcing the candidates they supported in advance and, as time went on, states connected their popular vote totals to the anointed Electors of candidates.

Despite franchise expansion, the Electoral College has remained. One of the reasons is that the Constitution is virtually impossible to change, as you'll see later when we go over the amendment process. Another reason, though, is that, like the Senate, the Electoral College gives disproportionate power to certain states and regions.

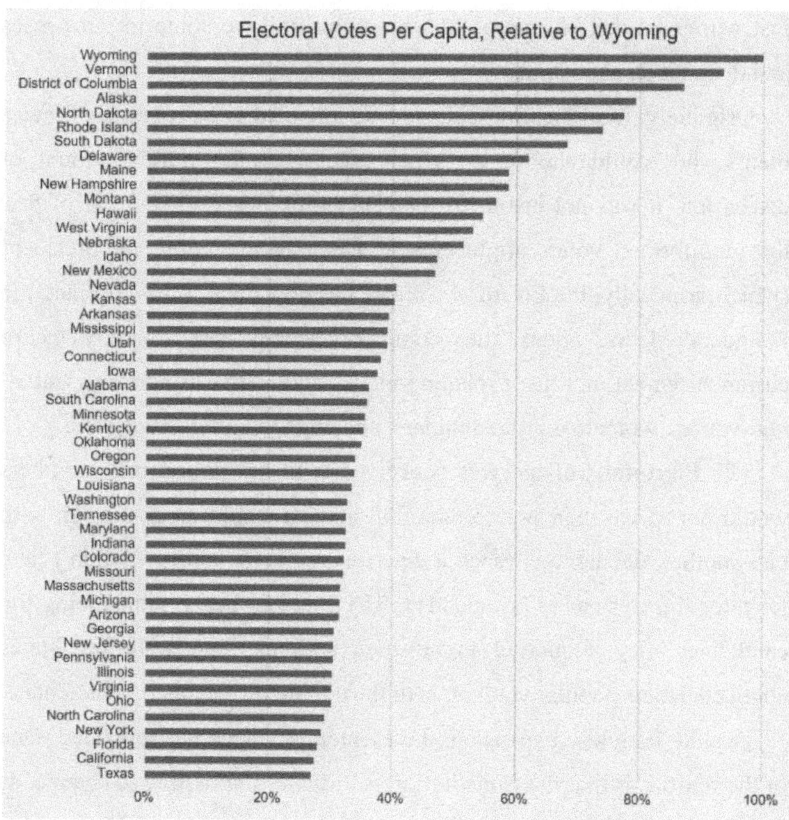

The Electoral College gives inordinate power to small states. Texas and California, for instance, have less than 30% of the electors per capita than Wyoming does. Courtesy of Matt Hoffman, hiphoff.com.

It's also extremely divisive. Though Barack Obama would like to believe that there are no "red states or blue states," the fact of the matter is that there are. More accurately, one could argue that we're a country divided in a different way: urban versus rural areas.

Here's a map of the last three presidential elections:

2008:

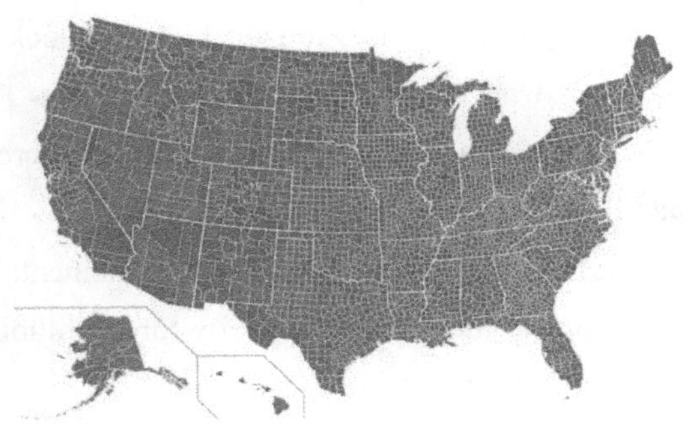

Credit: Robert Horning

2012:

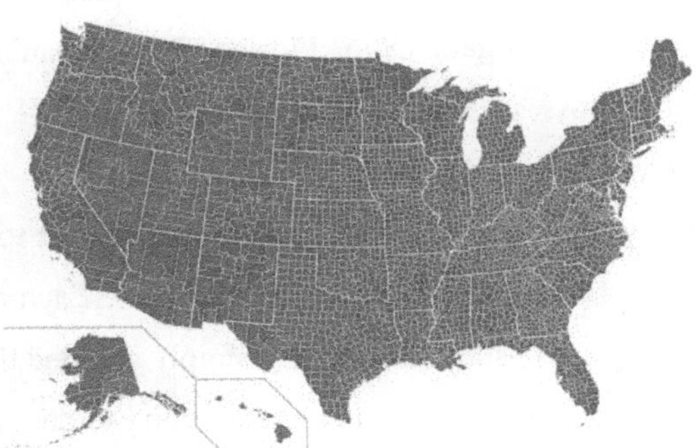

2016:

Credit: Ali Zifan

The blue areas are predominantly cities and suburbs. Looking it over, it's clear that Hillary Clinton's loss to Donald Trump looks fairly similar to Barack Obama's wins against John McCain and Mitt Romney. What made the difference? Well, about 80,000 votes spread across Wisconsin, Michigan, and Pennsylvania.

Think about how ridiculous that is for a moment: those 80,000 people's votes counted more than the nearly three million more people who chose Clinton over Trump.

And this disproportionate voting power has a huge effect on campaigning. As the *New York Times* pointed out about the 2016 presidential contest, "two-thirds of all public campaign events were held in just six states: Michigan, Ohio, Florida, Pennsylvania, Virginia and North Carolina; toss in six more and you've got 94 percent of all campaign events."

What point was there for Hillary Clinton to go down to Mississippi or Arkansas, or for Donald Trump to visit California? Each of them had no chance of picking those states up, so they simply avoided them.

And it has a huge effect on turnout. According to data from Associate Professor Michael McDonald of the University of Florida, states that are considered close or "toss-ups" receive much higher voting percentages. For instance, while just 43% of Hawaiians came out to vote, nearly 75% of Minnesotans did. While Texas and New York had just under 52% and just over 57% of eligible voters cast a ballot, respectively; Michigan and Florida each had 65.7%. Sure, some states, like Maryland (67.2%) and Massachusetts (68.3%) had reasonably high voter turnout despite their results being pretty much foregone conclusions. But when you examine the data overall (which you can do here), it becomes obvious that there is a strong correlation between voter turnout and swing-state status.

This detracts from our ability to determine whether a presidential election actually reflects the popular will of the people. The US lags behind most industrialized countries in this regard. Whereas less than 56% of the eligible voting population cast a ballot here in 2016, France had nearly 70% participation in their 2017 election, Israel had nearly 77% of its citizens vote in 2015, and Sweden hit 82.6% in 2014. This excludes countries with compulsory voting, like Australia (79%) and Belgium (87.2%).

Yet, amazingly, some conservatives pose false arguments claiming that the Electoral College somehow makes us more democratic. It's not surprising that Republicans would say this, considering that the Electoral College has upended the popular vote (or simply "the vote") four times since the Republican Party has been in existence, and each one of those times the Republicans came out on top. Let's summarize and address some of these false arguments and Electoral College myths.

Myth #1: The system was intended to work this way.

This false claim is meant to make it appear as if the Electoral College is some wise system that was instituted by the Founding Fathers. It's wrong on a few counts. The committee that designed the system did not link it to the popular vote and did not design it to be winner-take-all for each state. Alexander Hamilton, who, despite popular belief, was a supporter of the system but not its designer, wrote in Federalist #68 that the electors should be a group of "men most capable of analyzing the qualities adapted to the station," chosen by their respective state legislatures, who would in turn choose the president. It was a way of giving states some control and limiting federal power, and, furthermore, a way of avoiding the voice of the people. At the time, we were only a nation of some 3 million, only a small fraction of whom could actually vote, and it was feared that a demagogue could delude the people and become president. As noted earlier, Hamilton and other supporters did not intend for the electors to announce their preferences beforehand, but instead to meet, discuss the choices, and make a decision in the best interests of the country.

At first, the popular vote mattered not at all. Washington was chosen unanimously. During the Era of Good Feeling, James Monroe was reelected nearly unanimously, with a lone elector voting against him solely so that Washington would be the only person ever to win that distinction.

It wasn't really until 1824 that the popular vote played any part at all, with states utilizing it to determine their electors. That election, of course, would prove to be the first of now five times that the popular vote winner did not emerge victorious.

Myth #2: The College has protected us from bad choices.

Actually, you could argue quite the opposite.

The first mess came with the Election of 1800, during which Aaron Burr seized on a loophole in the College to try to get himself chosen as president. His effort failed in large part because of Hamilton, who intervened on behalf of his political enemy, Jefferson. When Hamilton later came out against Burr (then vice president) in his attempt to become governor of New York after the presidential election debacle, Burr challenged him to a duel and, let's just say, it didn't end well for Hamilton. The loophole was later closed by the 12th Amendment.

Fast-forward to 1824. While John Quincy Adams was indeed a better man than Andrew Jackson, who not only supported slavery, but is perhaps second only to smallpox when it came to killing Native Americans, the Election of 1824 tore up the country and led to accusations of a "corrupt bargain."

Furthermore, it didn't prevent Jackson from becoming president. He came back and was easily elected in 1828 and again in 1832. His presidency led not only to the Trail of Tears, but to a depression as well, due to his opposition to fiat currencies and his battles with Nicholas Biddle and the Second Bank of the United States.

The Electoral College would next be a deciding factor in 1876. While Rutherford B. Hayes clearly lost the popular vote to governor Samuel J. Tilden of New York, and seemed to have pretty clearly lost the Electoral College as well, several states were called into question. A Congressional committee was appointed to decide the matter. To make a long story short, this time a corrupt bargain was most definitely arrived at: Hayes agreed to withdraw federal troops from the South if given the presidency. The deal done, Hayes became president and the Ku Klux Klan, Jim Crow, and nearly a hundred years of terror, abuse, and government-sanctioned discrimination ensued. Thank you, Electoral College!

Next we come to the Election of 1888. This time Grover Cleveland won a somewhat narrow popular vote victory but was defeated in the Electoral College by Benjamin Harrison. Now, is anyone reading this going, "Thank goodness we got the brilliant Benjamin Harrison as president rather than Grover Cleveland!" Somehow, I doubt it. Most of you are probably saying, "Who the hell is Benjamin Harrison?"

And now we come to the Election of 2000. Thankfully, the Electoral College did us the favor of not upsetting the apple cart throughout the 1900s, but in 2000 it granted us none other than the great George W. Bush. He lost by about 500,000 votes, but the "wisdom" of the College gave us this brilliant, brilliant man, who proceeded to ignore warnings about Al Qaeda striking within the US, did nothing to stop the Katrina disaster or ease its after-effects, and – oh, yeah – started a disastrous war on false pretenses. He condoned torture, tried to appoint Harriet Miers to the Supreme Court, and promoted policies that led to a near-global economic meltdown and depression. His administration also exposed Valerie Plame and damaged our reputation internationally. Thanks again, Electoral College!

And now the Electoral College, in its "wisdom," has given us Donald J. Trump. What could go wrong?

Myth #3: The Electoral College is somehow more representative than a direct popular vote.

This one definitely doesn't pass the smell test. It essentially argues that, without the Electoral College, states like Florida, Michigan, Iowa, and Ohio would be ignored.

First off, there are people in those states. And if there was a direct popular vote, candidates would still visit them. But, more importantly, the argument ignores the fact that the Electoral College makes it so that candidates don't bother to campaign in states like New York, California, or Texas – states where the most people are. In fact, the fifteen most populated states hold about two-thirds of our overall population. Why disregard so many states?

This argument also falsely treats states as single-minded entities. About half of Michigan went for Hillary Clinton, yet that half didn't count in the vote because of the College. The same goes for Florida, Wisconsin, and Pennsylvania. The nearly half of New Hampshire that went for Donald Trump also didn't count. That's just silly, and not in any way a better representation than if all of the votes actually counted.

Myth #4: The Electoral College unites us.

Do we really seem very united right now?

As a matter of fact, the Electoral College is extremely divisive. Since Democrats can't win Mississippi in the current atmosphere, for instance, they never go there, and Mississippians don't get to see them. Democrats don't bother to try to win over Mississippians because the Electoral College makes them insignificant. If there was a straight popular vote, Democrats would find those areas of Mississippi where they felt they could get votes and would make appearances.

Of course, the typical counter-argument to this is that a straight popular vote would cause the candidates to spend all of their time in the big cities. First off, if that's where most of the people are, what's wrong with that? But you can only spend so many days or run so many ads in a big city anyway. Smart candidates and political operatives would look to go to pockets where they could find more votes.

Myth #5: The Electoral College protects us from cheating.

Actually, the Electoral College does the complete opposite. In a national vote with over a hundred and thirty million votes cast, a few hundred votes here and there wouldn't be likely to make a difference. But the Electoral College, with its winner-takes-all system, encourages cheating by making it possible to steal an election by trimming hundreds or thousands of votes in a close state. Florida in 2000 is a perfect example: Bush, who would've most-likely lost a full state recount, won by only 537 votes. Efforts by Republicans to purge voting lists certainly helped. This is the same reason that voter purges have continued, as have other forms of voter suppression, such as the closing down of polling stations, voter ID laws, and cross-checking to eliminate eligible voters.

Myth #6: The Electoral College protects the vulnerable.

Again, it does the opposite. Giving unequal voting power to some is not somehow fairer than making every vote equal.

In this past presidential election, it was minority groups who were most vulnerable – Muslims, blacks, Latinos, immigrants. Yet because those people tend to be concentrated in cities, they were less protected. Rural areas in Pennsylvania were able to cancel out the cities of Pittsburgh and Philadelphia. The same goes for Florida, Texas, and North Carolina.

Hillary Clinton won the popular vote – again, the only one that should matter – by over 2.8 million votes. Who is protecting those people?

* * *

Grover Cleveland did a really stupid thing back in 1888: he didn't call bullshit when he won the popular vote by over 90,000 and lost the Electoral College, giving us the great Benjamin Harrison as president. Had Cleveland made a stink back then, maybe we wouldn't have had to suffer through the presidency of George W. Bush or that of the current disgraceful occupant of the White House, Donald Trump.

So what can we do? Well, first off, any president (including *President Trump) who doesn't win the popular vote should not be treated with the same degree of respect as someone who does. An asterisk should be placed by his name and we should use the term "unelected president" every time we refer to him. Much like the extremist Republican Party refers to the Democratic Party as the "Democrat" party and the Estate Tax as the "Death Tax," liberals have to learn how to brand. And a president who wasn't actually elected should be branded as well – Unelected President Donald Trump sounds much better, or perhaps simply "Resident Trump." Either way, we certainly shouldn't be foolish enough to award him respect he in no way deserves.

We also have to push for two things at the same time: an amendment to the Constitution to get rid of the Electoral College and the approval by states of the National Popular Vote Interstate Compact (NPVIC).

As we'll get to later, amendments are extraordinarily hard to pass. But we have to push for one to abolish the Electoral College anyway. In fact, we have to demand it. Why? Because it's important. In fact, it's urgent. Or do you want to see Trump lose by six million votes next time and get to remain in office because he was "reelected" by the Electoral College?

Simultaneously, we have to promote the passage of the NPVIC with large-scale, coordinated campaigns. If you're not familiar with it, the NPVIC is an agreement between states that says that all of them will cast their Electoral College votes for whoever wins the nation's popular vote, no matter who is the victor in their particular state. The agreement only goes into effect once the Electoral College vote total of those states involved reaches at least 270 – a majority of the College. Right now it's been passed by eleven states and the District of Columbia and has 172 Electoral votes in the bag, meaning that it needs 98 more.

Of course, those 98 aren't going to be easy to come by: unsurprisingly, all of the legislatures that have passed the compact so far have been liberal-leaning ones. Not a single conservative state has supported the idea of everyone's vote being equal. We need to make their legislators answer for that, and the way to do so is by sending a strong message – through voting, protests, marches, telephone calls, emails, and whatever other peaceful means at our disposal. We need to turn up the pressure and make them feel the heat, because the College has got to go.

Maybe once it does, I can finally stop being mad at ole Grover.

2. Voter Suppression

Martin Luther King (far right) looks on as LBJ signs the Voting Rights Act. August 6th, 1965

Despite what you may have learned in grade school, the US did not start off as a magnificent democracy. When the Founders spoke of freedom, they meant freedom for themselves: white, male landowners.

That's not to say that we weren't a land and a people of promise. The words that the slave-owning Jefferson wrote about freedom would become a model for the world and would inspire generations to come.

But United States history is often presented in the classroom as a journey which was destined to culminate in egalitarianism and greatness.

Teachers make the mistake of teaching history as if it's a trajectory – a progression.

Except it's not really like that. Oftentimes, people go backwards, and the US is no exception in this regard. In fact, we've frequently gone in reverse.

Some examples:

After Chinese laborers risked their lives to help construct the railroads, we passed the Chinese Exclusion Act in 1882. That was at the same time that the Statue of Liberty was being constructed. I guess her torch didn't extend to Asia.

After we allowed waves of immigrants in between 1890 and 1911, we closed the door in the 1920s with the Immigration Acts of 1921 and 1924.

After we passed the 13th, 14th, and 15th Amendments, abolishing slavery, guaranteeing citizens' rights, and providing suffrage for black males, we proceeded to tolerate Jim Crow, white supremacist vigilantism, and institutionalized disenfranchisement.

And while it's true that we've made tremendous progress, we are now going backward, and one of the main ways we're doing so is through disenfranchisement. It is abundantly clear at this point that Republicans have engaged in a systematic effort to suppress voting. Republican leaders know that they would be out of power rather quickly if we had a fair, universal system. If everyone voted, and if every vote counted the same, they and their conservative policies would stand no shot. It's the same reason they maintain the Electoral College: not because they honestly believe in it, but because they know it would be more difficult for them to win the presidency without it.

Even in presidential election years, US turnout is only in the mid to high 50% range. This is no accident; it's by design.

How is it done? Several ways: voter ID laws, cross-checking, voter caging, voter purging, the closing of polling stations, the limiting of election times, and the creation of apathy.

Let's go over them.

Voter ID Laws

Mike Turzai, the Republican Pennsylvania House leader, infamously (and stupidly) declared that voter ID laws would allow Mitt Romney to win the state in the upcoming presidential election. He was wrong – Romney lost the state anyhow. Still, voter ID laws are not without their impact.

It's difficult to say for sure how many voters are turned away or discouraged by such laws. An analysis by the *Washington Post* determined that it may not have had as large an impact on the 2016 election as some people think. Yet the 2000 and 2016 presidential elections showed us how a very small shift in votes can have a massive effect, especially when one factors in the Electoral College. But it's not only presidential elections that must be considered: there are Congressional, local, and state elections as well.

Meanwhile, the supposed problem that advocates of voter ID laws claim they solve is nonexistent. Voter fraud is an extremely (and I mean extremely, extremely) rare occurrence. After all, who is going to risk a heavy fine and jail time just so they can say they voted twice? What's the likelihood that that one extra vote would make a difference?

Loyola Professor Justin Levitt, for one, thoroughly examined the issue and found just 31 believable cases of voter fraud out of over a billion ballots cast. Basically, this is a fictional problem invented purely as an excuse to make it harder for poor people to vote. Guess which party poor people tend to vote for? I'll give you a hint: it's not the Republicans.

As Professor Carol Anderson of Emory put it in a *New York Times* op-ed:

> Rampant voter fraud does not exist. There is no epidemic of illegal voting. But the lie is so mesmerizing, it takes off like a wildfire, so that the irrational fear that someone might vote who shouldn't means that hundreds of thousands who should can't cast ballots, in part because of the increase in voter ID laws across the country in recent years.

Cross-Checking

The practice of cross-checking allows Republicans to X voters off voting lists if they are registered in more than one state or county. This can typically happen when someone moves and is, of course, far from any indication that they plan to vote twice. As noted above, double-voting is truly a fictional problem to begin with, since the penalties for voting twice are so high and the benefits non-existent.

Yet, as this article from *Rolling Stone* points out, Republicans have used cross-checking to eliminate tens of thousands of voters from the voting rolls in an instant, as they did in Virginia. The "system" – if it can even be called that – was designed by Kris Kobach, who also designed the "system" of racial profiling that was used after 9/11. Mr. Kobach is the Secretary of State of Kansas whom Donald Trump asked to be on his Voter Integrity Committee, which quietly vanished after not being able to find any voter fraud, despite Trump's claim that 3-5 million undocumented immigrants voted illegally. Twenty-eight states use Kobach's "system," known as the Interstate Crosscheck System. It has identified over 7 million voters as "suspect."

How is that possible, you ask? Well, the Interstate Crosscheck uses mainly two criteria: a person's name and his or her date of birth. In a country of 320 million people, and 140 million or so active voters, you're going to get a lot of matches that way. As the *Washington Post* has pointed out, Kobach's "system" is likely to misidentify 200 cases for every one it gets right. That's a failure rate of over 99%. Another system, the Electronic Registration Information Center, or ERIC, does a much better job and also helps to register unregistered potential voters. Yet Republicans don't want to use that system, instead opting for Kobach's terrible one. Why? Because it's much more efficient in one respect: eliminating undesirable voters.

Voter Caging

This method is just as simple as it is outrageous. Republicans target an area filled with Democratic voters, then send out non-forwardable mailers to the homes in that area. Any mail that's returned is used as evidence that that particular voter should not be registered.

Of course, there are many reasons why a letter might be returned. It could be that the resident of the home it was mailed to moved to a different address within their voting district and hasn't informed the government yet. It could be that they were away for a while. It could be that they closed their PO box, etc. in order to avoid bills or debt collectors. It could be a typo on the envelope. The bottom line is: Republicans know that if they send out enough mailers they'll be able to eliminate a certain percentage of voters they'd rather not have on the voting lists, based only on this flimsy, flimsy evidence.

Voter Purging

Simply put, voter purging is the practice of eliminating voters from the voting rolls, mainly through two methods: felon lists and the "use it or lose it" approach.

By felon lists, I'm not referring to the mass elimination of minority voters through felony convictions (we'll get into that later). I'm talking about a method for eliminating non-convicts simply because they happen to have a similar name and details as a convict. In Florida in 2000, for instance, thousands of voters were kept from voting who could easily have swung the election to Gore and probably would have, had not a concerted effort by the Republicans and Florida's Attorney General, Katherine Harris, kept them from voting. The St. Louis Board of Elections similarly purged almost 50,000 voters that year. Like with cross-checking, the goal is to find a way to eliminate people from the rolls – they err on the side of disenfranchisement.

The "use it or lose it" approach, meanwhile, seeks to take away the voting rights of people who haven't voted in a while. Ohio is the strictest state in this regard, eliminating voters who fail to vote in two consecutive elections. Of course, this treats voting more like a privilege than a right, and is not only unfair but also patently ridiculous. Imagine a person skips one election because they're young, let's say, and not particularly enamored with voting. The next time around, they're tending to their sick mother in the hospital and can't make it to the polling station. Well, that's it for them! They're out!

The Brennan Center for Justice recently issued a report that found that between 2014 and 2016, nearly 16 million Americans were purged from voter lists. They compared that to another two-year period, 2006 to 2008, and found that it had increased by some 4 million. This is not an accident: it is a systematic effort to reduce the amount of voters – especially minority voters.

The Closing of Polling Stations

One of the easiest ways to stop people from voting is to make it incredibly inconvenient. When I vote, in my mostly white neighborhood, I'm in and out within ten minutes every time. Yet, in many places, voting is an all-day affair. That's no accident: the purpose is to discourage people from voting. Keep in mind: the US does not give people time off for voting (Election Holidays have been proposed, but, as Osita Nwanevu has pointed out for *Slate*, we can't be sure whether or not such a thing would increase turnout, though she also noted that "35 percent of registered voters who failed to vote in 2014 specifically cited work and school conflicts as impediments."). Unlike other countries, we don't automatically register people to vote or allow for same-day registration.

We make voting much more difficult than it has to be. The Republicans have figured out that they don't need to take away someone's vote directly; they've replaced the violent version of Jim Crow with a more surreptitious statistical Jim Crow. A key victory for them in this regard was *Shelby v. Holder* (2013), which allowed them to close 868 polling stations throughout the South, largely gutting the Voting Rights Act.

The less polling stations there are, the more inconvenient it is for voters the Republicans don't want voting. And even if these voters are willing to travel, the lines at the polling stations (once they finally arrive) can be long. In 2012, for instance, the average wait time across Florida was forty-five minutes. In some places, voters are waiting several hours.

Apathy

The overall goal is for Republicans to make people likely to vote against them lose interest in voting altogether. After a while, with many realizing that their vote won't count for much due to the Electoral College or gerrymandering (up next), and many finding it difficult to vote due to long lines at polling stations or voter ID laws or voter purging, many just give up. The GOP also tries to poison the political atmosphere at times by creating false equivalencies, as they did with Hillary Clinton and Trump. "They're both terrible!" some said, unable to distinguish character traits with all the noise. The idea is to convince people that all politicians are bad, untrustworthy, and corrupt, so that they just don't believe in anything or anyone anymore.

* * *

These methods of disenfranchisement, along with the lack of uniform voting standards, were why the Electoral Integrity Project ranked the US last among Western democracies when it comes to the quality of elections. The Variety of Democracies project, out of the University of Gothenburg in Sweden, reached a similar conclusion, ranking the US well below other industrialized democracies and 46th out of 161 countries worldwide.

Ask yourself: What is more important to a democracy than having free and fair elections?

3. Gerrymandering

Original "Gerry-mander" cartoon, *Boston Gazette*, March 26th, 1812

Redistricting to cancel out votes is nothing new; in fact, it's about as old as the Constitution itself. Virginia governor Patrick Henry tried to do it to James Madison way back in 1788, only to see Madison prevail despite Henry's efforts. In 1812, Massachusetts governor Elbridge Gerry took the tactic to the next level when he signed into law a redistricting plan designed to give the

Democratic-Republicans more seats in the legislature. The resulting salamander-like district that was created led the *Boston Gazette's* Elkanah Tisdale to create the image of the "Gerry-mander," and hence a new term was coined.

So gerrymandering (pronounced with a soft-G, though Gerry's name had a hard-G, like "goat") has indeed been around for a long time. But technological innovations that allow political operatives to map out districts with incredible accuracy have made it possible for Republicans to bring gerrymandering to entirely new and disgusting levels. Political maps can now be created that literally cut through neighborhoods, carving out districts favorable to the GOP and ensuring that it can maintain its grip on power. Whereas before politicians could only gerrymander by general area, now they can do it house by house. Demographic and survey data help them determine with a high degree of accuracy how someone is likely to vote and to include or exclude that person in a district based on that data. Keep in mind that there are two ways to disenfranchise voters: the first is to make it difficult or impossible for them to vote; the second is to make their votes powerless.

The tactics are known as "cracking" and "packing."

Cracking involves breaking up a district's voters in a way that dilutes their votes. For instance, if there's a district that's 55% Democratic, you split it up so that it's only 42% Democratic, placing many of the previous district's Democratic voters in a Republican stronghold where their votes won't make a difference. Instead of winding up with one House seat, Democratic voters get nothing.

Packing, on the other hand, involves creating a district stuffed with the opposing party's supporters, once again diluting the power of their votes.

For instance, if there are three districts held by Democrats who each won their seats with around 52% of the vote, you redraw the districts so that one district has over 80% Democrats and the others have safe Republican majorities.

This is how Republicans have managed to maintain a ridiculously disproportionate lead in the House.

After Obama's victory in 2008, the Republicans went back to the drawing board. There was a concerted effort to win state offices, called REDMAP (for Redistricting Majority Project). As Elizabeth Kolbert pointed out in a column for *The New Yorker*, in 2010 Republicans realized that Democrats held both houses in twenty-seven states, and one of the houses in another six states. But the Democratic majority in several of these states was rather thin, and the GOP saw vulnerability.

Republicans sank $30 million into state races, with much of it arriving in the wake of the *Citizens United* decision, which had opened the financial floodgates. A substantial amount came from corporate donations, and most of it arrived just weeks before Election Day. The GOP was able to pour funds into polls, ads, and deceptive mailers, some of which spread out and out falsities. Democrats across the country didn't know what hit 'em, and they didn't have much time to respond to all of the accusations being leveled against them.

By gaining control of state legislatures, Republicans were able to redraw Congressional districts in a way that greatly favored them.

In 2016, for instance, Republicans got just 1.1% more votes than the Democrats in the House, yet they managed to win 55% of the seats, while the Democrats only received 45% (241 to 194). That's a 47 seat lead! To make matters worse, incumbents tend to win, so the Republican lead of

1.1% in voting was probably simply a benefit of the corrupt system that's been set up to begin with.

An analysis by Michael Li and Laura Royden of the Brennan Center for Justice, which they detailed in a piece for the *New York Times*, demonstrates exactly how uneven the system is and the daunting prospects facing the Democrats in 2018:

> Even the strongest blue wave may crash up against a powerful structural force in American politics: extreme gerrymandering....We conducted an analysis to measure how hard it would be for Democrats in each state to win additional seats under these gerrymandered maps. The results are sobering. In 2006, a roughly five-and-a-half-point lead in the national popular vote was enough for Democrats to pick up 31 seats and win back the House majority they had lost to Newt Gingrich and his Contract With America 12 years before.
>
> But our research shows that a similar margin of victory in 2018 would most likely net Democrats only 13 seats, leaving the Republicans firmly in charge. Just to get the thinnest of majorities in the House, Democrats would need around an 11-point win in the national popular vote. They haven't come close to winning by that much in a midterm election since 1982.

And they ain't just whistlin' Dixie: in 2012, Democrats won well over a million more votes than Republicans in the House, yet the GOP wound up with 234 seats to the Dems' 201. That sound like a fair system to you?

This can be solved, so long as we have the political will to do it. Other countries have independent commissions that determine their voting districts in order to prevent the drawing of districts from becoming politicized.

There's also the idea of proportional representation: rather than have one person elected in each district, there can be larger districts that elect several candidates. If a district is large enough, a third or fourth place finisher can still win a seat. This method would lead to more minority-party voices being heard and help to eliminate the two-party domination that currently exists in the US.

District lines could also simply be harder to change and therefore not as susceptible to political whims.

Out of 60 countries analyzed by election consultant Lisa Handley, only two – the US and France – had both no proportional representation and no independent commissions drawing district lines. Forty-three of the 60 have some sort of election commission to handle district delineation, including 22 that have commissions created for that express purpose.

In the US, it's a self-perpetuating system: self-interested politicos have lines drawn in a way that favor them and their party and therefore get them more representation, which in turn allows them to maintain the biased system. Unfortunately, as with many of the things in this book, it would probably require large-scale public pressure to force these politicians to change their ways.

4. Money in Politics

The "Brains" (Boss Tweed) - Thomas Nast, *Harper's Weekly*, 1871

The last two presidential elections have been the most expensive in history, and, yes, that includes adjustments for inflation. In today's dollars, Jimmy Carter and Ronald Reagan spent less than $300 million combined for the 1980 election. By comparison, the 2016 presidential election cost over $2.5 billion, and the total cost of all of the campaigns, including those for Congress, was approximately $6.8 billion. The cost for a winning House seat right now is around $1.5 million. In the Senate, it tops $10 million. If you factor in outside money, it's almost $20 million.

Despite the notoriety of *Citizens United*, it was actually more like an exclamation point at the end of a long line of cases that brought about unlimited campaign spending, with the first being *Buckley v. Valeo* in 1976. In *Buckley*, the Supreme Court arrived at a somewhat convoluted decision. In the wake of Watergate, legislation had been passed to limit campaign donations in an attempt to thwart corruption. The court upheld the direct donation limits, but said that no limits could be placed on what individuals spend outside of direct donations, so long as no coordination exists between the individuals and the campaigns. In this way, it was a precursor to *Citizens United*, which extended this "right" to corporations and nonprofits.

The court said that the direct donations were reasonable because they were needed to protect the "integrity of our system of representative democracy." Yet the court did not recognize the danger of allowing individuals to keep their expenditures secret – dark money, as we would say. Nor did it recognize that money allows some voices to drown out others, declaring that "the concept that government may restrict the speech of some elements of our society in order to enhance the relative voice of others is wholly foreign to the First Amendment, which was designed to secure the widest possible dissemination of information from diverse and antagonistic sources."

It was a majority decision joined by Thurgood Marshall, the first black Supreme Court justice and a civil rights hero. If Marshall approved of a decision, my natural tendency is to think it must be right. But, looking back, it's easy to see the Supreme Court's mistake in *Buckley*. While protecting the First Amendment is crucial to free speech, the justices made the error of not recognizing the potential of their decision to do the opposite: to limit free speech.

Think of it this way: Imagine you're at a minor league sporting event. The owners of the venue allow everyone to cheer for their respective team and favorite players. One day, though, a man shows up with a bullhorn. Since there was no policy against bringing a bullhorn to a game, the owners allow it. But then some people start bringing more and more expensive bullhorns. One man brings a bullhorn that costs $600,000 (he's a big fan) and uses advanced technology to drown out all other sounds so that only his voice can be heard. The others there can still cheer, but no one will hear them. They simply can't afford to keep up. In fact, the man's bullhorn is so powerful that even the team managers can't be heard, and so the players just take instructions from the man, who promises them all sorts of things if they'll only do what he says. And so the owners of the venue decide to impose a new rule: no more bullhorns, because the $600,000 bullhorn is making it impossible for others to be heard and is ruining the game. Seems reasonable, no?

Well, not according to the Supreme Court. Ever since *Buckley*, the court has looked at money as speech, not recognizing that it could actually be used to drown speech out. They reached a similar decision in 1978 with the *First National Bank of Boston v. Bellotti* case, when they struck down a Massachusetts law that limited corporate influence in elections. But in 1990, the court seemed to contradict this notion, this time in a decision that Marshall agreed with. In *Austin vs. Michigan*

Chamber of Commerce (1990), the court took note of the "serious danger that corporate political expenditures will undermine the integrity of the political process." *Citizens United* overruled the *Austin* decision, once again allowing unlimited corporate spending on elections.

Since *Citizens United*, spending by Super PACs has gone from less than $63 million in 2010 to over $1.1 billion in 2016, as shown here on the site Open Secrets. Groups that are purely political in purpose can set themselves up as charities, raise money in secret, and bestow cash upon candidates.

The problem with *Citizens United* and the torrent of money it's unleashed is mainly that it operates with a wink and a nod. Is money free speech? Well, no; but it can be used for that purpose. Imagine, for a moment, that you were legitimately raising money for a cause you believed in. Would you want to be told that you can't spend $10 million to fight global warming? Or to battle the tobacco companies? Or to fight corporate influence?

What if you were an executive at a corporation that was under attack from a politician who was spreading falsities? Should the corporation be able to use its funds to fight back? You might say no, but what if the corporation was Starbucks and the politician was Donald Trump? Would that change how you feel? It's not so clear-cut then, is it?

The first failure of *Citizens United*, then, isn't that it allows groups to raise and spend funds in a way they deem proper, but that it allows them to do so incognito. It would be more reasonable to insist that all donations – or all above $10,000, say - be made public, so that the people can know who is influencing their political leaders.

The second failure is that there is no serious mechanism to ensure that campaigns are not coordinating with outside groups or dark money donors – the wink and a nod aspect. It has to be clear that funds are being spent on causes and not candidates. No mixing of campaign figures and outside groups with unlimited spending power can be permitted. We cannot have situations wherein a campaign exec leaves a campaign to form a big money group to support the very same candidate, then receives a job in that candidate's administration once the election is over. No one can honestly believe that such a thing is a coincidence.

The third failure is that it simply isn't comprehensive enough; the court could've left it to Congress to carve out specific rules for corporations, granting them some leeway, but not treating them the same as nonprofits or individuals. You might say, "What a minute! If corporations were treated differently in certain regards, wouldn't the corporations simply form nonprofit groups to make the same arguments the corporation is making?" Well, yes. In fact, forming 501(c)(3)s is already a popular way to secretly give unlimited funds. But you would force the corporations to abide by the rules of a nonprofit, and since it would all be out in the open, they wouldn't be allowed to hide their intentions so easily. There are times that corporations have a legitimate vested interest or even a moral cause motivating them, and that's fine. But it must be out in the open so that we can avoid the great danger of allowing big money to corrupt our system.

The threat of such unrestricted spending cannot be overstated. Despite the inordinate amount of free media Donald Trump was able to conjure up, he's an ideal example of money buying influence and billionaires buying candidates. Trump only needed the support of a wealthy few in order to compete. Billionaire Robert Mercer, for one, not only gave millions to Trump but also invested $10 million in the neo-racist site *Breitbart*. The family of Donald Trump's completely inexperienced Secretary of Education, Betsy DeVos, may have given as much as $200 million to Republicans, according to her own testimony. The DeVos family also gave numerous contributions to the senators who were voting on her confirmation.

Trump's inaugural was in and of itself a prime example of wealthy individuals and corporations buying influence. Though they only spent perhaps half of it, his inaugural committee raised around $107 million. Sheldon Adelson alone Sheldon-ed out $5 million. According to the *New York Times*, over 48 corporations gave at least $1 million. One-tenth of the money came from energy companies, including numerous donations from coal mining execs. Soon after, Trump signed a law that ended the ban on coal waste in our waterways. Would he have done so anyway? Well, who knows? But we shouldn't be left to wonder.

Politicians, meanwhile, are making a killing after they leave office and in between political jobs. Barack Obama recently made a deal to get $400,000 to give a speech to Wall Street. Bill and Hillary Clinton made over $153 million in fifteen years, just giving speeches.

People like Kellyanne Conway are hitching their futures to candidates because politics has become a lucrative business. After working for a politician, they can get network gigs and publishing deals.

And after members of Congress rule on legislation affecting companies, they can go to work for those same companies and make a bundle. K Street and Wall Street firms come calling. There's supposed to be a two-year ban on joining such firms (and in some cases longer), but these bans are easily gotten around by referring to a former Congressman or woman as a "consultant" or some other euphemistic title. In fact, the list of people from Congress who have joined lobbying firms alone is astounding. One study found that, on average, they increase their salaries by more than 1400%.

It's doubtful, of course, that Donald Trump will seek to get a job on K Street once he's out of office. He does in fact donate his presidential salary (currently $400,000, plus travel and other expenses) each year, but that's for two important reasons: 1. It would probably look terrible for someone claiming to be a billionaire to take taxpayer money. And 2. Trump's blatant violations of the Emoluments Clause of the Constitution is probably netting him a helluva lot more than the salary. (For more, read chapter 28, Legalized Corruption.) I would not find it surprising, though – and neither would you, I would venture – if Trump looks to make a killing on speeches after his presidency. My guess is he'll look to get a million dollars a pop.

Public service should not be about getting rich. So how do we fix it? Well, there are some simple steps that could be taken and then some more difficult ones. Democrats are part of the flawed system and are not immune to it. Like Republicans in Congress, they spend inordinate amounts of time raising money from donors and many take jobs they shouldn't once they leave office. But at least the Democrats are more amenable to changing the system, so installing more of them in office makes it more likely that we'll see reasonable rules to try to put an end to the "revolving door" that allows lawmakers to turn into wealthy lobbyists (or "consultants"). As an electorate, we need to insist on rule changes to prohibit such behavior.

Public shaming is also a good technique, and we need more of it – not just from sites like Open Secrets, but from networks like NPR, CNN, MSNBC, and PBS (somehow, I'm not counting on Fox).

Of course, the hardest step right now is changing the Supreme Court. In time, though…in time…

5. Vulnerable Elections

Credit: DonkeyHotey

Unless you've been sleeping under a rock for the past couple of years, you're probably aware that a country called Russia interfered in our presidential election. But there's actually a lot more to this than you may realize. Yes, Russian trolls led campaigns on Facebook to spread falsehoods and help Donald Trump. Yes, they were on Twitter. And yes they hacked the DNC and used damaging emails from Clinton campaign chairman John Podesta to damage Hillary Clinton.

But are you aware that the Dems weren't the only ones hacked? As

James Comey testified to Congress in January of 2017, "there was evidence of hacking directed at state-level organizations, state-level campaigns, and the RNC – but old domains of the RNC, meaning old emails they weren't using. None of that was released."

It's interesting enough that old emails from the RNC were not released – that in and of itself makes one wonder. But it's also interesting that the Trump campaign or newer RNC systems weren't hacked at all. Is it because the Trump people were just too smart for that? Unlikely. If anything, they may have benefitted from simply being a smaller campaign. Still, one would think that repeated efforts by the Russians would've been successful when the guardians of Trump secrets were the likes of Trump lawyer Michael Cohen and son-in-law Jared Kushner.

But Comey also noted that state level organizations were hacked, and that's true. He was referring to voter information databases and not voting machines, but as Kim Zetter recently pointed out for the *New York Times Magazine*, the voting machines and systems themselves are actually much more vulnerable than people realize: despite what many politicians and pundits proclaim, voting machines "are in fact accessible by way of the modems they use to transmit vote totals on election night. Add to this the fact that states don't conduct robust postelection audits…and there's a good chance we simply won't know if someone has altered the digital votes in the next election."

Zetter goes on to say:

> There are roughly 350,000 voting machines in use in the country today, all of which fall into one of two categories: optical-scan machines or direct-recording electronic machines. Each of them suffers from significant security problems.

With optical-scan machines, voters fill out paper ballots and feed them into a scanner, which stores a digital image of the ballot and records the votes on a removable memory card. The paper ballot, in theory, provides an audit trail that can be used to verify digital tallies. But not all states perform audits, and many that do simply run the paper ballots through a scanner a second time. Fewer than half the states do manual audits, and they typically examine ballots from randomly chosen precincts in a county, instead of a percentage of ballots from all precincts. If the randomly chosen precincts aren't ones where hacking occurred or where machines failed to accurately record votes, an audit won't reveal anything — nor will it always catch problems with early-voting, overseas or absentee ballots, all of which are often scanned in county election offices, not in precincts.

Direct-recording electronic machines, or D.R.E.s, present even more auditing problems. Voters use touch screens or other input devices to make selections on digital-only ballots, and votes are stored electronically. Many D.R.E.s have printers that produce what's known as a voter-verifiable paper audit trail — a scroll of paper, behind a window, that voters can review before casting their ballots. But the paper trail doesn't provide the same integrity as full-size ballots and optical-scan machines, because a hacker could conceivably rig the machine to print a voter's selections correctly on the paper while recording something else on the memory card. About 80 percent of voters today cast ballots either on D.R.E.s that produce a paper trail or on scanned paper ballots. But five states still use paperless D.R.E.s exclusively, and an additional 10 states use paperless D.R.E.s in some jurisdictions.

Zetter also noted that just three companies control 80% of the voting machines: Electronic Systems & Software, Dominion, and Hart InterCivic. Moreover, the machines and their internal systems belong to the companies, and they're not exactly forthcoming with information. After the 2004 election, for instance, there were multiple discrepancies in

Ohio, which could've turned the Electoral College in John Kerry's favor, but the Kerry campaign was unable to access the records of the machines. The late intellectual Christopher Hitchens pointed out some of the irregularities in a 2006 article for *Vanity Fair*:

> In Montgomery County, two precincts recorded a combined undervote of almost 6,000. This is to say that that many people waited to vote but, when their turn came, had no opinion on who should be the president, voting only for lesser offices. In these two precincts alone, that number represents an undervote of 25 percent, in a county where undervoting averages out at just 2 percent. Democratic precincts had 75 percent more undervotes than Republican ones.
>
> In Precinct 1B of Gahanna, in Franklin County, a computerized voting machine recorded a total of 4,258 votes for Bush and 260 votes for Kerry. In that precinct, however, there are only 800 registered voters, of whom 638 showed up. Once the "glitch" had been identified, the president had to be content with 3,893 fewer votes than the computer had awarded him.
>
> In Miami County, a Saddam Hussein–type turnout was recorded in the Concord Southwest and Concord South precincts, which boasted 98.5 percent and 94.27 percent turnouts, respectively, both of them registering overwhelming majorities for Bush. Miami County also managed to report 19,000 additional votes for Bush after 100 percent of the precincts had reported on Election Day.
>
> In Mahoning County, *Washington Post* reporters found that many people had been victims of "vote hopping," which is to say that voting machines highlighted a choice of one candidate after the voter had recorded a preference for another. Some specialists in election software diagnose this as a "calibration issue."

Zetter noted a similar "glitch" issue had occurred in Florida in 2000: while everyone was concentrating on hanging chads and the recount effort, many people missed what happened in Volusia County. Al Gore's vote total experienced a sudden drop after one of Volusia's precincts reported that he had somehow received *negative* 16,022 – that's right: a negative vote total. Moreover, the socialist candidate had gotten nearly 10,000 votes – especially remarkable considering that the district had just 585 registered voters and only 219 had voted that day. The problem was later attributed to a memory card error, but what caused the strange result has never been fully explained.

After the 2000 election, there was an effort in Congress to bring about voting reform. But, oddly enough, cybersecurity was not made an issue. The Help America Vote Act (or HAVA) of 2002 provided $3.9 billion for states to update their voting machines, advocating that they get rid of the old punch-card systems and lever-pulls. Democrat Rush Holt repeatedly tried to amend the bill over the next several years in order to add cybersecurity measures, but his efforts didn't get very far. Stenny Hoyer, one of the bill's sponsors, admitted to Zetter that he had failed to foresee the problem that could result from the lack of a paper trail that came with such machines.

"I didn't think Rush was correct," he said. They had been told that the machines were extremely reliable. "Now I think in retrospect we were obviously wrong, because our premise was the machines were not subject to being hacked. And now we know."

Congress's latest spending bill does provide $380 million to states to update their voting systems and replace old machines, but the new machines have the same vulnerabilities as the old ones, it seems. The Election Assistance Commission, created by HAVA, is setting up new standards, but won't be able to apply them and test them on voting machines for two years or more. Meanwhile, the Trump administration seems strangely unmotivated to take action, despite the fact that Trump's own intelligence heads have warned that the vulnerabilities could impact the 2018 and 2020 elections.

Many of the problems with election vulnerabilities could obviously be fixed if we simply had the will power to fix them. HAVA should certainly be amended to insist that all voting machines provide an adequate paper trail and that audits don't take place in select precincts, but in all state precincts when a vote is close or discrepancies exist. Of course, even if HAVA isn't amended, states can independently take actions to ensure that their voting systems are safe and that results are easily reviewable.

When it comes to our presidential elections, of course, much of the danger could be eliminated by eliminating the Electoral College, as noted earlier. Russia was aware that our system made it possible for just a few hundred more votes in the right place to turn an election, as happened in Florida in 2000. This time, less than 80,000 votes in three key states made the difference, the popular will of the people be damned.

But our voting system also suffers from a lack of standards and uniformity. Other countries have national, uniform voting systems. But here in the United States we take the "States" part of our name a bit too seriously and allow states to make their own rules for federal elections. It's ridiculous, of course. There should be federal rules regulating how elections are run in order to prevent voter information from getting out, prevent voter purges and the closing of polling stations, set fair and open registration standards, and guarantee the security of our voting systems.

In the Gerrymandering section, I recommended a national voting commission to draw district lines. The same commission could also set up voting standards that would apply across the nation. Voting is too important to be left to the states and to the whims of party partisans.

Unfortunately, one of the greatest threats against our elections is just plain apathy, much of which is caused by the fact that many people feel their votes simply don't count for much. One of the reasons for that is our Senate, which by its very nature creates a system of disproportionate representation.

6. The Senate

Tilts to the right.

Despite what you may have learned in school about how great our system is and what a fantastic compromise the Founders made when they created the House of Representatives and the Senate, the fact is that the Senate is a completely disproportional body. The top nine most populated states have approximately the same population as the bottom forty-one, yet those nine states get only eighteen out of a hundred senators. The top fifteen states contain about two-thirds of the population of the US, and yet they get just thirty senators while the remaining 30% of the people get seventy. How can an institution wherein two-thirds of the people only get 30% of representation be called democratic?

We treat the institution of the Senate as if its existence should never be questioned – as if it was handed down by the wise Founding Fathers and is somehow sacrosanct. But that's preposterous. The truth is that the

Senate shouldn't exist, and that we'd be much better off with a proportional representation system.

While political pundits praise the Senate as the "cooling off point" for legislation, comparing it to a saucer that collects overflowing coffee, they often forget how much progress the Senate has prevented from happening. The Senate and the three-fifths compromise in the House, for instance, gave the South inordinate power before the Civil War and kept slavery around for decades. The Senate voted down women's suffrage in 1887. And the Senate of today makes it nearly impossible to pass a public option or single-payer health care, make Puerto Rico a state, or fix our corrupt tax system (which we'll get to later).

Currently, the Democratic caucus (including Bernie Sanders and Angus King) have two less seats than the Republicans. Yet, when you add up the state populations that they represent, it becomes clear that the Democratic caucus represents over 40 million more people than the Republicans do. Here's how it breaks down:

States with two GOP senators and their populations:

Alaska – 737,000

Arizona – 6,731,000

Arkansas – 2,966,000

Georgia – 10,100,000

Idaho – 1,634,000

Iowa – 3,107,000

Kansas – 2,904,000

Kentucky – 4,413,000

Louisiana – 4,650,000

Mississippi – 2,994,000

Nebraska – 1,882,000

North Carolina – 9,944,000

Oklahoma – 3,878,000

South Carolina – 4,832,000

South Dakota – 853,000

Tennessee – 6,549,000

Texas – 26,960,000

Utah – 2,943,000

Wyoming – 584,000

Total: 98,661,000

States with two Dem senators and their populations:

California – 38,800,000

Connecticut – 3,597,000

Delaware – 936,000

Hawaii – 1,420,000

Illinois – 12,880,000

Maryland – 5,976,000

Massachusetts – 6,745,000

Michigan – 9,910,000

Minnesota – 5,457,000

New Hampshire – 1,327,000

New Jersey – 8,938,000

New Mexico – 2,086,000

New York – 19,750,000

Oregon – 3,970,000

Rhode Island – 1,055,000

Virginia – 8,326,000

Washington – 7,062,000

Total: 138,235,000

States with one of each and their populations:

Alabama - 4,849,000

Colorado – 5,356,000

Florida – 19,890,000

Indiana – 6,597,000

Missouri – 6,064,000

Montana – 1,024,000

Nevada – 2,839,000

North Dakota – 739,000

Ohio – 11,590,000

Pennsylvania – 12,790,000

West Virginia – 1,850,000

Wisconsin – 5,758,000

Total: 79,346,000

State with a GOP and an Independent (caucuses with the Dems) and its population:

Maine – 1,330,000

State with a Democrat and an Independent (caucuses with the Dems) and its population:

Vermont – 627,000

Total for GOP: 138,999,000

Total for Dems and Independents: 179,200,000

Difference: Dems represent 40,201,00 more people

Ironically enough, in the case of *Reynolds v. Sims* (1964), the Supreme Court decided that states could not have disproportionate representation such as that which exists in our own Senate. The court recognized that having a county with forty times the population of another have the same representation made no sense. And yet, in the US Senate, one voter in Wyoming is equivalent to 66 voters in California, since California has 66 times Wyoming's population. Think about that: 66 times the population, yet they both get two senators. In fact, California has more people than the bottom twenty states, yet they get forty senators and California gets two. Is that democracy? Is that a republic in any true sense of the word?

7. Filibusters and Holds

Ted Cruz once read *Green Eggs and Ham* on the Senate floor. Credit: DonkeyHotey

Sometimes my fellow liberals make the mistake of thinking that the filibuster is some magnificent protector of democratic ideals – that it prevents bad legislation from passing. And although that's most certainly happened at times, the truth is that the filibuster has done a great deal more to hinder progress than to help it along. As the House of Representatives figured out over 200 years ago, the filibuster is a drag on democracy, and not in a good way. The House banned it back in the early 1800s, yet it's endured in our antiquated Senate.

Many progressive measures have fallen victim to the filibuster. Southern Democrats used it to prevent anti-lynching legislation in 1922, 1935, 1938, 1948, and 1949. Harry Truman was also thwarted by the filibuster in other civil rights areas, including an employment anti-discrimination bill he proposed and an anti-poll tax measure (this was before the 24th Amendment outlawed poll taxes in 1964). Some Democrats and Republicans also tried to use the filibuster to stop the 1964 Civil Rights Act, though fortunately fell short. But for a while it was a bit too close for comfort. Hubert Humphrey had to run around making sure the Johnson faction had the votes to stop the filibuster, which required a two-thirds vote for cloture at the time (now a "supermajority" of 60).

Other destructive uses of the filibuster include: defeat of an 1846 proposal that would've banned slavery from any territory purchased from Mexico; a South Carolina senator using the filibuster to extort $47,000 out of the Senate for his state; and Republicans using it in 1987 to stop a campaign finance bill that would've limited campaign donations to senators and allowed for public financing.

The use of the filibuster has grown dramatically since the 1970s and reached new heights under the Obama administration, as Republicans showed a willingness to use it for every possible reason, including filibustering (or threatening to filibuster, which often has the same effect) a ridiculous number of judicial and other appointments. On top of that, they also used the filibuster to kill gun control, the DREAM Act, the Buffett Rule, Immigration Reform, and the American Jobs Act, which would've taxed the wealthy to help provide jobs for middle and lower class Americans.

The filibuster is obviously blatantly undemocratic. Of course, as noted in the previous section, the Senate itself is undemocratic – less populated states already get an inordinate amount of power, and, of course, the majority of those states are conservative. But the filibuster makes the situation much worse. Think about it: the bottom twenty states, plus one more senator, can put a halt to legislation. The bottom twenty states have a population around 35 million, combined – out of 325 million people in the country. If you count the bottom twenty-one, it's about 38 million – again, compared to 325 million in the country. Out of those twenty-one states, thirteen are solidly Republican, four are solidly Democratic, two lean Democratic, and two are fairly evenly split. Just from those thirteen solidly Republican states, the GOP starts off with twenty-six votes for a filibuster of any Democratic measure. Those thirteen states, by the way, have a combined population of about 25 million people.

Like the Senate itself, the filibuster gives inordinate power to less populated states. The overall effect of the filibuster, therefore, is to compound the problem of unequal representation that already exists in the Senate.

But wait – it gets even better. For many things, the filibuster isn't even required. One senator – yes, *one* senator – can, on his or her own, hold up many pieces of legislation.

Can't be, you say. But it's true. It's called a "hold." And here's how it works:

In order to speed up business in the ultra-slow Senate, the Majority Leader maintains what are known as "unanimous consent agreements" that regulate how a bill is brought to the floor. Basically, these agreements state that no one has any objections to the processing methods of the legislation (such as how much debate time will be allowed).

The idea of the "hold" didn't really become popular until the 1960s. It allows any senator to voice objection to their respective party leader about a bill's process, and to place a hold on the bill, preventing it from coming to the Senate floor. What's perhaps most amazing is that the senator doesn't even have to go on the record as holding up the bill; it can be what's known as a "secret hold." Efforts were made to get rid of the secret hold in 2007, but the parties later disregarded the rule changes, which were easy to get around to begin with. Holds essentially give any senator veto power. Many senators have used them to stop judicial appointments.

So let's review: The Senate is (inherently) a vastly disproportionate body with incredibly unequal representation; the filibuster makes that inequality even worse, allowing a minority of senators to hold up legislation; and the "hold" gives veto power to individual senators, many of whom have used it to indefinitely delay important appointments.

The Senate could change the filibuster and hold rules (and has at times), but changes are difficult in the Senate because entrenched power likes to stay entrenched. If only we could get rid of the Senate….Perhaps a Constitutional amendment could do that. Well, that's not so easy, as you'll soon see.

8. The Amendment Process

At long last! Alice Paul celebrates the passage of the 19th Amendment. Because of our ridiculous amendment process, it took women 133 years to gain the right to vote, and even then it was extraordinarily close.

Not only is our government extremely flawed, it is also extremely hard to alter. The Constitution requires two-thirds of both the House and the Senate, plus three-quarters of the state legislatures in order to be amended. When we first started as a country, that meant ten states were enough to pass an amendment – ten small legislatures to go through. Now it means thirty-eight large ones. Worse than that, though, is the fact that the amendment process treats every state the same, no matter how big or small. That means that, theoretically, the thirteen smallest states could keep an amendment from getting passed. Those thirteen smallest states currently represent less than fifteen million people, out of a country with 325 million people in it. That's just ludicrous.

In our current circumstances, it means that a series of red states like Wyoming, North Dakota, Alabama, and Mississippi can keep progressive amendments from passing, even though such amendments have the support of the much broader population. As noted earlier, the bottom twenty states have a smaller population than California, yet each one counts just the same as California does when it comes to the amendment process. Thirteen of those states are solidly red. Such an arrangement makes any sort of truly progressive amendment, such as guaranteeing health care as a right, virtually impossible.

We've only amended the Constitution twenty-seven times, but really the number is much lower than that when one takes into consideration several factors:

- The first ten Amendments (the Bill of Rights) were essentially agreed upon ahead of time, and were therefore part of the deal for the Constitution's original passage.
- It took a war and a great deal of shenanigans (to say the least) to (fortunately) pass the 13th Amendment. Those shenanigans included the Lincoln Administration helping set up more favorable state legislatures and offering, essentially, bribes for votes in the House.
- The 14th and 15th Amendments were able to be passed largely because the Union still held a great deal of control over the South.
- The 18th and 21st Amendment (regarding Prohibition) do nothing

but cancel each other out.

Some Amendments did such mundane things that we can't exactly mark them as progressive or unifying. The 12th Amendment, for instance, simply clarifies the procedure for electing the president and vice president, while the 20th Amendment just moves up the start dates for the presidency, vice presidency, and Congressional sessions.

This is not to say that we haven't passed some important ones. In addition to the obviously important 13th, 14th, and 15th Amendments, the 16th Amendment gave us the income tax; the 17th gave us the direct election of Senators; the 19th provided for women's suffrage; and the 24th got rid of poll taxes.

But when you do the math, you find out that we've only passed fifteen amendments since 1791 (discounting the 18th and 21st). We now haven't passed an Amendment in twenty-six years, and the prospect for passing one, despite important Constitutional issues (such as money in politics) is practically nonexistent at this point.

Of course, many would argue that our Constitution is up to interpretation, and that we've seen changes to it through the courts. But such interpretational change can only take us so far, and even that is in danger of being undone by strict constructionists on the Supreme Court. In fact, with Kavanaugh taking over Kennedy's seat, you can be sure that judicial activism will decrease.

We need a better, more reasonable system for passing amendments, and one that does not include state legislatures. Other countries aren't anywhere near as restrictive when it comes to altering their constitutions. In France, for instance, amendments go through both their houses, then get approved by national referendum. Alternatively, amendments can simply be passed by a three-fifths joint session of the French congress. Germany only requires two-thirds of each of its houses to approve of amendments. Most amendments to the South African constitution can also be passed with a two-thirds majority of representatives. Since 1997, South Africa has passed seventeen amendments. Seventeen. In that time, we've passed none.

And we need them.

9. Squelching Protest

Miami police on hand for a protest, 2003

"Reflexive control" is a Russian concept that involves making people believe that they are in control and exercising options when, in reality, they're not: their options have been limited, their voices muted, and the information they receive has been filtered. One way this is accomplished is through control of the media. Vladimir Putin is popular in Russia – many Russians like him. But that's largely because he controls the media and rids himself of any possible opponents. The Russians who support Putin think that they're doing so willingly, but really they're doing so because they have an option of one. Reflexive control essentially involves having the trappings of democracy – the appearance of democracy – but no real democracy.

An example: If there are four candidates for president, say, in Madeupistan, and one, through efforts by the current "president," has been charged with money laundering, another can't get on TV, a third has been put up to drain votes from the second, and the last is a "president" who has been in power for a dozen years and gets to appear on TV whenever he wants, control the news cycle, and give out money as he pleases, guess who's going to win? It looks like there were four choices, but really there weren't.

There are protests in Madeupistan, but they're not covered on TV. There's no need to brutally crack down on the protestors because they won't get any attention anyway. They can easily be ignored and waited out, since their protest will have no affect on entrenched power. Could that happen here in the US? The truth is, it already does.

After every mass shooting we hear the standard line about "thoughts and prayers," and then nothing or practically nothing is done. After Parkland, student activists led massive protests throughout the country. But the kids had to go back to school and eventually the news cycle moved on. Sadly, little was accomplished: Florida governor Rick Scott signed a bill to raise the age at which you could buy a gun from 18 to 21 and imposed a three-day waiting period, but that was all. Congress took no action whatsoever, and the Florida legislature easily defeated another bill that would've banned assault rifles.

Occupy Wall Street is another good example. All that camping out, all the protests across the country, and what was the result? Well, nothing pretty much.

I'm not blaming the protestors. The fact of the matter is that they had jobs and families and responsibilities to get back to. After all, 78% of Americans report that they are living paycheck to paycheck. That fact alone makes it difficult to sustain a protest.

When the March on Washington occurred in August of 1963 and Dr. King gave his "I Have a Dream Speech," it was a huge event that attracted national attention. Politicians said, "Wow, 250,000 people came out." And that meant something. Now we have marches that dwarf that, yet politicians simply wait for the tide to pass. Why? Well, they know that eventually people will have to get back to those jobs, families, and responsibilities, and they don't have to worry about the anger of those people since gerrymandering, unlimited campaign donations from rich donors and corporations, and solid party control have made it so that they're often not truly answerable to the people. Plus, as noted earlier, uneven representation in the House and Senate, along with filibusters and holds, make it easy for conservatives to defeat progressive causes. They can just ignore them.

It's truly reflexive control because those marching feel like they're exercising free speech, but really they're exercising it in a bubble: that speech will never truly be heard. Politicians will often just pay the protest no heed whatsoever and sometimes it won't even be covered by networks like Fox "News."

In fact, Fox is excellent at promoting its own brand of reflexive control: Fox viewers think they're making up their minds, but what's really happening is that they're being fed propaganda and told that it's "fair and balanced." It's selective information designed to make viewers reach a certain conclusion. In this way, they're not like CNN or MSNBC. Those stations can be biased at times, but both at least feel bound by a dedication to journalism, even when they fail at it; Fox does not. Fox hosts like Sean Hannity and Jeanine Pirro are personal friends of the president, dishing out his messages, and will never offer critical information. The oligarch Murdoch stirs up anger for ratings. Essentially, Fox has become the propaganda arm of the Republican Party, and of Donald Trump. And Fox crushes the other news networks in terms of viewers, helping people "decide."

When it comes to protesting, we'd like to believe that our voices matter, but often they don't. Often they're ignored or sidelined. We pride ourselves on our First Amendment, but the First Amendment does not make us completely free to speak our minds.

Nearly a hundred years ago, in *Schenck v. United States*, the Supreme Court established the "clear and present danger" doctrine. From this decision we get Oliver Wendell Holmes's famous analogy, stating that freedom of speech does not allow someone to shout fire in a crowded theater. But what's too often forgotten is that the case was about the right to protest a war – in this case, World War I – which was what Schenck had been charged with doing under the Espionage Act of 1917. Schenck, a socialist, had given out fliers encouraging individuals to dodge the draft. And Schenck wasn't the only one the Wilson Administration had charged: they brought numerous cases against people who did nothing more than exercise their free speech by opposing the war.

In *Brandenburg v. Ohio* (1969), the standard was altered somewhat to require "imminent lawless action." Since then, numerous cases have come before the court regarding the notion of dangerous speech. At times the court has held it up and at other times free speech has won out. In *National Socialist Party v. Village of Skokie* (1977), free speech emerged the victor, as it did in *Snyder v. Phelps* (2011). However, *Schenck* has never been overturned, merely reinterpreted, and it is still considered applicable law.

What should also be kept in mind about *Schenck* was that Schenck had been told he couldn't mail out fliers to men eligible for the draft. He couldn't recommend that those men resist what he considered to be an unconstitutional law. Basically, he was kept from appealing to his target audience.

This is often the case with protests today. They are frequently placed in designated "protest areas" or "free speech zones," away from where the protestors want to be. They're kept away from their target audience or from the very people they might be protesting. Police effectively limit the impact of their protest by telling them that they have to be two hundred feet back or on the other side of town. You can speak, so long as you're not too loud and no one can see you.

Worse still, many wrongfully believe that protests should always be polite and non-confrontational. That notion, of course, is preposterous. The very purpose of a protest is to get attention; to make some people feel uncomfortable and force them to reconsider. Here is what Dr. King said in his "Letter from Birmingham Jail":

> You may well ask, "Why direct action, why sit-ins, marches, and so forth? Isn't negotiation a better path?" You are exactly right in your call for negotiation. Indeed, this is the purpose of direct action. Nonviolent direct action seeks to create such a crisis and establish such creative tension that a community that has consistently refused to negotiate is

forced to confront the issue. It seeks so to dramatize the issue that it can no longer be ignored. I just referred to the creation of tension as a part of the work of the nonviolent resister. This may sound rather shocking. But I must confess that I am not afraid of the word "tension." I have earnestly worked and preached against violent tension, but there is a type of constructive nonviolent tension that is necessary for growth. Just as Socrates felt that it was necessary to create a tension in the mind so that individuals could rise from the bondage of myths and half-truths to the unfettered realm of creative analysis and objective appraisal, we must see the need of having nonviolent gadflies to create the kind of tension in society that will help men to rise from the dark depths of prejudice and racism to the majestic heights of understanding and brotherhood. So, the purpose of direct action is to create a situation so crisis-packed that it will inevitably open the door to negotiation.

Of course this is correct. The point of a protest is to stir to action, and no, you don't have to be polite to do so. Protesting public figures who have supported racist and bigoted policies at restaurants, for instance, is not only perfectly acceptable, it's the right thing to do. Should protests take place outside of Paul Ryan's house? You bet. Should they take place outside of Sean Hannity's palatial home on Long Island, where his kids could see? Yes, indeed. Protests should take place where they can be most effective. And if you want them to be effective, you can't simply do them in the manner Republicans have prescribed.

Alice Paul was considered a radical. She was, after all, a militant feminist who demanded suffrage immediately. And where did she go? Right outside the White House. In her case, it was a silent protest, but Woodrow Wilson had to look out his window day after day and see Alice and her fellow suffragettes. Eventually, he came around to supporting a woman's right to vote and helped get the 19th Amendment passed.

At the time, people criticized the way Alice Paul did things. They said she was being uncivilized. What she was being, of course, was effective. The same goes for Martin Luther King, by the way. A 1966 Gallup poll found that 63% of Americans had an unfavorable view of Dr. King. While 12% of respondents reported having a highly favorable view of the reverend, 44% had a highly unfavorable view of him. To them, he was a rebel-rouser, a troublemaker, someone causing problems. But King understood the situation better than all of those people and knew what he had to do.

Yet too many Americans have been convinced that speaking out is somehow unseemly. You can disagree, we're told, but you can't question someone's character, no matter how much they lie or how obvious their self-serving motives; you can protest, but only in certain designated areas; and you shouldn't ever make the target of your protest feel uncomfortable.

Nonsense, of course. Liberals should shed themselves of these notions if they want to be effective. And we should thoroughly reject the idea that we have to speak how conservatives tell us to. We'll get to that next.

10. Restricted Speech

George Carlin in the 1970s. He just didn't give a fuck what the FCC said. Credit: Kevin Armstrong

Puritanism has been haunting America since the earliest days of European colonization. As we'll get into more later, whether you like it or not, the United States is not an entirely secular nation. Forty-four men have been president (Grover Cleveland is counted twice, making Trump the forty-fifth), and all but one, JFK (a Catholic), were Protestants. Forty-four men, forty-four Christians. We are a nation dominated by Christianity, and our laws, language, and mannerisms reflect our Puritan past.

This streak of Puritanism has been affecting us for hundreds of years now. It's one thing, of course, if certain people want to limit themselves and treat the word fuck or the word shit as if it's taboo and never to be uttered. It's another thing entirely, though, when they try to apply such rules to everyone else, making it so that there's no cursing on TV, on the radio, or in schools.

Wait! you say. *Schools? Did he say schools? Does he mean elementary, middle, and high schools?* No. I mean preschool, kindergarten, elementary, middle, high schools, vocational schools, and any other school you can think of. And I'm not suggesting that children shouldn't be disciplined for poor behavior; I'm simply saying that cursing alone doesn't make for it.

Imagine a scenario, if you will: Vera, a school bully, goes up to another little girl named Emily in the schoolyard and says, "Emily, you are just so fat and ugly!" She keeps repeating it, and Emily starts to cry. Another little girl, Sarah, sees what's going on, walks up, and says to Vera, "Hey, why don't you fuck off?" Vera, chicken-shit bully that she is, immediately slinks away. Sarah then turns to Emily and says, "Don't listen to that idiot, you're fucking beautiful!" Emily immediately brightens.

But a teacher hears it and grabs Sarah, dragging her into the principal's office. Sarah tells the principal the entire story. Emily is called in to confirm it and does. What is the result? Vera is told not to tease people, but Sarah receives five days detention for using "such language." She must also agree never to curse again or be suspended. And yet, she did nothing wrong.

Smaller kids are no different. There's no rhyme or reason to how we try to control their language, even when they've said nothing wrong. No one has been able to explain to me why it's OK for a four-year-old to say "poopie" or "caca," yet not OK for him to say "shit." "Mama, I made a shit" is no worse than "Mama, I made a caca."

This is not just a matter of personal choice – we've codified language – codified how people are allowed to speak.

In *FCC v. Pacifica* (1978), the Supreme Court decided that the FCC has the right to make decisions about "obscene" or "indecent" material and to ban it from the airwaves. The case involved a routine performed by comedian George Carlin over the radio that was about "filthy words" that could not be said on TV. Carlin said the words were: shit, piss, cunt, fuck, cocksucker, motherfucker, and tits. A man who had been listening with his son complained and the FCC took action. The court sided with the FCC, and since then the FCC has limited what we can see and hear over our airwaves.

According to the FCC:

Title 18 of the United States Code, Section 1464, prohibits the utterance of any obscene, indecent or profane language by means of radio communication...

Profane language includes those words that are so highly offensive that their mere utterance in the context presented may, in legal terms, amount to a nuisance. In its Golden Globe Awards Order the FCC warned broadcasters that, depending on the context, it would consider the F-Word and those words (or variants thereof) that are as highly offensive as the F-Word to be profane language that cannot be broadcast between 6 a.m. and 10 p.m.

Consider for a moment what this is saying: in a country that prides itself on free speech, the FCC is not going to allow us to hear the word "fuck" over the airwaves, even though there is no evidence that this word truly hurts anyone. It's also going to decide what words may similarly be "offensive" and could potentially go after broadcasters or individuals for uttering them. This seems like a clear violation of the doctrine of separation of church and state, as the FCC's decision-making appears to be largely geared toward religious sensibilities.

And the FCC's influence goes beyond its authority. Even cable subscription services, which are, by and large, not regulated by the FCC, still tend to apply FCC standards. Networks such as CNN, TBS, and even FX censor their material. Popular podcasts also often warn about cursing, as if we need to ready ourselves or make sure no children will hear those "dirty words" because, as everyone knows, if children hear curses, they immediately turn to booze, heroin, and violence. They become degenerates. They hear a curse and go, "Well, that's it for rules and civility! Time to go rob a liquor store!" It's ridiculous, and yet we allow it.

And it's not just cursing. Our self-imposed Puritanism also often prevents us from simply telling the truth. Trump surrogates like Jason Miller or Kellyanne Conway can go on TV and lie with impunity, unafraid that anyone will call them out for it. After all, that would be *unprofessional*! Not true, of course; what it would actually be is correct.

Government and self-imposed language restrictions are some of the ways that our freedom of speech is being done-in by our own self-destruction. Another is by the slow death of professional journalism.

11. An Insufficient and Undermined Media

Credit: DonkeyHotey

A healthy, free press is essential for any democracy. Even before the US was its own country, the concept of a free press was upheld in the famed case of John Peter Zenger in 1733. Freedom of Speech is enshrined in our 1st Amendment.

But now that freedom is under attack, including by our president and his administration. Donald Trump has repeatedly attempted to undermine our institutions by calling reputable sources “fake news,” and by selectively disenfranchising them in favor of pseudo-news groups more favorable to him, such as Breitbart and Newsmax. We are currently experiencing propaganda media like that which used to exist in the 1800s, when political parties had their own newspapers and stuck to scripted narratives. The president, meanwhile, continues to spread falsities through social media, using Twitter as his own personal propaganda machine.

Since the election of Donald Trump, Reporters Without Borders has lowered the US on its World Press Freedom Index from 41st to 45th (out of 180 nations). The UK, by contrast, ranks 40th, Germany 15th, and Norway 1st. RWB cites insufficient protection of whistleblowers (which preceded Trump) and Trump's declaring that the news media is the "enemy of the people" as part of the reasoning behind the ranking. This is hardly a great result for a country that prides itself on its First Amendment.

Let's be clear: professional journalism is not dead, but it is, at the least, down on the mat and being counted out. As Ryan Holiday has pointed out in his tell-all, *Trust Me, I'm Lying*, the era of reliable, subscription journalism has been largely stamped out by an oppressive demand for page hits at any cost. American attention spans have gotten shorter and articles have gotten shorter to accommodate them. Holiday quotes Nick Denton of the now defunct *Gawker* telling a prospective writer that pieces should be "one hundred words long. Two hundred, max." And that "any good idea can be expressed at that length."

But it's not simply the internet. Fox "News" is truly little but a propaganda network that was created to stoke people's anger with irrational fears. If you're going to turn on that channel tonight, I can save you the time: host after host will agree with Donald Trump. They'll condemn Democrats in the harshest of terms and cry out about the "mainstream media," a term which they use to condemn those who don't share their extreme right-wing agenda. Fox "News" is so terrible, in fact, that a Farleigh Dickinson poll from 2012 found that viewers who used it as their sole news source knew less about current events than people who watched no news at all (though the American people as a whole also did pretty terrible, frankly).

But Fox isn't alone. Donald Trump also has Chris Ruddy's Newsmax network and David Pecker's American Media on his side. You might recall that Pecker was kind enough to buy the Karen McDougal story that might have been incredibly damaging to Trump. It was a clear case of "catch and kill," as they call it, to stop the story from getting out. Pecker has described himself as a close friend of Trump's, as has Ruddy.

And the propaganda has worked! Forty-eight percent of Republicans now believe that "the news media is the enemy of the American people," while only 28% say it is not. Seventy-nine percent of Republicans agreed that "the mainstream media treats President Trump unfairly."

It's pretty clear that these propaganda networks are having an enormous impact.

And other networks, though definitely not on the propaganda side of things, have too often sold-out for ratings. CNN, now a target of the Trump administration, helped Donald Trump get to the presidency in the first place by presenting extremists like Kayleigh McEnany and Jeffrey Lord as if they were reasonable people and by replacing journalism with panels. The network could seek out information by interviewing scientists, professors, and economists, but they'd much prefer to go for ratings by engaging in faux debates.

To make matters worse, the media can't seem to get out of the Overton window. Certain topics are either taboo or just beyond the range of possibilities they're willing to consider. When was the last time you heard a panel discussion on CNN about whether or not we should replace the Constitution? Or make Puerto Rico a state? Or legalize prostitution? Do they ever have a discussion about religion and its effect on our politics? Of course not.

To make matters worse, networks practice a form of etiquette that bends to fabricators and condemns truth-tellers. No matter how much a Trump surrogate – be it Rudy Giuliani, Sebastian Gorka, or any other Trump stooge lies, dissembles, and misleads, no anchor or fellow panelist is permitted to call out the lie or call that person a liar. In fact, many anchors go out of their way to let viewers know that they're friends with the political figures they're interviewing. Even Rachel Maddow did this when she interviewed Kellyanne Conway during the 2016 campaign, despite the fact that Conway was supporting a bigot for president. She even went so far as to congratulate her for becoming the head of Trump's campaign. More recently, none other than Chris Cuomo – CNN anchor and brother of Democratic Governor of New York Andrew Cuomo – when interviewing Rudy Giuliani, made sure to let us all know what good friends they are, in the most sycophantic of fashions. If this doesn't both disgust and concern you, it should.

Part of the reason for this is that the media and those they cover have become far too cozy. This isn't a completely new problem: any politician with any sense at all tries to buddy up with reporters. JFK, for one, cultivated close relationships with the media and benefited from biased coverage.

But now the media and the political class have almost blended into one. To begin with, too many of them started out as political people before crossing over to the networks – George Stephanopoulos, Nicolle Wallace, Chris Matthews, Mike Huckabee, Jeanine Pirro – to name a few. Many more, of course, appear as frequent panelists and guests on show like *Anderson Cooper, 360.* Before CNN fired him, Jeffrey Lord was on Cooper's program practically every night. Now Cooper fills up his panel with Republican and Democratic "strategists." Cooper knows what he can expect from many of them, since their answers are incredibly biased. He himself once joked to Lord that he would find a way to defend Trump if the president took a shit on his desk in the Oval Office. And yet he continued to have him on his show. Why?

As Mark Leibovich brilliantly detailed in his pre-Trump era book, *The Town*, there's simply too much hobnobbing. D.C. has become too much like L.A., with everyone trying to get on TV. Rather than reporters viewing politicians and their subordinates as people to keep tabs on, they view them as friends to get quotes from.

One of the worst examples is the White House Correspondents Dinner. Not only has the entire affair become a cultural joke, attended by Duck Dynasty cast members and Don Lemon alike, but it's truly a travesty for professional journalism. The attendants act as if they're all just actors coming out from behind the camera for a while. Or sports stars who are really all friends, because although they appear on opposing sides on TV, it's really just in good fun and there's no hard feelings.

It's preposterous, of course. Someone should tell the anchors at CNN, Fox, MSNBC, and elsewhere: these people are not your friends. Nor should they be. Reporters should treat political figures like deer treat lions: watch them carefully and never get too close.

This is not to say that there aren't still great journalists out there doing fantastic work. Some fine reporting about the Trump administration has been produced by the *New York Times*, the *Washington Post*, the *Wall Street Journal*, *Bloomberg*, the AP, and (yes) even CNN, as well as numerous others.

But the overall dynamic has shifted, in part because of failures by the networks themselves, in part due to social media and its impact, and in part from the unrelenting attacks from the president and his media propaganda machine. Considering all of that, it should come as no surprise that our democracy is suffering from another great ill: an uninformed electorate.

12. An Uninformed Electorate

A healthy republic requires an informed electorate. If the people are uneducated, they are ill-equipped to participate in the democratic process. An uninformed electorate can easily be duped by demagogues and charlatans, as we're seeing now.

According to Pew, 67% of Americans get at least some news from social media, with 20% using it as their main news source. 45% get at least some of their news on Facebook, and we know how that worked out in 2016….

But it's not just that people consider social media a worthwhile resource – it's *why* they do. Social media – be it Twitter, Reddit, Facebook, or what have you – is usually short and sweet. People don't want to take the time and read and go into details. That's not to say that someone can't start off hearing something on Twitter and then look into it – there's no denying that social media can be great for reaching people. And some of those people will take the time to investigate what they hear.

Unfortunately, though, many won't. And one of the main reasons for that is that we're becoming a society that just doesn't read.

Now, wait! Before you dismiss what I'm saying like I'm a crotchety old man complaining about how "things were better in my day," be aware of two things: One, I'm actually just 38, so "my day" wasn't all that long ago. And Two, I've got the numbers to back it up.

The Bureau of Labor Statistics reports that the average American spends some 2 hours and 47 minutes watching TV on a typical day, and only 19 minutes reading for leisure. It's true! See for yourself. If you figure that the average American life span is approximately 80 years, that means that, on average, we spend over nine years watching TV (not including sleep time). You can do the math yourself: 2.75 hours a day (rounding off), times 365 days a year (keeping it simple), times 80 = 80,300 hours of TV in a typical American lifetime. Divide that number by 24 and then by 365 and you get over 9 years of television. Now for reading: .32 hours a day (rounding), times 365, times 80 = 9,344. Divide that by 24 and by 365 and you get just over a year.

Of course, you also have to keep in mind that some people (like you, perhaps, since you're reading this book) raise the average when it comes to reading while their opposites tend to watch more TV. In other words, people who do more reading usually tend to watch less TV, whereas people who watch more TV tend to do less reading. In all likelihood, then, many Americans are probably spending twelve or thirteen years of their lives watching TV and only a few months reading.

And the numbers are worse for younger people than older ones: according to the BLS, the average American 75 and older reads for 51 minutes a day, while the average 20-34-year-old read for just 7 minutes! Now, to be fair, older people have more leisure time, it's true. But look at that difference! (And if you're going, "Well, what about reading things like texts?" – No, they don't count and No, they shouldn't.) Back in 1978, Gallup surveyed American adults and found that only 8% hadn't picked up a book in a year. In Pew's latest study, that number stood at 24% – it's tripled! And just from 2004 to 2017, the number of Americans 15 and older who cracked open a book just for their own interest went from about 28% to 19%.

We're just not reading!

And we're not hacking it academically either. The Programme for International Student Assessment (PISA), designed by the Organization for Economic Cooperation and Development, measures the skills of students around the world by testing fifteen-year-olds in math, reading, and science. It's most recent round of tests in 2015 included just over 70 countries. The US ranked 24th in reading, 25th in science, and 38th in math – just above the average scores for OECD countries in the first two categories and well below the average in the third – pretty atrocious for the world's wealthiest nation.

Our college graduation rates aren't much better: only 54.8% of entering college freshman graduate within six years. According to the Census Bureau (2017), only 33.4% of our population, twenty-five and older, has obtained a bachelor's degree or better.

Academically, our college system certainly isn't terrible, and I don't want to detract from my own argument by exaggerating. When all tertiary learning is included (college, vocational schools, etc.), the US doesn't fare too poorly, ranking 6th. In fact, eight out of ten of the highest ranked universities in the world are in the US.

Yet the US used to be the ranked #1 in terms of college graduates with an associate degree or better. And now, several countries have bypassed us. Worse still, we're now 11th or 12th (depending on how you use the data) when just comparing 25-34-year-olds.

Why is this happening? Well, for one, college costs are becoming prohibitive for many, especially if you can't finagle some sort of scholarship. Also: many high school grads who were pushed up before they were ready are finding that they just can't hack it in college and are dropping out. Many college kids also have to choose between working and going to school, and so they put off college, maybe forever.

But academic performance is not the only problem. There's also a dangerous trend of simply not accepting science or believing in the importance of education anymore. According to Pew, 58% of Republicans or those who lean Republican said they have a negative view of the impacts of going to college; only one-third of Americans fully accept evolution; less than half of Americans believe that humans are driving global warming. A National Science Foundation survey found that a quarter of all Americans think the Sun goes around the Earth. In a HuffPost/YouGov poll, 45% of Americans said that they believe in ghosts. Over 70% believe in angels.

Probably not big fans of science

This type of ignorance plagues the decisions we make, affecting the votes we cast and the policies we support. For instance, despite the widely-held belief that welfare fraud is rampant, it's actually less than 2%. Yet the impact of such a misguided notion is probably responsible for the fact that 33% of Republicans think the government does too much to help the poor.

As many have pointed out, we seem to have entered a post-truth society, wherein a large portion of the populace believes that facts are simply one way of seeing things. And a democracy without facts is not a successful democracy.

How did this happen? Well, our inadequate educational system has combined with an anti-intellectual movement to create a poorly equipped electorate.

Let's talk some more about that educational system…

13. A Weak Educational System

A strong educational system is key to a thriving democracy. Without it, we risk reflexive control, wherein choices are limited, upward mobility is largely stagnant, and a general malaise sets in amongst the voting public, leading to nonparticipation and a failure of citizens to exercise their civic duties.

The US used to rank well ahead of other OECD (Organization for Economic Cooperation and Development) nations in terms of college graduates. In 1995, we were ahead of all other OECD countries. But by 2014, we ranked 19th out of 28. Our number of college graduates had not dipped – it had in fact slightly increased. But other nations had caught up with us and surpassed us, and the average percentage for all OECD countries had nearly doubled, from 20% to 38%.

Liz Weston, interpreting the results for *Business Insider*, noted:

"Twenty-nine percent of American men and 17 percent of American women had less education than their parents, compared with the OECD average of 19 percent for men and 13 percent for women. Twenty percent of U.S. men and 27 percent of U.S. women had more education than their folks, compared with the OECD average of 28 percent and 36 percent, respectively."

The OECD report found that the US is considered a country with "less equitable access" to higher education. Whereas other nations allow young people to attend college for free or at least not force a tremendous amount of debt upon students, the US system is more restrictive.

Still, our colleges themselves are fairly good: students at our universities engage in healthy competition with one another, standards are generally rigorous, professors tend to be highly qualified, and a great deal of fine research comes out of our institutions.

But some of the better aspects of the college educational system are lacking in our K-12 system. Colleges have not suffered from the "self-esteem" movement, which is based on no empirical evidence and has done a vast amount of damage, as I noted in an article for the *Daily News*. In college, if you fail, you fail – there is no "social promotion." As a general rule, students get no credit for "effort" in college – either they understand the course material or they do not. And although grades in college may be inflated, they are generally not based on how much a teacher likes a student – oftentimes professors don't even know which student's exam they're grading. Heck, much of the time it's a TA doing the grading anyhow.

Unfortunately, the standards upheld at most colleges don't trickle down to K-12 schools. Most US schools base their teaching methods on unscientific traditions rather than on more efficient methods established by research. For example, many schools are now employing a "sight word" system to teach reading, even though there is no empirical research to back it up and it hasn't produced any improvements. In fact, according to the National Assessment of Educational Progress, known as "the nation's report card," only 37% of our high school seniors are proficient in reading. But it gets worse: the proficiency number for high school seniors was just 25% in math, merely 22% in science, and only 20% when it comes to geography. Heck, only 12% were proficient in US History! That's the country they live in! When it comes to civics, just 24% made the cut, meaning that, by and large, they don't understand how their own government works. How, then, are they going to participate in it?

This is a serious issue. An uneducated country is a country in which the people will be uninformed and unaware.

Uneducated Americans is how we got to Donald Trump. But that's not all: it also helped cause the housing crisis in 2008 and subsequent Great Recession, has led to a disbelief in climate change, and has led to an overall inability of Americans to decipher fact from fiction, which has done tremendous damage to the state of our politics.

Our educational system is also incredibly discriminatory: it largely favors the wealthy, who tend to be disproportionately white. The main reason for this is that the entire system is based mainly on property taxes. Sure, the federal government can give grants to help correct the inadequacies, but they don't go nearly far enough in doing so. It would make much more sense to have a federal system that guaranteed each child an equal opportunity education. There's two reasons it doesn't happen, though: the first is the real estate lobby and the second is that well-to-do white people would largely freak out: They bought homes in pricey neighborhoods in part so that their kids could get better educations. If all of a sudden the government tried to level the playing field, many of them would probably be quite angry.

And yet, when you look at the best school systems in the world, they tend to be the best, in part, because they are able to direct resources to where they're most needed. Japan's system operates through prefectures, which are kind of like states, unlike our system, which goes more by localities. The result is that poor Japanese children receive extremely similar educations to wealthier ones.

In Finland, the entire system is nationalized. Finland also, unlike the US, takes seriously the latest developments in educational research. They make sure that their teachers were themselves top students. And, not surprisingly, they thoroughly kick our ass in global educational assessments.

As described by *Smithsonian* magazine:

> Finland's schools are publicly funded. The people in the government agencies running them, from national officials to local authorities, are educators, not business people, military leaders or career politicians. Every school has the same national goals and draws from the same pool of university-trained educators. The result is that a

Finnish child has a good shot at getting the same quality education no matter whether he or she lives in a rural village or a university town. The differences between weakest and strongest students are the smallest in the world, according to the most recent survey by the Organization for Economic Co-operation and Development (OECD).

In contrast, the IMF found that excessive poverty in America creates "disparities in the education system, hampering human capital formation and eating into future productivity."

Some of it also comes down to the respect given to teachers by society. If you think about it, investing in teachers should be a no-brainer – we should want the best people teaching our children. Insisting on highly qualified teachers and paying them high salaries makes a great deal of economic sense. After all, they're helping create our future. If, on the other hand, you allow uneducated people to teach our children, then the children won't receive stellar educations, and we'll have less students growing up to become brilliant doctors, engineers, and inventors. We'll basically be shooting ourselves in the foot, which is what we've been doing for generations now.

We're not getting the most out of our students. And worse, we're not always promoting the most qualified people.

14. Lack of a Meritocracy

In high school I had a Health teacher everyone called Fritz. Fritz was a bearded, liberal guy with gray-white hair and square glasses. He was skinny and energetic and would run around the room eliciting answers from students whether they had raised their hands or not. His classroom was pretty much an open discussion forum, where no issue was off the table.

I believe it was the first day of class that Fritz asked us why we were there. The question took most of us aback, since we weren't quite sure what he was asking. Why were we in his class? Well, we had to take Health and it fit in our schedule. But that's not what he meant. I remember the exchange went something like this:

"Why are you in school?" he asked.

"In high school?" we said.

In school at all, he explained.

"To get good grades," some said, with others nodding along.

"And why do you want to get good grades?"

"To get into a good college."

"And why do you want to get into a good college?"

"To get a good job."

"And why do you want to get a good job?"

"To make a lot of money, I guess."

"And why do you want to make a lot of money?"

"So that we can get stuff?"

"So that you can get stuff. OK. What kind of stuff?"

"A big house…a nice car maybe…"

"A nice car?"

"Yeah."

"Like a Porsche or a Mercedes?"

"Yeah."

"So, let me get this straight: the whole purpose of all of this – all of your schooling, from age four till age twenty-two – or longer if you go on to become a doctor or lawyer or something like that – all of those years of schooling, all of those hours you put in, all of that time from your life, is simply so that you can someday – maybe twenty-five, thirty years from when you start – *someday* – you can drive a really nice car?"

There was silence.

Fritz was right. A lot of those kids didn't really understand the purpose of getting an education, and many kids still don't understand the purpose today. To them, education is simply a time investment with a financial reward at the end.

Now, I have nothing against earning money – money is important – you'll need it to own a home, to pay for food, and to live a less stressful life. But if you're one of the young people getting an education right now and you think it's all about driving a Porsche one day or being able to vacation every year in the Bahamas, you've got it very, very wrong.

So what is education about?

Your education should be about expanding your mind, broadening your horizons, and embracing new ideas. It should be about satisfying your curiosity. And if you don't have any curiosity, you probably shouldn't go to college at all. Your education should help make you a greater asset to society, and you should emerge from school better prepared to understand others and do more for them.

And your education also shouldn't end. Ever.

If you leave education in your rearview mirror when you leave college, you're going to spend the rest of your life growing ever more ignorant. Education should continue throughout your lifetime, and if you don't know a lot more now than you did last year, you're doing something terribly wrong.

Unfortunately, many kids do go to college with the wrong idea. They're career-oriented, rather than learning-oriented. This is part of the reason why we often don't end up with the best people in their respective positions: they're eager to increase their bank accounts rather than being eager to increase their knowledge base.

In his book *Excellent Sheep*, Yale professor William Deresiewicz outlines the failures of our meritocracy, questioning how much of a meritocracy it truly is. The criteria for getting into America's top schools is biased and often ridiculous, he argues. Kids are expected to actively participate in five or six clubs in high school, play an instrument, and get straight-A's. Not that grades don't matter – they do. And surely good grades are a sign of higher intelligence. But most of the Ivy League schools give credit for school activities, yet no credit for working at McDonald's to help pay for clothes for yourself; they (like other schools) give preference to legacies – those whose parents or grandparents or siblings have attended the university, despite the fact that no other country on Earth engages in this obviously discriminatory practice; they give favor to those whose parents may have donated a building or to those who look like they'll have more promising financial careers. If you want to be the world's best nurse, you can forget about going to Harvard, Yale, or Dartmouth.

Deresiewicz argues that we're churning kids out like robots, many of whom lack passion and have no true direction. They only know that they want to make money. As he wrote for *The New Republic*:

I taught many wonderful young people during my years in the Ivy League — bright, thoughtful, creative kids whom it was a pleasure to talk with and learn from. But most of them seemed content to color within the lines that their education had marked out for them. Very few were passionate about ideas. Very few saw college as part of a larger project of intellectual discovery and development. Everyone dressed as if they were ready to be interviewed at a moment's notice.

Despite what many believe, Deresiewicz says, the best people do not necessarily rise to the top. In fact, usually it's those who took the fewest risks and made sure never to offend anyone. Yes, there are the Steve Jobses and Jeff Bezoses of the world who take tremendous risks and get paid off with enormous dividends. But those are the exceptions. In most workplaces, you don't get ahead by challenging the boss, but by agreeing with him.

College is no different. They're not necessarily looking for truly inquiring minds, but far too often are seeking what Deresiewicz classifies as a "return on investment." Let's face it: colleges have huge endowments – tens of billions of dollars worth when you're talking about some of the elite universities. They're looking for future alum to fill those coffers.

I don't mean to sound overly sinister here, and neither, I'm sure, does Mr. Deresiewicz. Surely there are still young people out there who are willing to challenge societal norms and are motivated more by what is right than by what is profitable. If I didn't believe in young people, I probably wouldn't have written this book. And no, I don't think that our universities don't take into account personal hardship, individual achievement, and expressions of curiosity. They still appreciate hearing that kids want to learn for learning's sake. It would also be wrong to blame one university or even a group of them for this problem; it's a systematic problem with a history.

Surely, though, colleges could take certain steps to help create a more meritocratic system.

They can start by ending legacies. Giving an edge to legacies is an antiquated practice that helps maintain the status quo for the wealthy and upper-middle class and has no societal benefit. Frankly, it should be outlawed on a national level for what it is: class discrimination. No student should ever receive preferential treatment just because granddad also attended Princeton. It's ridiculous, and a way to keep minorities out of top schools. (Affirmative Action, unfortunately, has not helped much when it comes to reverse this trend, as we'll get to later in the Racism section).

We're also suffering from an epidemic of grade inflation. Between 1998 and 2016, the average GPA for students at private high schools who took the SAT rose from 3.25 to 3.51. That's an 8% jump for a GPA that was probably already inflated. At suburban high schools, GPAs rose from 3.25 to 3.36, a 3% jump. But in city public schools, the average went from 3.26 to 3.28 – almost no change whatsoever. Keep in mind that that's only for those who took the SAT, and that, percentage-wise, considerably more wealthy and middle-class students take the SAT or ACT than poorer students.

You can imagine how this grade inflation occurs: First off, many teachers want to give kids A's because they like them personally and want them to succeed. It's understandable. The teachers are aware that the grades they give kids will have an impact on their lives, and so they give extra-credit projects or bonus questions on tests so that their students will score highly. Each teacher is also aware that the grades they give often reflect on their own job performance: if a teacher gives out too many poor grades, he or she can expect to be questioned by the principal. If all the students seem to do well, the teacher is praised. A teacher who grades objectively risks being unfavorably compared to their fellow educators. And the last thing a teacher wants is for a suburban mother to come up to the school to complain about them because they're "too hard," "unfair," or "doing a poor job" in some way.

Sadly that does happen. It stems from a feeling of entitlement: some suburban parents cannot accept that their kid simply didn't make the grade. It can't be their child, they reason, and so it must be the teacher or the school. And they will raise bloody hell to get what they want. Whereas poor parents working two jobs just to make ends meet don't have the time, resources, energy, or inclination to make such demands.

And so the well-to-do kids' grades are inflated and they come to expect nothing less. One Harvard professor caused some controversy in 2013 when he questioned the grade distribution at that esteemed institution: He said that he heard a rumor that the most common grade given at the school is an A-. The dean corrected him: the median grade is an A-, he said. The most common grade given is an A.

We're in an age where every kid gets a trophy and too many who come from well-off backgrounds expect to succeed no matter what. Once again, to quote Deresiewicz:

> The prospect of *not* being successful terrifies them, disorients them. The cost of falling short, even temporarily, becomes not merely practical, but existential. The result is a violent aversion to risk. You

have no margin for error, so you avoid the possibility that you will ever make an error. Once, a student at Pomona told me that she'd love to have a chance to think about the things she's studying, only she doesn't have the time. I asked her if she had ever considered not trying to get an A in every class. She looked at me as if I had made an indecent suggestion.

We're not producing inquiring minds; we're producing careerists – people who want to go into law or politics, even, in order to get rich. Kids who want to go work on Wall Street because that's where the money is. And the worst part is that we as a society have condoned it; we've developed an ends-justify-the-means mentality – "He who dies with the most toys wins," as Malcolm Forbes said. We celebrate reality TV stars who act with callousness and worship the wealthy as if they are gods to be emulated.

As an educator, I've often had kids tell me that they don't feel they should learn more than what's going to be on the test. Worse still, the parents seem to be OK with this. Reading drops off for American kids around eleven-years-old because after that parents tend not to care if they're learning and inquisitive, so long as they're getting good grades. (Sadly, as noted earlier, the parents often don't read themselves, so who are they to criticize their children?) We have kids cram information into their heads so that they can get a high score on a test, then let them forget it all. They often don't learn much other than how to game the system. We're teaching them how to do the least possible and still "succeed."

The Opt-Out movement is a good example. Realizing how far behind we had fallen, business leaders, philanthropists, politicians, teachers, administrators, and child psychologists worked together to set up certain standards for students to meet, known as the Common Core. The program wasn't perfect by any means, and needed some revisions. But overall it was a reasonable set of standards that had been years in the making, with efforts led by the 100% charitable Gates Foundation.

But a problem arose: suburban parents began to complain that the test was "unfair" or "too stressful." Why? Well, many of them couldn't bear to hear that their children might not be excelling as much as they thought. In fact, as the National Assessment of Educational Progress had indicated and as many educators familiar with the inflated-grades phenomenon already knew, a lot of these kids weren't nearly as advanced as some of the parents wanted to think. In fact, a lot of them were truly behind in terms of reading and mathematics.

And so these parents – almost entirely white and suburban – fought against the Common Core and its testing requirements. Some conspiracy-minded Opt-Outers claimed that the effort was led by testing companies looking to make a profit (it wasn't, of course; they just got the windfall from it). Others said "no test can judge my child!" (They're wrong, obviously – tests, which have no emotions, do a better job of gauging children's abilities than parents or teachers, who have emotional investments.) And so they refused to allow their kids to take the test: they "opted-out." And school administrators and politicians, rather than push back, largely caved, allowing parents to choose to not have their kids take important diagnostic exams. It's as silly as refusing to have your kid take a medical test because you're afraid you might get bad news. There has been no empirical evidence that the Common Core tests are in any way traumatic for kids or that they cause any damage whatsoever. Yet if you read anecdotes online, you'd think having a kid take a state-orchestrated test is akin to giving them Chinese water torture.

It comes down to expectations. Many parents look at school grades and college admissions as if they're grades for the parents themselves. If young Emily doesn't get into a top school, they've failed as a parent, they figure. And so everything must be done to ensure that Emily winds up at Harvard or Yale or Northwestern. They'll bully teachers if they have to, pay for tutors and college admissions advisors, and pressure friends to write letters for kids they barely know.

And what is the result? Well, we get kids of privilege in positions they're in no way suited for. Imagine a kid, if you will, with mediocre grades who winds up at UPenn; then at his wealthy father's business; then uses his father's connections to secure loans and receive political favors; then causes numerous bankruptcies and gets special arrangements from the courts to pay off his debts; then starts a dubious company on the stock exchange just to pay off his debts and rebuild himself, while investors lose out; then participates in numerous scams that cheat people out of their money, yet avoids prison time somehow; is a consistent tax cheat as well; and, on top of all that, repeatedly shows himself to be a racist, bigot, and sexist, even going so far as to admit that he has blatantly sexually assaulted women.

What would become of such a white, wealthy, Christian male in America?

Well, he's president of the United States.

Trump is the epitome of our plutocracy: a man who hasn't finished a book in fifty years and has the verbal skills of an eight-year-old.

But Trump's not alone. Sure, he benefitted from nepotism, the privileges of wealth, and a white-male-dominated society, but so did others. His kids, for instance. Something tells me that Donald Trump Jr. wasn't somehow uniquely qualified to run the Trump Organization, though one could argue that his singular disregard for morality may have inclined him to the position. Nor did Ivanka or Eric earn their positions by anything but birth. And son-in-law Jared is about as qualified to serve in the White House as Mickey Mouse is to be Secretary-General of the UN.

Trump, by the way, wasn't the only president we've had recently who was woefully unsuited for the job and helped along by nepotism: George W. Bush, though not the racist Trump is, was obviously in way above his head and was nothing but a walking disaster. He's an ideal example of nepotism at work – talk about a guy who was in no way prepared to take on a job, yet took it on with swagger. The result was a disastrous war in Iraq that left hundreds of thousands dead; the Hurricane Katrina fiasco that resulted in 1800 deaths; the global financial crisis, which the administration deserves at least some of the blame for; and backwards environmental and tax policies – just to name a few.

When we fail to tax wealth appropriately and allow dynasties to be created, we wind up with utterly unprepared people in important positions. And they appoint their friends to other important positions. And the cycle goes on.

It's actually alarming how many people who should be authorities on a subject don't know what they're talking about – English teachers who can't put together a proper sentence; political pundits who don't know the first thing about the history or topic they're discussing; news anchors who think journalism is about presenting "both sides" rather than about getting at the facts.

We have movies "based on true stories" that are only true if by "based" they mean 99% bullshit. We have "museums" dedicated to teaching "Intelligent Design," which is designed to fool people who aren't too intelligent or would rather not know facts. And we have senators who think that global warming isn't real because they have seen it snow.

We'd like to believe that the most intelligent, most qualified people rise to the top. But what more often happens is that those people – the ones who question things or don't go along with the program – are frequently relegated to the back. In their place are the people who go along, don't question, don't upset anyone, have a rich parent, are overly aggressive, and don't let morals get in the way of their financial success.

We should be rewarding good character, perseverance, honesty, and integrity. Instead our laws, tax system, colleges, and courts largely favor the established class. Nepotism in government and in business has run rampant, and less qualified people have wound up in positions of tremendous power and influence.

The truth is, there isn't much of a meritocracy in America. A legitimate meritocracy would require a great deal more socialism.

Why is that?, you might ask.

Because a meritocracy requires a much more level playing field than currently exists in the United States. To have a true meritocracy, you would have to guarantee each child access to a high-quality education; we don't. To have a true meritocracy, you'd have make sure that everyone has access to health care, so that no one would have to worry about going bankrupt due to a stay at the hospital. To have a true meritocracy, you'd have to address the wealth gap and make the rich pay their fair share, do more to end class and race discrimination, and improve the social safety net so that no one would get caught in the economic abyss of poverty and immobility.

The pity of having no true meritocracy isn't simply that you wind up with people in positions of power and influence who shouldn't be there, but also that so many who should have their chance won't get it – inspired business leaders with no access to capital; brilliant writers who can't get published; honest politicians turned away by the system; talented engineers overstepped by the mediocre; creative students denied entry into elite universities because of unfair admissions practices; sincere, hardnosed journalists who can't compete against those willing to sell-out to the lowest common denominator; and on and on and on. These people will often never receive their opportunity to shine, while the sons and daughters of the well-placed and wealthy will get a ticket stamped "Automatic Entry."

It's not so hard to score if you're born on third base. But we're supposed to be "The Land of Opportunity," no? Everyone is supposed to have a decent shot at success, right?

Well, let's examine that notion some.

15. We're No Longer the "Land of Opportunity"

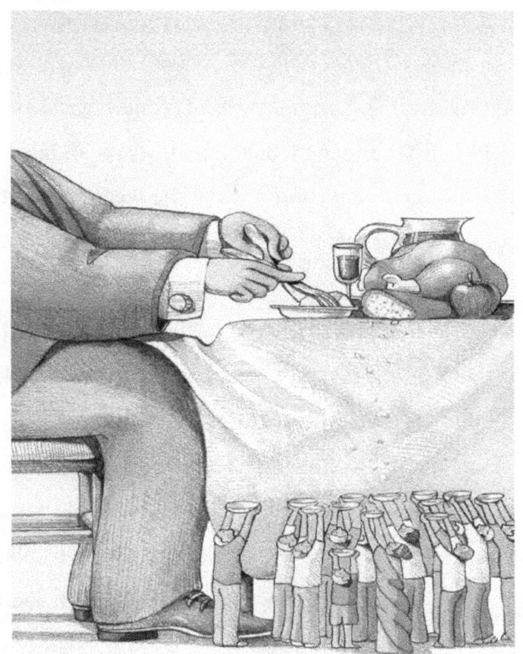

According to the Brookings Institution, 42% of those born in the bottom fifth of the economic ladder in the United States will remain there as adults, and only 8% will ever make it to the top fifth. In European countries, by contrast, the first number tends to be 25% to 30% and the latter 11% to 14%. In America, if you're born poor, you tend to stay poor.

While calculating real wages can be a tricky business, depending on whether you employ the CPI or a GDP price deflator, it's undeniable that many of the gains since 1970 have gone to the upper 10% and the upper 1% in particular. With the destruction of unions (coming up later), the lower and middle classes have seen their portions of the pie shrink. The average CEO at the top 500 companies makes 250-300 times what the average worker makes (depending on whose stats you use). Between 1980 and 2015, while the bottom 90% of Americans saw just a .03% gain, the top .01% of Americans – our richest – saw an increase of 322%. The richest 10% of Americans hold 76% of the wealth. And the minimum wage, which, for some reason, isn't tied to inflation, has effectively shrunk.

This wasn't just happenstance. As you'll see in the next section, our politicians are much more responsive to the wealthy than the rest of us. Tax policy ridiculously skews in favor of corporations and the rich. And workers are seeing fewer and fewer protections.

The wealth gap now is the worst it's been since before the Great Depression, and it's only getting worse. During the 2016 election, Bernie Sanders said that we have to decide whether we want to be a democracy or an oligarchy. On that account, he most certainly isn't wrong, as the numbers are truly alarming.

Conservatives often falsely equate the mere *possibility* that a poor person can succeed in America with the notion that everyone somehow has a reasonably fair shot. They'll say, "Anyone can succeed in America, so long as they're willing to work hard."

Now, if by "can" they mean that it's not literally impossible, maybe. But that's not usually how they express it: instead, they tend to believe that it's formulaic: work hard, save, seize your opportunities, and you will succeed. Of course, it's complete nonsense. Many people work hard and have no real shot to ever own their own business, own their own home, or comfortably retire.

Conservatives' belief that everyone has a pre-ordained path to success, if only they take it, ignores the fact that for many people that path is a cakewalk, while for others it's a minefield. When some manage to maneuver through that minefield and come out on top, Republicans often take the wrong lesson from it. It's like Mark Twain said, "We should be careful to get out of an experience only the wisdom that is in it and stop there, lest we be like the cat that sits down on a hot stove lid. She will never sit down on a hot stove lid again, and that is well. But also she will never sit down on a cold one anymore." Republicans prefer to concentrate on encouraging people to manage minefields rather than figuring out how to remove mines.

In the UN's "Report of the Special Rapporteur on extreme poverty and human rights on his mission to the United States of America," Special Rapporteur Philip Alston put it succinctly:

> Defenders of the status quo point to the United States as the land of opportunity and the place where the American dream can come true because the poorest can aspire to the ranks of the richest. But today's reality is very different. The United States now has one of the lowest rates of intergenerational social mobility of any of the rich countries. Zip codes, which are usually reliable proxies for race and wealth, are tragically reliable predictors of a child's future employment

and income prospects. High child and youth poverty rates perpetuate the intergenerational transmission of poverty very effectively, and ensure that the American dream is rapidly becoming the American illusion. The equality of opportunity, which is so prized in theory, is in practice a myth, especially for minorities and women, but also for many middle-class White workers.

If somehow a poor black kid growing up in America manages to escape the mines of endemic poverty, neighborhood crime and gang violence, inadequate schools that leave him woefully unprepared, drugs, racism, low expectations, food insecurity, lack of proper health care, and the twelve million other problems that can spring up, he still might be faced with prohibitive costs for a college education. Adjusted for inflation, the average cost of tuition at a four-year public university for the 1987-1988 school year was $15,160 (2017 dollars). What was it for the 2017-2018 school year? $34,740. Keep in mind, both numbers have been adjusted for inflation, meaning that, in real dollars, there's been almost a 130% increase. In fact, just in the past ten years, the average cost of tuition and fees at a four-year private university has increased over $7,000, from $27,520 to $34,740. It's outdone inflation by over 3%. Public universities are still a much better deal, with the average cost of tuition and fees running $9,970. But for the 1987-1988 school year, it was $3,190 (adjusted for inflation). It's more than tripled!

Now, to be fair, these are the "sticker price" rates. When you account for grants and scholarships, the average price comes down considerably, to $14,530 for private institutions and $4,140 for public ones. BUT!

Three things: 1. The other numbers cited were also the "sticker price" rates. 2. The cost of both public and private institutions have been steadily going up for the past several years, and scholarships, grants, and financial aid haven't kept pace. 3. The figures are only for tuition and fees, and don't take into consideration room, board, and books, which can also be incredibly steep.

In the end, what you find is that poor and middle class kids often have limited options. Some must decide between going to school and going to work. And the more elite a university, the more you can expect to pay. It becomes a vicious cycle of oligarchy.

Home ownership isn't much different. When adjusted for inflation (2018 dollars), the median home value in 1940 was a little over $50,000. Today it's $217,000 (according to Zillow). Meanwhile, list prices are far above that: Zillow notes that the average list price is $279,500, while the median price houses sold for was $231,700. In certain areas, it's considerably worse, of course. In New York City, for instance, the median income is less than $51,000, while the median selling price of a home is $568,300 and the median list price is $848,000.

We'd like to believe that becoming wealthy has a lot to do with skill, pluck, and perseverance. In truth, though, there's a lot more luck than we'd like to admit. Those people who bought homes in the 1940s, 1950s, and 1960s, truly had no idea the amazing investment they were making. My grandmother once told me that she bought her house in Franklin Square, New York for about $5,000 back in the 1940s. Today a typical house in Franklin Square is valued at about half a million (don't worry – I didn't see any of it).

"The Land of Opportunity" is often more "The Land of Get Here

First." In his book *Outliers*, Malcolm Gladwell points out that fourteen of the seventy-five richest people who ever walked the Earth were all born within nine years of one another, including John D. Rockefeller, the richest person who ever lived (until Jeff Bezos surpasses him in his quest for world domination). They had the good fortune to be born during a time of incredible economic opportunity: railroads were booming, the oil industry was growing, steel was making skyscrapers possible. Rockefeller, for one, was a hard worker, of course, but he was also born at the right time, in the right country, with the right gender, and had the right religion for becoming successful in America. And all his descendants had to do to be successful was be born with the last name Rockefeller.

Those people, like my grandmother, who bought a house at the right time, had an opportunity that no longer exists for many Americans. Homeownership peaked in 2004 at 69.4% of households, fell to 62.9% in 2016, and is now just over 64%. If you happen to be part of the 36% of American households living in a home you do not own, you're really up against it, especially since the median asking price for rentals doubled from 1995 to 2017, going from just under $450 a month to over $850 a month (and yes, that's adjusted for inflation – 2017 dollars). The national minimum wage is still $7.25 an hour, yet the National Low Income Housing Coalition estimates that "in order to afford a modest, two-bedroom rental home in the U.S., renters need to earn a wage of $21.21 per hour."

It's time for another striking number: 94%. That's the percentage of new jobs created between 2005-2015 that went to "alternative work arrangements," according to a study conducted by Lawrence F. Katz of

Harvard and Alan B. Krueger of Princeton. This has come to be known as the "Gig Economy": rather than obtaining permanent jobs with union benefits and health care, workers are being forced into unstable positions with little or no bargaining power. And right now there's about 23 million of them.

Katz and Krueger define "alternative work arrangements" as "temporary help agency workers, on-call workers, contract workers, and independent contractors or freelancers." According to the study, from February of 2005 to late 2015, the percentage of all workers engaged in such work rose from 10.7% to 15.8%. And that's how we arrive at our 94% number. That means that 94% of new workers have less rights than workers had three generations ago. While surely some degree of freedom comes with this new Gig Economy, don't be fooled: much of the benefit goes to management and corporations, who save huge sums on taxes because they can issue 1099s rather than W-4s. A race to the bottom ensues, with freelancers competing to undercut each other's prices in order to find work. Companies, meanwhile, avoid many of the costs of doing business, pushing those costs onto the "independent contractors" instead.

Of course, the contracts these companies provide to such workers are not only completely inadequate, but oftentimes are utterly unconscionable. Yet they're upheld by the courts, since the idea of an unfair playing field no longer seems to apply (we'll touch on that more later).

You might say, *Well, why doesn't the worker simply find another, more permanent job, then?* And the answer (as indicated by the 94% figure) is that often those jobs just aren't there to be found. Workers are left in a take-it-or-leave it position, and feel compelled to sign away basic rights and privileges just to get by. It's part of the reason why 78% of Americans are living paycheck-to-paycheck.

Such an unfair power dynamic leads to incredible instability for workers and ridiculous levels of concentrated wealth.

16. Income Inequality

In a capitalistic society, more money equals more freedom. Money ensures the exercising of rights and privileges. It provides for better health options, increased freedom of speech, and greater influence. Vast disparities in wealth inherently lead to vast disparities in freedom. If such disparities are not addressed, a strain on freedom will automatically exist.

The United States has the worst income inequality among industrialized nations. You can see for yourself by viewing the map feature of the WIID – the World Income Inequality Database. Right now, the top 1% in America own more wealth than the bottom 90%, and that gap is growing. In 2016, the median household income in the US rose to $59,039. It was considered a significant rise, but still: it barely beat out 1999, when the median income was around $58,665. So, since then, the median income overall – for all US families – rose $374, or about six-tenths of one percent (.0064). If you go back to 1990, it did a bit better: the median income in 1990 was $53,350. That means it grew $5,689, or not quite 11% in 28 years. (All numbers adjusted for inflation.)

Now let's look at the upper 1%. In 1990, their average yearly income was just under $729,000. By 2015, it was almost $1.365 million. It grew about 87% in 25 years! A typical 1% household currently has a net worth of about $10.4 million. When you look at the top .01% - the richest of the rich – during the same time period, their average yearly income went from just under $3 million to over $6.7 million. That's an increase of over 220%! (See for yourself.) The top 10% now collect more income than the bottom 90%. They now own more than 77% of the wealth in this country. And if you happen to be in that top .01%, your family – on average – will make 198 times what a family in the bottom 90% brings home. It's not surprising when you consider that the bottom 90% has essentially seen no rise in income since 1980. That's right: None – since 1980. In 1980, they averaged $34,062. By 2015, it was $34,074 – a statistically insignificant .03%. If you go back to 1980 for the upper .01%, you'll find that they averaged just under $1.6 million; now they average over $6.7 million. Their income increased over 320%. Another way to think of it is that each of those people got a raise of about $204,000 each year. In contrast, workers in the bottom 90% averaged a raise of 34 cents a year. That's not a typo or an exaggeration – that's literally what it works out to. It's why the wealthy now control just as much wealth as they did right before the Great Depression.

The higher you go on the income ladder, the greater your annual growth. If you're in the bottom 20%, you'll see essentially no growth or you'll see your annual earnings decline. If you're in the top .001%, you'll see an annual growth rate of about 6%. It used to be the opposite: the poor and middle class used to see the greatest percentage of growth. This makes sense, if you think about it: the lower your income, the larger percent increase any growth at all will make. If you get a raise from $25,000 a year to $26,000 a year, you just saw 4% growth (a $1,000 raise on $25,000). For someone making $25 million a year, they'd have to make a million more dollars the next year to see a 4% increase.

At this point, it's not simply a wealth disparity; it's wealth hoarding. As the *New York Times* reported, the average CEO now makes 275 times what their workers make. Live Nation's chief exec, Michael Rapino, made over $70 million in 2017. If you're a typical worker at that particular company, you'd only have to work about 2,900 years to make that much. Really – the median income for a Live Nation worker was just over $24,400 a year, meaning that it would take you only 36 lifetimes or so to match Mr. Rapino.

In his special report to the Human Rights Council of the UN, envoy Philip Alston noted:

> The trajectory of the United States since 1980 is shocking. In both Europe and the United States, the richest 1 per cent earned around 10 per cent of national income in 1980. By 2017 that had risen slightly in

Europe to 12 per cent, but massively in the United States, to 20 per cent....

High inequality undermines sustained economic growth. It manifests itself in poor education levels, inadequate health care and the absence of social protection for the middle class and the poor, which in turn limits their economic opportunities and inhibits overall growth.

Alston observed "dramatic contrast between the immense wealth of the few and the squalor and deprivation in which vast numbers of Americans exist." He called America "a land of stark contrasts," noting that we have 40 million in poverty, yet over 550 billionaires. Trump's new tax plan, meanwhile, he said, "will worsen this situation and ensure that the United States remains the most unequal society in the developed world. The planned dramatic cuts in welfare will essentially shred crucial dimensions of a safety net that is already full of holes. Since economic and political power reinforce one another, the political system will be even more vulnerable to capture by wealthy elites."

He's right. A 2015 study from Princeton professor Martin Gilens and Benjamin Page of Northwestern found that politicians are essentially unconcerned with the preferences of the poor and middle class – it doesn't matter whether 10% of them support a certain position or 90% – but are extremely responsive to the upper 10% of the population: the more of them that want something, the more likely it is to happen.

We should be challenging this excessive opulence, but Republicans have somehow sold Americans a narrative that they're being ripped off by the poor. A Pew survey from 2017 found that 34% of Americans feel that the poor are poor because of a "lack of effort." Only 43%, meanwhile, said that the rich were rich because of certain advantages. The poll divided very much along partisan lines: whereas only 19% of Democrats said the poor suffered from a lack of effort, 56% of Republicans felt that was the case. Sixty-six percent of Republicans said the rich are rich mainly because they work harder (compared to 21% of Republicans who attributed it to fortunate circumstances).

Keep in mind that the Supreme Court has equated money with speech, and ignored inequality in the process. Its recent decisions have cut sharply into unions, which have traditionally been voices for the working class.

An unfair tax system, a political class largely dependent on donations from wealthy individuals and corporations, and the destruction of workers' rights have paved the way for massive economic gaps. And for those who argue that a person should simply "pull themselves up by their own bootstraps," they should realize that bootstraps are nowhere near good enough any longer: The financial obstacles that the average worker faces are so enormous, that a rope and a ladder – or maybe even a few ropes tied together – would be more like it. They are often suffering not just from unfair employment situations, but from tremendous, tremendous debt.

17. The Stranglehold of Personal Debt

Americans are currently $13 trillion in debt. I'm not referring to the national debt, which is now nearing $22 trillion. I'm talking about the personal debt American citizens have from mortgages, student loans, credit cards, and more. If you average it out among US adults, it comes to about $52,000 per person. Even if you include children, it still works out to about $40,000 per person. Eighty percent of Americans, meanwhile, have at least some debt.

Most of it, of course, is mortgage debt – almost $9 trillion worth. People moving into houses is, generally speaking, a good thing. But as we talked about in chapter 15, home prices keep going up. In order to meet those increases, many Americans are forced to take on more and more debt. Even the average person 75 and up still has some $34,500 worth of it. The average American 35-54, meanwhile, owes over $130,000. And the average debt per household that has debt is also over $130,000, according to NerdWallet.

Of course, mortgage debt isn't the only problem. As noted earlier, tuition costs and fees keep rising, forcing students to take on higher student loan debts. In 2017, Americans owed more than $1.3 trillion in student loans alone. According to Pew, 37% of adults under thirty have student loan debts, with a median level of $17,000. In any given year, an average student will take out $6,600 in loans and will accrue $22,000 in debt by graduation. And according to Ben Miller of the Centers for American Progress, who studies postsecondary education, the problem is much worse than we think. As he noted in an editorial for the *New York Times*, the crisis has largely been disguised by poor tracking and student loan deferment.

There are two ways to measure whether borrowers can repay those loans: There's what the federal government looks at to judge colleges, and then there's the real story. The latter is coming to light, and it's not pretty.

Consider the official statistics: Of borrowers who started repaying in 2012, just over 10 percent had defaulted three years later. That's not too bad — but it's not the whole story. Federal data never before released shows that the default rate continued climbing to 16 percent over the next two years, after official tracking ended, meaning more than 841,000 borrowers were in default. Nearly as many were severely delinquent or not repaying their loans (for reasons besides going back to school or being in the military). The share of students facing serious struggles rose to 30 percent over all.

Collectively, these borrowers owed over $23 billion, including more than $9 billion in default.

Nationally, those are crisis-level results, and they reveal how colleges are benefiting from billions in financial aid while students are left with debt they cannot repay.

Miller also noted that for-profit colleges are among the worst offenders, with 44% of borrowers experiencing loan distress, including 25% who default.

These debts affect graduates' psyches and their ability to earn and pursue their dreams. Twenty-one percent of 25-39 year-olds who are employed and have student loan debt have two jobs, compared with just 11% of those without such debt. These indebted young people also feel less financially secure: only 27% of them reported living comfortably, compared with 45% of those without outstanding loans.

So what can we do about it?

Well, first off, we could keep interest rates low for students. The point is not to make a profit, but to benefit society and reap the rewards later. Investing in students is one of the best investments we can make.

Second, we need to do a better job of advising students what career paths are best for them and make sure they understand the kind of debts they're taking on.

Third, we need to shut down for-profit colleges that take advantage of students. Unfortunately, under Trump's secretary of Education, Betsy DeVos, we're actually doing the opposite: DeVos has not only allowed these bogus institutions to continue to operate, but is in fact encouraging them.

Fourth: We need free college education. Some places, like my home state of New York, are already trying it: If you live in New York and your parents make less than $125,000 a year, you don't have to worry: you can attend any state university for free, and many of them, like Stony Brook,

Binghamton, and Geneseo, are quite good. Other countries, of course, have had free college education for a long time. You shouldn't have to choose between missing out on higher education and going into severe debt. That's an awful choice to foist upon students, and one that keeps the rich rich and the rest of us struggling to catch up.

How about credit cards?

Well, when it comes to credit cards, young people might actually be able to boast a little: the average 18-24-year-old has a balance of $2,000 on their credit cards, while the average American has $6,375 worth of credit card debt. According to CNBC: 43% of Americans have been carrying a credit card balance for over two years, and the average credit card debt per household is almost $17,000. Interest payments alone total nearly $1,300 per annum.

So what can we do about that?

To start, we need the Consumer Financial Protection Bureau to actually do its job. Trump stooge Mick Mulvaney, who is supposedly running the agency, literally asked for zero dollars for its budget.

We also need the agency to have teeth. We've somehow bought into the idea that anything that happens to a debtor is fair game because they incurred the debt. That idea is not just nonsensical, but dangerous: when you sign up for a credit card, you shouldn't be promising to go into years of debt and pay usurious rates if you happen to fall behind.

There's also tax debt. It's estimated that 30 million Americans fail to withhold enough from their pay for income taxes. Many of them probably do it to make ends meet. But it means that millions who fail to make up the difference will be hit with penalties and interest. It's not hard for the amounts to pile up and for many people to fall into tax holes they can't climb out of. Tax breaks that favor the wealthy also make it more likely that less well-off Americans will fall behind. One way to help correct this would be for the government to offer tax services, which we'll get into more later on.

Another major cause of debt is, of course, medical emergencies. The amount of bankruptcies caused by medical problems is a bit difficult to estimate, with the key being determining what the "cause" was (in other words: Did a medical expense cause the bankruptcy, or was it just one of many factors?). Still, CNBC estimates that medical emergencies cause over 640,000 bankruptcies a year, and affect around 2 million people (counting the immediate families of those who go bankrupt). NerdWallet says that 17% of credit card debt is also related to emergency medical expenses.

It's part of the reason why access to insurance is one of the keys to a well-functioning republic: if you don't have healthy citizens, you won't have a healthy democracy.

18. Insurance

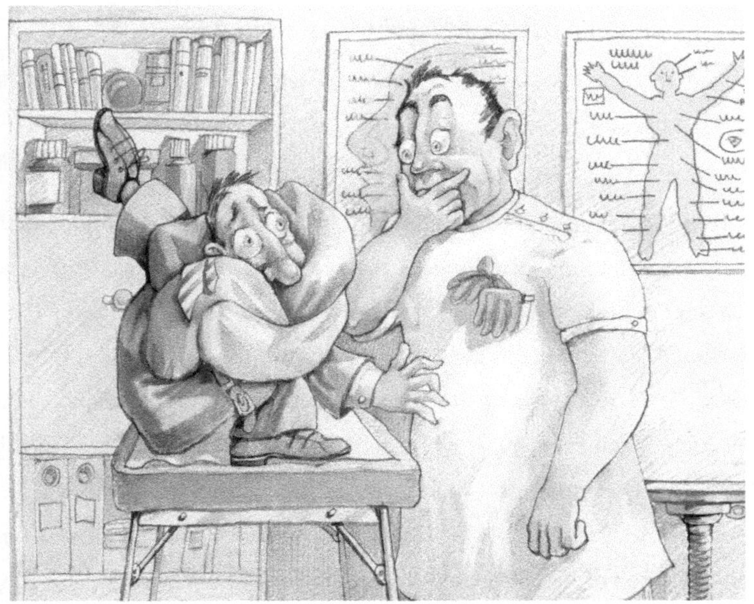

So, why is a healthy citizenry such a vital aspect of democracy? Well, to begin with, dead people don't vote. And, oftentimes, neither do sick people.

But it's more than that. Remember: the primary function of government is to keep its citizenry safe. For that purpose, most developed countries recognize a fundamental right to health care; the US, sadly, does not. In that regard, the United States government is failing to provide perhaps the most basic service to its people: to ensure their overall well-being.

"Health care is not a commodity. The goal of a health care system should be to keep people well, not to make stockholders rich. The USA has the most expensive, bureaucratic, wasteful, and ineffective health care system in the world."

That's a quote from Bernie Sanders, introducing an article in the medical journal the *The Lancet* that found a fifteen-year difference between the life expectancy of the upper 1% and that of the lower 1% in the United States. Lack of health insurance isn't the only cause for this, of course – there's also overall better nutrition and (perhaps) better educational achievement – yet another reason why we shouldn't be placing an enormous debt-burden on students. But the authors of the report acknowledged that a "Medicare for all" type of plan would alleviate much of the difference and a great deal of unnecessary suffering. This, however, would require our political class to recognize health care as a basic human right.

Yet while our politicians consider it important to protect us from terror, many do not seem as concerned about protecting us from heart disease. Of course, terrorism is a real threat and we must constantly be vigilant: if a terror group was able to successfully detonate a "dirty bomb" in a downtown metropolitan area, the casualties would be enormous.

But your odds of dying in a terrorist attack are about 1 in 46,000, while your odds of dying from heart disease are 1 in 7, as are your odds of dying of cancer. That means it's over 6,500 times more likely that you'll be done in by heart disease than terror. For all the talk and energy devoted to worrying about attacks from refugees, meanwhile, the odds of being killed in a terror attack committed by a refugee are estimated to be 1 in over 46 million – considerably worse than your odds of being killed by lightning (1 in approximately 175,000), by an asteroid (1 in 1.6 million), or in a shark attack (1 in 8 million). And for those of you wondering about your odds of getting killed by terrorists who are illegal immigrants, it's approximately 1 in 138 million.

Now, the federal government spends over a trillion dollars a year on health care, through Medicare, Medicaid, and other health programs. The conservative Cato Institute, meanwhile, has estimated that the US has spent approximately $2.8 trillion on anti-terror campaigns since 9/11. If you do the math, you'll find that's about $165 billion a year devoted just to anti-terrorism.

That's not to say we shouldn't continue our anti-terror efforts. But we should also put things in perspective. As terrible as 9/11 was, it pales in comparison to the amount of deaths we experience each year due to our horrible health system. Prior to Obamacare, a study out of Harvard Medical School and Cambridge Health Alliance found that approximately 45,000 people a year died in America due purely to lack of health insurance. As Trump and the Republicans seek to dismantle the Affordable Care Act, you can expect that thousands will continue to die needlessly, though the unnecessary nature of their deaths will probably go unnoticed by many. An analysis by the OECD recently ranked twenty nations based on childhood death rates; the US came in dead last. They estimated that 600,000 American kids have died since 1961 due purely to lack of proper health care. Had one-tenth of that amount of children been killed in a terror attack, the nation would rightfully be outraged. Yet we ignore it when it doesn't happen in a massive explosion but quietly in schools, hospitals, and poverty-stricken homes every day. It's both incredible and appalling. We seem to be the only advanced industrialized nation on Earth that allows its citizens to die simply because they can't afford proper health care.

Our system is inadequate and extremely inefficient. Overall, $3.3 trillion is spent on health care in the US, with state and federal spending constituting about 45% of that. Yet not everyone is covered and many citizens are one medical emergency away from bankruptcy. We spend more than twice as much as the UK does per capita, yet the British live longer: 81.2 years (on average), compared to just 78.6 years in the US. We outspend Switzerland by 31%, yet the Swiss have an average lifespan of 83.7 years. We outspend Japan by more than two-to-one as well, with the average lay-out in the US being over $10,300 per person, while it's around $4,500 per person for the Japanese; yet the average lifespan for a Japanese person is 84.1 years! They're living five and a half years longer than us and spending less than half of what we're spending on health services!

Why is this?

Well, to begin with, these countries – like all major industrialized nations – consider health care a right, and their national governments ensure that all of their citizens receive proper health services. The US system, meanwhile, is tied up with businesses, through which a fifth of all people still get health insurance. Others have to purchase private insurance. And there's no guarantee that you'll be covered when something goes wrong – that's up to the insurance company.

In countries like the UK, citizens can choose to supplement their government-provided insurance with additional services. But they have peace of mind because they know that they don't have to: the government has an interest in their remaining healthy and no one is denied care. But too many of our politicians are doing the opposite: rather than shore up health benefits and look to extend them to as many people as possible, they're sabotaging efforts to do so and abdicating their responsibilities with policies that favor the wealthy and eschew common sense.

Once again, to quote Philip Alston's special report to the UN:

> Health care is, in fact, a human right. The civil and political rights of the middle class and the poor are fundamentally undermined if they are unable to function effectively...The Affordable Care Act was a good start, although it was limited and flawed from the outset. Undermining it by stealth is not just inhumane and a violation of human rights, but an economically and socially destructive policy aimed at the poor and the middle class.

Insurance, and therefore life itself, has largely become a privilege for those of means. The problem is compounded by the endemic poverty that plagues our nation. Let's talk about that next.

19. Poverty

A homeless man in outside of the United Nations in New York.
Credit: C.G.P Grey

W*hy poverty?*, you may ask. *Sure, it's terrible, but is it really antidemocratic?*

Yes. For several reasons:

First off, poverty and education are related. Poverty is education's worst enemy. While some, like Ben Carson, like to preach that anyone can make it out of poverty if they just work hard enough, the truth is that

that isn't always the case. And, moreover, it ignores the tremendous uphill climb that poverty creates.

There's a former MLB pitcher named Jim Abbott. His stats wouldn't exactly blow you away: more losses than wins and a 4.25 Earned Run Average. But he made it to the major leagues! Certainly he was a success. He even pitched a no-hitter with the Yankees! And here's the amazing thing: Jim Abbott was born without a right hand! That's right: if you look up his stats, it'll say (a bit unnecessarily, I think), "Bats: Left. Throws: Left." And that's because left was his only option!

Abbott has an amazing story. He deserves all the credit in the world – really. But should we then start thinking that everyone who's born missing a hand has an equal chance of becoming a major league athlete as everyone born dual-handed? Should we treat his handicap as if it's no handicap at all? Or did Jim Abbott have to work much, much harder than others to be able to play in the majors?

Conservatives often tend to dismiss tremendous obstacles simply because it's *possible* to overcome them. For them, it's easier to say "You should've done more to pull yourself up" than to actually address the institutional and societal problems that hinder people's progress, and that includes endemic poverty.

Grow up poor and there's no doubt that you'll be lacking in educational resources. I know from firsthand experience: I've worked both as a New York City middle school teacher and as a tutor for the wealthy. One poor kid from Brooklyn I worked with who was living with her grandmother because her mother had gotten HIV from a needle, put it to me bluntly. She said, "How can we concentrate on school with all the shit we got going on in our lives?"

Many of the kids were missing a father. Some were missing a mother. Some were missing both. I saw kids being raised by an aunt or uncle or even an older sibling. I would hear teachers and administrators try to absolve themselves by saying that the trouble was that the kids weren't being raised right at home – that the parents or guardians just didn't care enough. But that of course wasn't the case. To me, it was implicit racism, since almost all of the kids were black or Hispanic. Sure, there were those parents or guardians who could've done more or should've done more – some who had given up on their kids, which is a sad thing to witness. But there were also plenty who would come to me and tell me that they just didn't know what to do: they were working two or three jobs, living in run-down neighborhoods, and simply didn't see a way to get out of the vicious cycle of poverty.

I had kids in my class who were dealing with gang violence, drugs, lack of resources, lack of guidance, and the dangerous racism of low expectations. One time, a lady who spoke with kids around the school about drugs came in to do her spiel. She asked the kids, "How many of you know where you could buy drugs?" As I recall, every hand went up, and there were about thirty kids there that day. When she asked how many knew where they could buy a gun, almost every hand went up. They were 8th graders.

Some mistakenly think that the advantage wealthy or middle class people have over the poor when it comes to education is that their money allows them to provide greater educational resources. But that's not what's making the major difference. The biggest factor is actually time. That's right: economically secure parents (or guardians) are able to spend more time with their kids, which means they can do homework with them, read with them more, take them to museums, etc.

Another big factor is security: food security, feeling safe, feeling economically secure. Kids who have to keep moving around and have no sense of stability or have to worry about where their next meal is coming from are bound to have educational difficulties.

The third giant factor is mentorship: as noted, poverty is a vicious cycle, and parents or guardians who received poor educations themselves are less able to pass on information and learning skills to their kids. If you graduated from Tufts University, you probably won't have trouble explaining algebra to your child. But if you yourself didn't make it through high school, you're probably not going to be able to help them much. Less educated parents tend to have weaker vocabularies, tend to share with their children less, and may even avoid doing homework with kids if they feel embarrassed about their own abilities.

Keep in mind that these problems didn't suddenly materialize: poverty has a history and that history is mired in racism and bigotry. When slaves were finally set free at the end of the Civil War, there was no stipend. Uncle Sam didn't pass any G.I. Bill-type legislation for the slave. Millions were left in poverty. Sure, there were those who tried to help: the Radical Republicans of the 1860s and 70s (who passed the 13th, 14th, and 15th Amendments), right-minded religious groups like the Quakers, government organizations like the Freedman's Bureau, and, of course, black leaders who fought for equal rights and started organizations and universities to fight back.

But Rutherford B. Hayes sold out the black population when he made his corrupt deal for the presidency, removing federal troops from the South and opening the door for nearly a hundred more years of segregation, terrorism, and disregard. Those blacks that found jobs in the North fared somewhat better, but not much. There were lynchings in Wisconsin as well as Mississippi, keep in mind. And many Northern cities were segregated as well, socially, economically, and at numerous private establishments.

Much of the difference between white families and black families, in terms of wealth, has to do with real estate. Older white families who have been here since the founding or before have had the advantage of having land and wealth passed down through the generations. Even if they never had any land passed directly down to them, they've been the beneficiaries of a system that was built on the abuse of the native population and African slaves.

Some whites (and I am white) may object to this; they'll argue that their families came to this country with little more than the shirts on their backs, from places like Ireland, Germany, Italy, Poland, and Russia. My family did as well, in fact. But they came with skill sets, intact families, and often with the support of their communities back home. The slave did not. Slave families were often broken up; slaves were purposely kept illiterate; they did not have the chance to learn to be a tailor or a musician or jeweler, say; they could not join the police force, even after slavery had ended, for Jim Crow and ingrained racism prevented that. And, unlike Jews or Italians, say, whose children could easily blend in once language barriers were broken, blacks could not take away their blackness; they could do little to mitigate the prejudices against them. Hispanics are in a similar position in that regard.

This is not to take away credit from hardworking German, Swedish, and Russian immigrants who came to America with little or nothing and managed to succeed; it's simply to recognize a historical fact that is obviously linked to poverty.

Poverty plagues us, and disproportionately so when it comes to minorities. *I understand*, you say. *But how does that affect democracy?*

The simple answer is that poor people don't vote nearly as much. In 2015, a Pew study found that only 54% of the least financially secure people were registered to vote, compared to 94% of the most financially secure. Furthermore, they estimated that only 20% of financially insecure people were likely to vote, compared to 63% for the most secure.

There are multiple reasons for this. One, of course, is the impediments placed on voters by politicians who don't have the poor's interest at heart – voter ID laws, distant polling stations, etc.

Another is that poorer people tend not to be as politically engaged. It's naturally harder to vote when you can't get off work or you have kids to take care of or an elderly parent you have to care for. Or when you have to worry about just surviving: While the wealthy kids I've worked with can rest assured they'll get home safe and could concentrate on their upcoming science test, the poor ones had to be concerned about getting beaten up on the bus by a gang from a rival neighborhood. To give you an idea of how disproportionately this affects minorities, consider this: according to the CDC, black Americans are eight times more likely to be victims of homicides than whites. Say that to yourself: eight times more likely.

Poverty also causes many poor people to be ambivalent about politics. They feel like it doesn't matter who wins because their situation is unlikely to improve anyhow.

And finally, since poverty correlates with inadequate educations, poverty-stricken individuals oftentimes aren't up on the issues. They're not usually reading the *New York Times* or *The Atlantic*. They don't tend to listen to NPR (you can check it out yourself here – NPR listeners, for one, are 242% more likely to have post-graduate degrees). Republican politicians tend to ignore them, and Democratic politicians often take them for granted.

Money is a megaphone. As noted earlier, Supreme Court decisions, including, of course, *Citizens United*, have made it clear that the court considers money speech. Think about what that means for people who don't have it.

If you're poor in America, you're virtually invisible. You're also often taken advantage of.

20. The Systematic Exploitation of the Poor

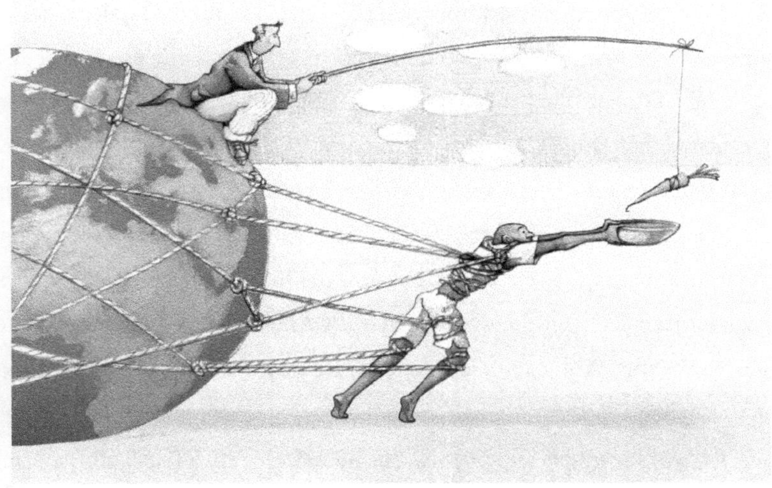

"Anyone who has ever struggled with poverty knows how extremely expensive it is to be poor."

–James Baldwin

Loan-sharking is illegal; unless, of course, banks or credit cards do it, then it's perfectly fine. The key is to replace the word "usury" with the word "fees," and then you're good to go.

And poor people sure get hit with "fees" in America – checking account fees, low-balance fees, overdraft fees. In fact, when it comes to overdraft fees, banks will often stack debits in such a way as to hit their poorest customers with more and more of these nonsense "fees." Let's say, for instance, that Dom has $900 in his checking account. He buys a couple of songs on iTunes for $.99, spends six bucks at McDonald's, and buys a book on Amazon for $8. He mailed his rent check to his landlord for $950, figuring it wouldn't be a problem because he'd be able to put in some cash he was owed for some contracting work he'd done over the weekend. Except the guy who was supposed to pay him had an emergency and Dom didn't get the money. Well, his bank can be happy about that because they'll make out like bandits: even though the songs and the purchases from McDonald's and Amazon came in first, they decide to process the rent check before the others. They hit Dom with a $35 overdraft fee. But they're far from done: they hit him with the same $35 fee for the six bucks he spent at McDonald's, again for the Amazon purchase, and twice for the two songs he bought. Each one of those songs didn't cost him ninety-nine cents, but about $36. In total, Dom gets hit with some $140 in "fees," $105 of which is complete and utter nonsense. Charging $35 for a $1 purchase is 3,500% interest – loan-sharks would be green with envy.

When Dom calls the bank to complain, he's told that there's nothing they can do. "It's just the system," a "representative" tells him. When he finally gets a supervisor on the phone, the supervisor tells Dom that it's his own fault – he agreed to their terms when he opened the account and, besides, he should be more careful.

Of course, since all banks have similar nonsensical terms, Dom really didn't have much of a choice. Banking is a necessity nowadays, and yet we allow the banking industry and others to prey on the poor.

As Karen Weese put it in an excellent piece for the *Washington Post*:

> For low-income families, these kinds of costs are everywhere.
>
> Let's say you clean houses or offices or hotel rooms for a living, or wait tables, or work in a child-care center or nursing home. Your income fluctuates depending on the hours your employer gives you week to week (or tips you get day-to-day), and your wages barely cover your expenses each month. Since your bank balance is not exactly flush (according to one analysis, the median checking account balance for Americans making less than $25,000 a year is $500), it only takes one glitch in your income or bills to throw everything off....

Weese notes that over a third of banks reorder purchases in order to hit patrons with more overdraft fees. And since most people don't even realize they're overdrawn for two or three days, those fees can really add up quickly.

> In only a few days, you could owe hundreds of dollars, creating a debt that, on your waitressing or child-care wages, will take months or years to pay back.
>
> If you throw up your hands and close your bank account...you will have to cash your check at a check-cashing establishment, where you will pay a fee for the service (usually a percentage of the check's value). Once you've got the cash in hand, you will need to turn it into money orders to pay your bills — and you will pay yet another fee for each one.
>
> Need to buy a car? You may only be able to get financing from a "buy here, pay here" car dealership that charges exorbitant interest rates (think 25 percent and up)...
>
> If you do buy a car, you had better drive carefully, because if you get a ticket and cannot pay, you could wind up in prison. Nineteen-year-old Kevin Thompson of DeKalb County, Ga., made an illegal left turn and spent five days in county jail because he could not quickly pay $838 in fees and fines related to the traffic stop. The ACLU

intervened, and the case was eventually settled, but the practice is widespread, as states and municipalities fund their budgets through the collection of fines and fees.

Meanwhile, companies like Walmart make enormous profits while their employees struggle to get by. Those who argue against welfare and a proper minimum wage often don't realize that the two are linked: we are subsidizing businesses that underpay their employees.

In order to get by, those employees will often seek out payday loans. These loan-sharking operations have sprung up throughout poor neighborhoods, preying on the indigent, immigrants, and minorities. If you think credit cards are bad, payday loans put them to shame, charging $15 for a $100 loan that only lasts perhaps two weeks, effectively working out to a 391% annual interest rate. Online payday lenders are even worse, with the median cost being $23.53 per $100 borrowed, or a 613% APR. Pew has found that the typical borrower will be forced to pay some $520 in "fees" on just $375 lent.

Not surprisingly, borrowers can't keep up and often default. They spend years trying to pay back a loan that might've started out as just a few hundred dollars. Meanwhile, payday lending (or prey-day lending, as perhaps it should be known), has become a $6 billion industry serving approximately 30 million people a year in the US.

Payday lenders also target members of our military, putting up payday loan centers near military bases. Heck, a quick map search found twelve payday lenders (or "cash advance" places) within five miles of Fort Knox! This was an enormous problem until the passage of the Military Lending Act, which forbid excessive interest loans to military personnel.

Payday lenders were also struck a blow by new rules issued by the

Consumer Financial Protection Bureau which require them to evaluate a borrower's ability to repay or limit loans to $500, with a limited time of indebtedness.

Hearing this, you might say, "Wow! The Consumer Financial Protection Bureau is actually doing its job? I can't believe it! I would've never thought Trump's interim head of the CFPB, Mick Mulvaney, would ever have supported rules that actually help common people."

But hold on – your never-thinking was actually right: Mulvaney (of course) did not support the rule changes – in fact, he's vigorously opposed them, even joining with industry groups to try to thwart them through the courts. The new rules preceded Mulvaney, and he's been fighting to stop them from going into effect.

But at least he hasn't opposed the efforts to stop people from gouging our brave men and women in the military…

Wrong again! He's done that too. The agency has canceled routine examinations to ensure that payday lenders aren't abusing members of the military.

And if you're wondering if Mulvaney's having received over $60,000 from the payday lending industry has anything to do with it, to be fair, many, many Congressmen and women have received a lot of money from the industry – over $11 million worth, in fact, as reported by Open Secrets.

So what can be done?

Well, first off, we have to acknowledge why payday loan places exist: the fact of the matter is that poor and lower-middle class people often have expenses they can't meet – medical bills, keeping the lights on, broken down cars – and they need access to capital.

But that doesn't mean they should become indentured servants. Colorado has crafted legislation that forces payday loan centers to allow borrowers to pay off loans over an extended period of time. It seems like only common sense, and it is.

We should also do away with the idea that payday loans are providing a vital service that can't be gotten elsewhere. The Center for Responsible Lending has called this notion a myth, noting:

> While fast cash and no credit checks make it easy for a consumer to get a payday loan, it usually only postpones the financial crisis for two weeks until the loan comes due. Because payday loans are targeted to people in financial trouble, there are few borrowers who can pay off their loan at that point. 91% of all payday loans are made to borrowers caught in a cycle of repeat borrowing with five or more payday loans per year.
>
> Borrowers, on average, receive 8 to 13 payday loans per year from a single payday shop. Typically these are loan flips - rollover extensions or back to back transactions loans where the borrower is basically paying a fee for no new money, never paying down the principal owed. The typical borrower's situation is even worse since borrowers often go to more than one shop (1.7 shops on average), therefore taking out 14 to 22 loans per year. In fact, **only one percent (1%) of all payday loans go to one-time emergency borrowers** who pay their loan within two weeks and don't borrow again within a year.

The center has also addressed the idea that payday loan interest rates have to be high due to the amount of risk the lenders are supposedly incurring:

> A payday lender would have to work hard to lose money, even though borrowers are generally low-income and have weak credit histories. Holding a "live" check as security gives a lender strong collateral and leverage over a borrower who, when faced with the threat of criminal prosecution and penalty fees, will keep paying renewal fees every two weeks when they cannot afford to repay the loan in full and walk away. With these renewals (or loan flips), they are never paying down the principal owed.

While some states (like New York, New Jersey, and Massachusetts) are more restrictive when it comes to payday loans, either banning them outright or limiting the interest that can be charged, thirty-two states still permit high-interest lending. Obviously, legislation at the federal level is required. And we need our federal agencies, like the CFPB, to do their jobs.

But we may need more than that: in order to best serve people who are targeted by payday lenders and banks, governments should consider opening up public banking institutions that can provide checking and savings accounts to their denizens. Seven percent of American households are considered “unbanked,” meaning that they don’t have any bank account whatsoever. Another 19.9% are “underbanked,” meaning that they have to depend on high interest check cashers. In fact, a 2011 report from the postal service’s Inspector General found that, on average, the underbanked spent over $2,400 a year using financial services. To cater to the needs of these underserved individuals, there's a movement afoot for municipalities to establish their own banks, which could result in massive savings for large cities. Los Angeles, for instance, paid $100 million in unnecessary bank fees in 2016.

This should be considered at the national level as well. After all, banking has become a necessity, and banks are essentially utilities, much like the phone company. As we saw in 2008, when the banks were about ready to collapse, it was tax payers who had to bail them out. Why, then, should banks not be treated like public services?

Moreover, we already have over 30,000 potential banking sites across the nation that could fill this gap, providing fee-free accounts, issuing debit cards, and even granting small loans to the unbanked and underbanked. They're called post offices.

Before you dismiss the idea, take note that we've done it before: from the Taft administration to LBJ's time in office – a period of some fifty years. And it worked just fine and could work again. In fact, 87 other countries do it, including Japan, the UK, and China.

That's why Senator Kirsten Gillibrand of New York is proposing a bill that would make post offices into banking institutions once more. It's an ideal plan that would allow poor people to receive banking services without being bled dry and give the postal system a chance to make a little bit of money in its quest to remain solvent. Of course, the latter is only a side benefit: the point is to provide an important service, not make a profit. A subway system doesn't have to make money – it just has to get people where they're going – and postal banking should be treated no differently.

You'll often hear people criticize the postal service as being outdated or unprofitable. But it's actually very efficient. Think about it: for less than fifty cents, you can still send a letter across the country and know it will arrive within a few days. More importantly, the postal service forces other, private services to compete with it, keeping their prices lower. It could do the same when it comes to banking, making Chase or Wells Fargo have to lower their fees to compete, and hopefully putting payday lenders out of business.

Predictably, Republicans will cry "socialism" and degrade the plan, as if subjugation by bankers somehow makes us freer. But there's no legitimate reason that the post office can't also operate as a bank, as it does in many countries.

Speaking of freedom:

We also have to get rid of debtors' prisons.

Debtors' prisons! you say. *Since when has the United States had debtors' prisons?*

Every time we put someone in jail for not paying a traffic ticket or for being unable to make bail for a minor crime.

For-profit companies harass defendants for minor infractions and states and municipalities are charging defendants more and more in order to make up for lost tax revenue.

In 2014, NPR led a year-long investigation that found some truly startling results: 43 states and DC billed defendants for a public defender; prisoners could be charged room and board in no less than 41 states; at least 44 states will charge convicts for probation or parole supervision; and many of those in jail are there purely because they can't afford fines. In Washington state, for instance, they found that a quarter of jailed inmates were there for that reason. Washington also charged the accused for jury trials – $250 for a panel of twelve – as remarkable as that seems.

One Texas judge, Ed Spillane, wrote in a piece for the *Washington Post* that he typically saw ten to twelve indigent offenders a day whose crimes were small, but who couldn't afford any potential fines. Rather than send them to jail, he used alternative sentencing, such as community service. Unfortunately, Spillane said, many of his fellow justices do not act in the same fashion, with some refusing to recognize that economic factors should be taken into consideration during bail hearings and sentencings.

It's part of what's led us to our next issue: mass incarceration.

21. Mass Incarceration

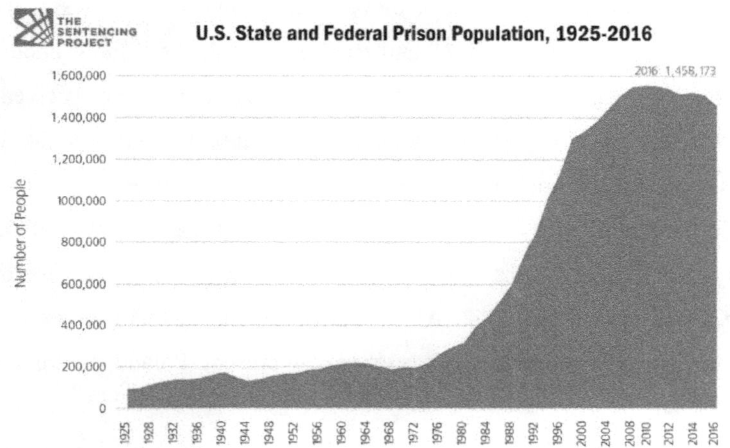

According to the World Prison Brief, the US currently ranks first internationally in terms of prison population rate: 655 people per 100,000 (if you only count adults, the number shoots up to around 860 per 100,000). Russia, with 430 people per 100,000 in prison, is 13th. The UK ties with several other nations for 104th, with 145 per 100,000. France comes in 147th, with just 101 per 100,000.

And despite what most Americans probably believe, we don't even come close to leading the world in terms of equality under the law. Out of 113 nations wherein the World Justice Project was able to conduct surveys and collect data for its Rule of Law Index, the US ranked 19th with a score of just .73 (most African nations and some others around the world, including Israel, were not included in the latest data from 2016).

Moreover, the US had some glaring points of concern, such as the "Equal treatment/no discrimination" question under the "Fundamental Rights" section, where we achieved an awful score of .52. For comparison, the UK got a .71 and Russia a .59. Unbelievably enough, Russia also beat us in terms of "Labor rights," where they received a score of .61 while the US came in at .58 (don't abscond to Russia just yet – its overall score – no surprise – was a .45 and its rank 92nd).

In terms of "Civil Justice," the US got a .67, giving us a rank of 26th. We got a .42 for "Access and affordability." France got a .62 and the UK a .52. Russia also got a .52. As for discrimination in this category, our score was a .48, meaning that it is extremely present. Poland, by contrast, got a .80.

In terms of criminal justice, the numbers are just as glaring: the US ranks 20th overall, receiving a total score of .65. We garner just a .37 for "no discrimination." That means, at least as far as people see it, the system is largely discriminatory. Canada, in contrast, gets a .60, as does Italy. The UK receives a .69.

In case you're wondering, the WJP's top five countries for rule of law are (in order): Denmark (.89), Norway (.88), Finland (.87), Sweden (.86), and the Netherlands (.86).

But it's not simply that we're losing to other nations; our overbearing and ineffective "correctional system" doesn't seem to be very good at correcting. Basically, it's not so much a correctional system as a punishment system. It's understandable, of course. After all, victims and families of victims want to feel that perpetrators are being punished. But that doesn't necessarily make for effective crime deterrence.

The US prison population is currently between 2.2 and 2.3 million people, but even that doesn't paint an accurate picture of the scope of the problem: Every year between 10 million and 11 million people go to jail. 6.1 million Americans cannot vote due to a felony conviction. (And yet they still have to pay taxes – taxation without representation.) One in nine men born in 2001 will do time, and one in three black men. In fact, approximately 70% of the prison population is made up of minorities. Since 1980, spending on prisons has grown tremendously, sentences have gotten longer, and many more people have been locked up for drug offenses. And believe it or not, just as many people have a criminal record as have a college degree – at least 70 million. And once you have a criminal record, it can become extremely difficult to get a job, acquire credit, or make a life for yourself. In a way, every criminal record is a life sentence.

Worse still, the system is used for political means. Felons usually can't vote while they're incarcerated, and some can't even vote once they've served all their time, effectively taking away their most important right and eliminating them from any political consideration. (Only Maine and Vermont allow felons to vote.)

The effect of this mass disenfranchisement was particularly apparent in Florida during the 2000 Presidential Election. Everyone was so caught up in the Supreme Court and the recount that few noticed that the GOP had used incarceration and racism to steal the election as well. Here's an excerpt from the report issued by the United States Commission on Civil Rights after the election:

Florida's overzealous efforts to purge voters from the rolls, conducted under the guise of an anti-fraud campaign, resulted in the inexcusable and patently unjust removal of disproportionate numbers of African American voters from Florida's voter registration rolls for the November 2000 election.

The purge system in Florida proceeded on the premise of guilty until proven innocent. In 1998, the Florida legislature enacted a statute that required the Division of Elections to contract with a private entity to purge its voter file of deceased persons, duplicate registrants, individuals declared mentally incompetent, and convicted felons without civil rights restoration, i.e., remove ineligible voter registrants from voter registration rolls. This purge process became known as list maintenance. Once on the list, the process places the burden on the eligible voter to justify remaining on the voter rolls. The ubiquitous errors and dearth of effective controls in the state's list maintenance system resulted in the exclusion of voters lawfully entitled and properly registered to vote.

African American voters were placed on purge lists more often and more erroneously than Hispanic or white voters. For instance, in the state's largest county, Miami-Dade, more than 65 percent of the names on the purge list were African Americans, who represented only 20.4 percent of the population...whites were 77.6 percent of the population but 17.6 percent of those purged.

The commission also noted that, for various reasons, black voters were ten times more likely to have their votes discounted than whites, effectively turning the election.

Four states currently do not restore voting rights even after a convicted felon has completed all of his sentence: Iowa, Kentucky, Virginia, and Florida. In Virginia, Democratic Governor Terry McAuliffe restored voting rights to over 170,000 convicts in 2016. Similarly, New York governor Andrew Cuomo signed an executive order restoring voting rights to people on parole. Florida has unfortunately gone in the other direction, currently maintaining a list of 1.5 million "felons" who are not allowed to vote. Some are actually incarcerated, some have already done their time and probation, and some should've never been on the list in the first place. Over 20% of Florida's black population, who would otherwise be able to cast a ballot, are unable to vote due to the restrictions. (And keep in mind that Donald Trump won the state by about 120,000 – approximately 1.3%.)

As explained in this pleading editorial from the *New York Times*, the process for restoring voting rights in Florida for those whom it's been taken away from is nothing short of ridiculous, involving, among other things, having to make a personal plea to the governor. That governor, Rick Scott, has only granted around 3,000 requests in seven years. His predecessor, Charlie Crist, restored the rights of some 150,000 people. At one clemency hearing, Scott practically admitted to the randomness of Florida's system saying, "We can do whatever we want." After a federal judge ruled Florida's voting restoration system unconstitutional, a spokesman for the governor said, "The governor believes that convicted felons should show that they can lead a life free of crime and be accountable to their victims and our communities." Yet all it took for one convicted felon to have his voting rights restored was for him to tell Scott that he had voted for him illegally, moments after which Scott reinstated the man.

As of now, Scott's administration is appealing the federal decision. Before there will be a ruling on it, a ballot initiative in November will ask Florida voters (the ones who can still vote, that is) whether or not voting rights should be restored once a convict has done all of his or her time (with the exception of those who have committed murder or sexual assaults). Hopefully, Floridians will make the right decision. Polls currently indicate that they will.

Yet the law won't do anything for those currently incarcerated or for those still on probation or parole. To make matters worse, felons are often counted as part of the population of the county in which they're incarcerated, rather than from where they're from. So not only are they not allowed to vote, but they're being counted for population purposes and not represented. This gives inordinate power to many counties with prisons.

* * *

We also suffer from a one-size-fits-all approach for smaller crimes and infractions and, oftentimes, when it comes to bail. As Alec Schierenbeck pointed out in his piece for the *New York Times*, "A Billionaire and a Nurse Shouldn't Pay the Same Fine for Speeding," fines for misdemeanors and traffic tickets have a disproportionate effect on the poor. First off, a nurse, as opposed to a big shot stock trader, is more likely to be driving her own car to work to begin with and therefore more likely to get a ticket. But whether she speeds or he does, the fine is the same. The stock trader can stuff the ticket into the glove compartment of his Porsche and pay it that night before he heads to the 21 Club for dinner. To him, it will make no financial difference whatsoever. But the nurse might be severely hurt. Yet no consideration is given to a person's financial position. Surely, there should be a minimum penalty. But a judge should be able to hit a billionaire with a $100,000 fine for speeding and make the nurse pay just $30. And, as noted in the previous chapter, many people (sadly) wind up in jail over traffic infractions and an inability to pay.

The same, of course, is true for bail. Bail was originally designed to decongest the jails and allow those awaiting trial the chance to do so at home. But it's clear that bail has become biased against the poor.

Jamycheal Mitchell of Virginia, a 24-year-old schizophrenic, was charged with stealing a can of soda, a Snicker's bar, and a piece of packaged cake from a 7-Eleven. The total value of the items was about $5. His bail was set at $3,000. He was tossed in jail and left there to rot. He was found dead in his cell four months later. The cause is still being investigated.

Mitchell's a unique example, sure. But there are plenty of others. According to the ACLU, about half a million people are in jail in the US simply because they can't afford their bail. Pretrial incarceration also leads to higher conviction rates. The ACLU cites a study that saw increases in conviction rates for non-felonies go from 50% to 92% and rates increase for felonies go from 59% to 85% when a person is detained before trial. That's right: just being incarcerated makes it more likely that a person accused of a crime will either plead guilty or be convicted by a jury. That, of course, could be a good thing in certain instances. But it's also a recipe for forcing poor people to cop to crimes they may not have committed.

Part of the problem, of course, is that many of the poor aren't properly represented, resulting in an excessive amount of plea deals (around 95% of cases) being agreed to. Funding for public defenders has consistently gotten cut throughout the states, with the typical public defender trying to juggle hundreds of cases. National statistics about public defenders are difficult to come by, but here are some illuminating examples:

- In Missouri in 2016, the public defender's office had 82,000 cases; lawyers were expected to handle between 80 and 100 cases a week
- In New Orleans, 60 public defenders are responsible for 20,000 cases a year
- In 2013, a Florida court ruled that public defenders can apply to turn away indigent clients if caseloads are too heavy; in Miami, public defenders were already handling 400 cases each

And yet public defenders are the attorneys of record in most criminal cases. That's right: the Justice Department estimates that 60 to 90 percent of criminal defendants cannot afford an attorney. Once again, we can see the connection between poverty and incarceration.

To be fair, there are some good things occurring in our prison system as well. Racial discrimination has decreased somewhat: as the Marshall Project has pointed out, the overall black male population has dropped some 24%, while the female black population has been cut in half. Yet blacks are still imprisoned five times as much as whites, and one out of ten black kids has a parent who is incarcerated. And although it's improved, the racial gap remains incredibly disproportionate, with blacks still outnumbering whites in prison, despite the fact that whites make up over 76% of the population and blacks just 13%.

What can be done?

Well, first off, as suggested in the previous chapter, not every infraction needs to result in jail time, and people's economic means should be considered during sentencing. We also need to properly fund public defender offices. And, of course, we should never allow political considerations to play a part in whether or not someone is incarcerated. And if they are incarcerated, it shouldn't mean they can no longer vote.

Think about this for a moment: convicts serving time in prison still maintain their freedom of speech, do they not? That freedom may be limited in certain ways (e.g. they can't wear whatever clothing they'd like), but it's not eliminated. Their right to vote – perhaps the most important right we have, since it determines whether or not we're a democracy – shouldn't be taken from them either.

Of course, when this is said, right away people's minds go to murderers. Should murderers still have the right to vote? I would contend that they should, much in the same way that even the worst people maintain their freedom of speech. (By guaranteeing free speech for a neo-Nazi, we're protecting that right for ourselves as well.) But it should also be kept in mind that murderers only make up about 9% of the prison population (in all, approximately 40% of inmates are there for violent crimes). The rest are there for things like property crimes, drug offenses, prostitution, insurance fraud, burglary, etc.

If we take away prisoners' right to vote, we make incarceration into a political weapon. We also push them out of society and give them little hope of returning to it. By removing a person's right to vote, we're essentially saying to them, "We no longer respect you as a human being." We're inviting future criminal behavior.

We also simply have to reduce the amount of people we're sending to prison. The US has less than 5% of the world's population, yet 22% of the world's prison population. Something is definitely wrong. Opioid addicts belong in rehab, not jail.

And we need to end mandatory minimums and lengthy prison stays. Three-strikes-and-you're-out-type laws have to be struck out. Sending someone to prison for the rest of their life shouldn't be something we do cavalierly. And judges should always have the discretion to show mercy; while Congress and state legislatures can impose mandatory minimums in order to look tough on crime, judges, faced with individual incidents and special circumstances, should retain the ability to use – well – their *judg*ment to determine if someone really should go to prison. Remember: when we send someone to prison, we're not just sending them; we're sending their family, their friends, and their future to prison as well.

Sure, some people are going to have to go: there are many in prison who definitely shouldn't be walking about among us. But we don't want to create criminals either. If we send a kid to prison at seventeen because he stole a car and took a joyride, we're exposing him to prison gangs and potentially turning him into a hardened criminal.

We should also keep in mind that intervention works. Communities across the country have engaged in programs to recognize at-risk youth and steer them to the right path, and that must continue.

Education works also: if we're educating kids and giving them a legitimate chance, they're less likely to be attracted to crime. But, as noted earlier, poverty and educational needs have to be addressed simultaneously.

We also have to make it easier for released convicts to obtain jobs so that they can rejoin society. This is not such an easy one: from an employer's point of view, it's obvious why you would want to know if someone has a criminal history. But past mistakes shouldn't always mean that you don't get another chance. Perhaps a compromise can be reached, though: asking, say, if someone has committed a *violent* crime in the past ten years, is reasonable; if they'd like to work at a bank, asking them if they've ever been found guilty of embezzlement is also reasonable; but denying a thirty-five-year-old a job at a fast-food restaurant for a property crime he committed when he was eighteen is not, and I think most of us would agree on that. But we can't expect employers to sort all of this out; the law has to do it.

It comes down to this: Do you believe in such a thing as convict discrimination? If you've never been to jail, I want you to take a moment to think about something before you answer: think of all the things you've done in your life. Were there any that you could've been thrown in jail for? I know the answer in my case is Yes. And I know I've also known my fair share of criminals, some who were incarcerated and others who managed to never get caught.

What about you? Have you ever done drugs? Stolen anything? Participated in illegal gambling? Ever punch anyone or drive without insurance or damage property? Maybe trespass?

If you had gotten caught and been convicted of a felony, should you have had to tell people for the rest of your life – put it on an employment questionnaire and watch your dreams go down the drain? Should you have lost your right to vote and participate in our democracy?

George W. Bush drove drunk. Bill Clinton sexually harassed women. Donald Trump admitted to sexually assaulting women (plus did a lot of other things, including tax fraud). They each got to be president, yet a seventeen-year-old Chicago kid who gets caught running drugs should figure he'll never get a second chance?

And yes, we can blame poverty and the educational system and a "correctional system" that doesn't do much correcting. But we also have to consider the part our emotions and our prejudices have played.

And there's something else we need to consider: the role of the prosecutor in America.

22. Prosecutorial Zeal and Unfair Legal Practices

Since 1980, the US incarceration rate has nearly tripled, from around 300 people per 100,000 to approximately 860. It's decreased somewhat since 2008 – when it hit a thousand and a full 1% of the adult US population was behind bars – but remains the highest in the world.

So what happened to cause the rise in prosecutions? Some of it, surely, was due to the expanding war on drugs, which is now being scaled back in progressive cities like New York and Philadelphia. Some of it could also be attributed to an ideology that came out of the high crime era of the 1980s and early 90s: lock as many people up as possible to reduce crime. The mentality was that there were simply bad people out there, and if you got rid of them, society would be much better off.

But something else was at play as well.

In 1871 Congress passed a civil rights act intended to protect black citizens from abuse at the hands of the law. The relevant section, known as 1983, said that no person "under color of" the law of any state or territory (or in the District of Columbia), can deprive "any citizen of the United States or other person within the jurisdiction thereof…of any rights, privileges, or immunities secured by the Constitution and laws," and if they do, "shall be liable to the party injured in an action at law, suit in equity, or other proper proceeding for redress…"

There were no exceptions carved out. But then the Supreme Court got involved, first absolving legislators in the 1951 case of *Tenney v. Brandhove*, then prosecutors some twenty-five years later. Despite the 1871 law, prosecutors had continued to operate under the idea of "prosecutorial immunity" – the notion that they cannot be held responsible for wrongful acts they commit in pursuit of a prosecution. In *Imbler v. Pachtman* (1976), the US Supreme Court upheld that notion, making it clear that prosecutors warranted "absolute immunity." A decision by the 2nd Appellate Court in 1981 clarified this position, basing its reasoning on *Imbler*: "The falsification of evidence and the coercion of witnesses...have been held to be prosecutorial activities for which absolute immunity applies. Similarly, because a prosecutor is acting as an advocate in a judicial proceeding, the solicitation and subornation of perjured testimony, the withholding of evidence, or the introduction of illegally-seized evidence at trial does not create liability in damages."

You may want to read that again because it's fairly remarkable.

Basically, prosecutors can do whatever they feel like to get a conviction and not be held accountable, so long as they do it in the course of the prosecution (and not during an investigation or with statements to the press).

Now, no one is arguing that some immunity shouldn't be granted – so long as a prosecutor acts responsibly and doesn't exceed his or her authority or violate the Constitution. Intent, after all, does matter, and prosecutors who make mistakes shouldn't be held personally liable in the same way as prosecutors who intentionally send people off to rot in prison knowing full-well of exculpatory evidence. But the current law doesn't make that distinction: absolute immunity means that a prosecutor can become a crusader with an ax to grind and never have to worry about the innocence of their potential victim.

The University of Michigan keeps a "National Registry of Exonerations." Surely, these exonerations represent just a fraction of the innocent people who have been put behind bars. As of this writing, they've recorded 2,240 exonerations since 1989, 872 of which – 39% – were for murder. A hundred and twenty of those wrongfully convicted murderers had received death sentences. In 96 of those cases, official misconduct was involved. In fact, overall, official misconduct (lying, falsifying evidence, etc.) was involved more than half the time. The registry calculates that misconduct alone has resulted in over 12,000 years of life lost. And yet prosecutors who knowingly sent these people off to jail or to the death chamber cannot be held legally accountable. That is just plain ludicrous.

In fact, not only do these prosecutors face no criminal charges – they don't even get disciplined as prosecutors. Even when federal judges criticize prosecutors for misconduct, they're often obligated to refer the cases to state justices. And then nothing happens: In 2010, the Northern California Innocence Project reviewed 707 cases in which prosecutorial misconduct had been found over a period of eleven years. A total of six prosecutors were disciplined and 80% of the convictions were upheld.

Basically, prosecutors can get away with anything. As a matter of fact, most states have no review boards overseeing prosecutors whatsoever.

The United States, meanwhile, is the only country in the world that elects prosecutors. Because of this, American prosecutors are subject to the whims of the electorate, and have constant pressure to be "tough on crime." They tend to take an approach centered on punishing perpetrators rather than embracing a holistic view that that reduces criminal incidents and improves communities as a whole.

They're also not a very diverse group. While 70% of inmates come from minorities, 95% of prosecutors are white and 83% are male.

So what can we do about prosecutorial zeal?

Well, first off, prosecutorial immunity should be qualified, not absolute. While it's important to society to protect our prosecutors from frivolous lawsuits, it's also important to protect our people from abusive prosecutors. No one should be above the law – not the president, not our legislators, and certainly not prosecutors.

We also have to improve the review process. Prosecutors should not be allowed to act with impunity and should know their actions are subject to evaluation.

And we need to make efforts to diversify. Otherwise we risk inherent prejudices playing a factor.

But our criminal justice system is only one part of the problem. We also have an extremely flawed civil justice system that favors the rich, discriminates against the poor, and acts as a cudgel for corporate interests.

23. Our Inadequate Civil Justice System

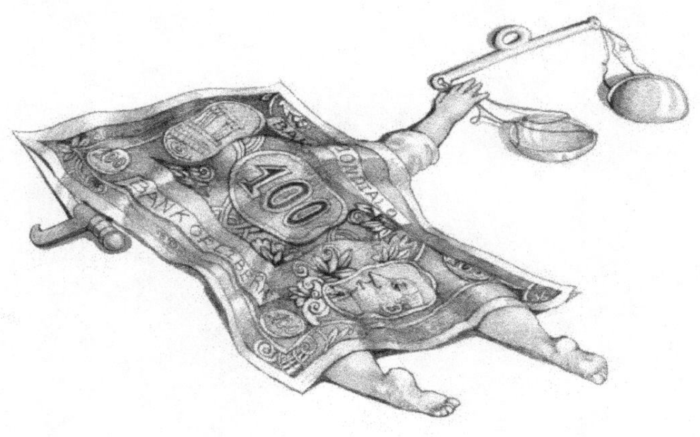

If you're a civic-minded person, you may be familiar with *Gideon v. Wainwright*. It was the 1963 case by which the Supreme Court, in a unanimous decision, established the right to an attorney in all felony cases. Justice Hugo Black, writing on behalf of the court, noted that lawyers in criminal matters "are necessities, not luxuries."

Prior to *Gideon*, the Supreme Court had mandated in *Powell v. Alabama* (1932) that defendants were entitled to attorneys in cases where they faced the death penalty. Before that, there essentially was no guarantee whatsoever that a defendant would receive a lawyer to help them navigate the charges against them.

Gideon, as important as it was, did not extend the right to an attorney to civil cases, no matter how dire. In 1981, the court had the chance to rectify that with *Lassiter v. Department of Social Services*. But in a 5-4 ruling along ideological lines, the court chose instead not to affirm such a right, asserting that attorneys were only required for criminal cases in which loss of "physical liberty" was at stake.

Since then – and especially in recent years – many legal scholars have questioned the wisdom of that decision. In 2006, the American Bar Association House of Delegates voted unanimously in favor of a "civil Gideon" rule, as it is known, which would provide attorneys for those facing severe repercussions from civil proceedings. After all, does a trial that may deprive one of their safety, their livelihood, or even their children not warrant proper legal counsel? Are we to believe that we should be guaranteed an attorney if we're facing jail time, but not if we're facing a severe loss of income or property or extreme reputational damage? Yet more than 80% of indigent people have to contend with civil proceedings without representation due to their inability to afford an attorney.

Of course, the greatest jeopardy posed by civil litigation may be the possibility of being thrown out of one's home. Yet most tenants face eviction hearings without counsel. A study from the Boston Bar Association, for instance, found that 90% of tenants facing eviction in Massachusetts went unrepresented.

According to Matthew Desmond, who founded Princeton's "Eviction Lab," we are in the midst of an eviction crisis. Approximately 2.3 million people were evicted from their homes in 2016. That's some 6,300 a day. As Desmond notes, when you lose your home, you also lose your stability, your community, and often your job. It doesn't just affect the renter being evicted, but their family, their friends, and the neighborhood itself, which may wind up with one less member of the PTA, one less childcare worker, or one less home health care nurse.

Meanwhile, as first noted in Chapter 15, asking prices for rentals have doubled since 1995, meaning that a higher and higher percentage of income has to go toward shelter.

But here's the real kicker:

Despite this enormous crisis, in most places, tenants are not guaranteed any right to counsel during a trial to determine whether or not they'll get to remain in their home or if their life and the lives of the members of their family will be upended because they've been tossed out. How important is this? Well, the Boston Bar study cited above found that tenants in the Quincy area who received representation were twice as likely to remain in their homes and were compensated for losses at five times the rate of those who did not. So the answer is: extremely, extremely important – life-changing, even.

Other countries have come to this realization as well, and most of them did so a long time ago. England provides free civil counsel to indigent defendants, as does Italy, Spain, Austria, Switzerland, Portugal, Sweden, Denmark, Belgium, and Holland. Way back in 1979, in the case of *Airey v. Ireland*, the European Union's Court of Human Rights stipulated that the indigent have the right to representation in civil matters, a decision that currently affects forty-nine countries under its jurisdiction. Outside of Europe, various nations have followed suit, including Canada, Australia, and Israel.

In the US, there are some organizations that provide free legal services for civil litigation, but they are so incredibly short-staffed and overworked that landing a lawyer from one of them is like hitting the Pick 4. And the odds that they'll be able to give your case the proper consideration are just as slim. While there are approximately 40 attorneys for every 10,000 people in the US, there's only one attorney for every 15,000 indigent people.

The good news is that there has been some progress on this front. Most states now waive filing fees if a civil litigant is indigent. According to ThinkProgress, twenty states encourage judges to avoid "legalese" when dealing with people representing themselves. Thirty-two allow court clerks to help out unrepresented parties. Twenty-three permit judges to assist those without counsel. And many states now provide access to an attorney if a parent is threatened by the state with the potential termination of parental rights.

In 2017, New York City Mayor Bill de Blasio signed into law legislation that devoted $90 million to guaranteeing free representation to indigent defendants in Housing Court. Like in Massachusetts, 90% of defendants in NYC's Housing Court were unrepresented at the time. New York state also has a general rule that allows judges to appoint attorneys for the indigent, as do Indiana and Massachusetts. Most states now have rules providing an attorney for anyone threatened with mandatory substance abuse recovery or removal to a mental health facility. Numerous states also provide free attorneys to the poor for matters before Family Court. (For a comprehensive list of state regulations regarding appointed counsel in civil matters, see "State Statutes Providing for a Right to Counsel in Civil Cases," from the Brennan Center.)

So, to at least some degree, states have made progress in this area. Yet not all states have embraced the idea of a "civil Gideon" rule to the same extent. Also, not all states publicize these rights to the same degree, and many poor people are unaware of them.

There's no reason why our federal government and federal courts can't recognize this basic right. While it's nice to know that an attorney will be provided for you in criminal cases (one who, due to their workload, may not be prepared to represent you – but an attorney nonetheless), it's not exactly comforting to think that you won't really have any way to take an HMO to court if they back out of your coverage. Or that you can't really fight back if Apple decides to sue you.

This doesn't just affect the indigent, either. As we'll get into later, our corrupted patent and copyright system is rife with abuse, permitting companies with teams of lawyers to extort money from hardworking, inventive Americans.

When it comes to civil litigation, the scales are definitely tipped in favor of Big Business. Credit card companies, for one, can take advantage of small business owners who have little recourse. Restaurant operators, for instance, have learned the hard way that challenging rules issued by the major credit card companies can not only potentially cost you business if they should decide to shut you out, but can also cost you tens of thousands in litigation if you're foolish enough to take them on. The Supreme Court even recently ruled that credit card companies can include anti-competitive clauses in contracts that prohibit merchants from steering customers to cards that may charge lower fees.

Right now the US civil justice system is more of a civil enforcement system in favor of Big Business, the golden rule being, "They who have the gold set the rules." The problem is that the federal court system – and some state court systems – often fail to recognize when there is an unfair playing field. They don't consider it their duty to protect the weak and indigent and not allow the powerful to take advantage of the rest of us. It would be like having to play a one-on-one basketball game for your life against LeBron James. Also: you're three feet tall.

"Civil Gideon" ought to be a Constitutional right, either established by amendment or (more likely) simply recognized by the courts. For that to happen, liberals will have to try to get the matter before the Supreme Court again. And if the court, with its current stolen-seat conservative slant, rules against us, we'll have to bring another case. And another. And another. Until we get the answer we want. It's how conservatives often do it, and it's what progressives should learn to do as well.

In the meantime, we have to dedicate ourselves to increasing the availability of Legal Aid for civil proceedings and concentrate on establishing the right to an attorney for civil matters in cities, towns, and states. While *Lassiter* was a setback, it does not prevent us from making progress at these levels; we can and we should.

We've now discussed poverty, mass incarceration, prosecutorial zeal, and our completely inadequate civil justice system. Next we'll discuss one of the major underlying factors for all of them: racism.

24. Racism

Black Lives Matter protesters, Washington, DC, November, 2015. Credit: Johnny Silvercloud

No country is immune to racism, but a thriving democracy should make people of all backgrounds feel equally welcome. The United States has, unfortunately, allowed prejudicial views to strongly affect its politics, its institutions, and its justice system.

As noted earlier, the World Justice Project gives the US a .52 when it comes to people believing that they are treated equally under the law, a truly atrocious score. Though the disparity between white and black incarceration rates has shrunk, black people are still imprisoned at five times the rate of whites and one in ten black children has a parent in prison, compared to one in sixty white children.

Although blacks make up only about 13% of the US population, they made up over 22% of fatal police shootings in 2017, according to the *Washington Post*. The Police Violence Report noted that out of 149 unarmed people killed by police in 2017, 49 of them (33%) were black and 34 of them (23%) were Hispanic (Hispanics make up approximately 17% of the US population).

This should not be exaggerated, nor be interpreted to mean that every cop is a racist. Many of them are very good people. Keep in mind that poverty disproportionately affects minority populations, and because of that it's to be expected that police would be called to minority neighborhoods at a higher rate than white neighborhoods. And if they're called to minority neighborhoods at a higher rate, they're more likely to kill unarmed members of those minorities at a higher rate as well. Still, it's important to understand that our system and culture tend to lead to higher percentages of minority incarceration and minorities being killed by police.

Minorities also receive disproportionate sentences. An analysis by the United States Sentencing Commission (which operates out of the Judicial branch) found that similarly situated black male defendants received, on average, sentences 19.1% higher than white male defendants (and yes, that's accounting for variables related to sentencing, such as prior criminal records).

Earlier (in the Mass Incarceration section) I noted how tickets disproportionately hurt the poor. Well, a study out of Stanford also found that tickets are disproportionately given to blacks and Latinos. According to the study, blacks were 20% more likely to receive tickets than whites, and Latinos were 30% more likely. Once stopped, each minority is also about twice as likely to be searched as whites, the study said. Guess it helps to be a white guy driving a Jaguar.

For a multitude of reasons, blacks and Hispanics are also vastly underrepresented in the nation's top schools, as the *New York Times* demonstrated when it did an analysis of the country's 100 best colleges and universities. The *Times* found that although African Americans make up 15% of the college-age population, they only make up 6% of freshman. Only 13% of freshman at the top schools were Hispanic, despite Hispanics making up 22% of the college-age population. The *Times* found that Affirmative Action hasn't helped at all: the numbers have actually gotten worse since 1980 when one takes into account population shifts. A switch in concentration to economic hardship rather than simply race would probably do more to help minorities and lead to less acrimony. Still, Affirmative Action on its own – whether race-based or poverty-based – would not in and of itself be enough to address the massive problems caused by our history of racism.

Again, not to oversimplify – there are a multitude of reasons that minority underrepresentation is occurring, including, of course, disproportionate poverty within both the black and Hispanic communities. And I'm not suggesting that admissions counselors are somehow unusually prejudiced – in fact, I accept that colleges tend to lean liberal and would probably prefer to admit more minorities.

But certainly racism plays a part in bringing these young people down to begin with. Many of them have had to suffer the soft bigotry of low expectations. Their opportunities have not been the same as their white peers. They've been kept out of neighborhoods with better school districts and often don't get the chance to enhance their applications with the same level of extracurricular activities as well-off white kids.

Speaking of opportunity: Want to hear a shocking number?

Ten.

That's about how much you'd have to multiply the median net worth of a black family to equal that of a white family. According to the *Washington Post*: "In 2016, white families had a median net worth of $171,000, compared with $17,600 for blacks and $20,700 for Hispanics." Even whites with less than some college education have a median wealth of $18,800.

How did this happen?

Well, much of it has to do with real estate, which has always been a great source of wealth for white families and one that is often a difficult barrier for minorities. In the case of black Americans, most of their ancestors were slaves and started out with nothing; there were no lands to pass on, no inherited wealth. Also: segregation – in the North as well as the South – kept blacks from owning homes and living in certain neighborhoods. That house with the white picket fence? It's not just the fence that tends to be white.

Despite these historic setbacks, there's ample evidence to suggest that many whites are pushing back against minority progress. Diana Mutz of UPenn found that, contrary to popular belief, the major motivator for Trump voters wasn't economic concerns, but racial ones. They were worried about losing their status as the majority power. Yes, shocking as it may seem, the people who voted for the guy who said that the first black president wasn't born in this country and pushed for banning all Muslims from entering the US were largely motivated by racism and bigotry. (Are you making your surprised face?)

We're also seeing a rise in white nationalism. It predates Trump, but he certainly didn't help. After the Nazi rally and subsequent murder of Heather Heyer in Charlottesville, the UN took the extraordinary step of issuing an "early warning" to the Trump administration regarding its refusal to adequately address hate groups. Such a warning had previously only been issued to Iraq, Kyrgyzstan, Burundi, Ivory Coast, and Nigeria within the previous decade.

On Fox "News," white victimhood is played up on a regular basis. White people are the real ones discriminated against, Rupert Murdoch's network would have you believe – working class whites have to contend with minorities wanting handing-outs and liberal smartie-pantses who think they know better than anyone. Who speaks up for the white man? Only Sean Hannity and his ilk, of course! (And perhaps that great American hero, Rush Limbaugh, who serves America every day by dishing up nonsensical controversies, lies, and utter absurdities to his 14 million listeners, raking in some $14 million a year.)

Of course, compared to the racial animosity which exists in countries such as India or South Sudan, or the intolerance of a Saudi Arabia or Myanmar, the US is relatively advanced. And other industrialized countries certainly have their issues with other cultures as well (e.g. France, when it comes to Muslims).

But such comparisons should not undermine the scope, complexity, and wide scale negative effects of racism and bigotry in America. Our country was built on the backs of slaves working lands stolen from Native Americans. We systematically abused and exploited minorities throughout our history, and the racial issues subsequently caused by such treatment haven't vanished with the advent of the iPhone. It seems almost ironic that the election of the nation's first black president was followed by the Electoral College's selection of a white supremacist to succeed him in that office. But history is often like that; not so much an arc as a winding path that often winds backwards.

25. Sexism

As of 2018, just 84 of the 435 voting members in the House of Representatives are women and only 23 women in serve in the Senate. That means women make up just 20% of Congress. And that's the high water mark! Never in our history have more women served in our legislative body. But 20%? Is that really the best we can do? According to the Inter-Parliamentary Union, the US ranks 102nd in the world when it comes to women serving in national legislative bodies. That's right: 102nd. We not only rank behind industrialized countries like the UK (41st), France (16th), and Denmark (24th), but behind Ethiopia

(18th), Bolivia (3rd), and Costa Rica (7th). The US has also never had a woman as head of state (although Hillary Clinton did receive more votes than Donald Trump). We've only had one woman – ever – Nancy Pelosi – as Speaker of the House. Meanwhile, India, the UK, Australia, Israel and others have had women lead their governments.

Like racism, sexism can be both direct and indirect, and sometimes hard to pinpoint. Did sexism play a role in the 2016 presidential election? Well, most-likely: while the percentage of women who voted for Clinton in 2016 was relatively the same as those who voted for Obama in 2008 and 2012, the number of men shifted greatly: Obama lost men by seven points to Romney and won them by one point against McCain; Clinton lost men to Trump by twelve points. Keep in mind that Trump was an absolutely atrocious candidate. I mean this seriously – many people like to say that about Hillary Clinton, but, if you're being honest, despite her flaws (and they did exist), it was obvious that Clinton was a vastly superior candidate to Trump. Yet men went for him by twelve points while no more women went for her than had gone for Obama. You would've thought, at the least, that she would've dominated the women's vote, but she didn't. There are three main reasons for this: One, the overall divisiveness of the nation made many women identify more as Republican or Democrat than as a woman; Two, issues of white identity trumped gender identity; and Three, there are a fair amount of women who are also prejudiced against women. That last one is perhaps the hardest to swallow, but is sadly true. Sexism is so ingrained in us that a fair minority of women maintain sexist, discriminatory views themselves.

Because of that, women often take themselves out of consideration. Certainly that's true when it comes to running for office, but it's also true in other fields. According to the Bureau of Labor Statistics, nationally, women make up just over 34% of legislators, 16.2% of engineering/architectural jobs, and only 13% of police officers. And often they do even worse when it comes to managerial positions. For instance, only 8.7% of engineering/architecture managers are women.

Part of the reason women are underrepresented in scientific fields is that they are discouraged from pursuing them in the first place. Despite receiving a higher percentage of college degrees than men, women only account for a quarter of STEM degrees. Many young women feel that they're not cut out for those subjects, even though they're more than capable. They've learned since the time they were little not to pursue such interests.

Let's face it: we concentrate far too much on beauty when it comes to females and it's doing damage. Girls are often judged more on their aesthetic qualities while boys are judged by their athletic abilities and their intelligence. We sign boys up to play sports, while girls tend to do dance and beauty contests. We would never consider contests to judge how handsome boys are, yet we force girls into beauty pageants all the time. And dance, despite the fact that it is a legitimate art form and can be great for exercise, has been hijacked: every girl is forced to dress exactly the same, forced to put on makeup, and forced to pose for ridiculous pictures. For most girls who do dance lessons and recitals in the US, it's become largely aesthetic. We're teaching girls that beauty trumps all.

It's probably why so many women were willing to vote for a man for president who literally admitted on tape to sexually assaulting women. They accepted the notion that "all men talk like that" and were able to ignore it because so many of them have been programmed to believe that such behavior is somehow normal or acceptable. They accept that men see them as objects of beauty. They've learned it from a young age.

How often do you hear fathers describe their girls as "princesses?" What does a princess do? Well, nothing. In the storybooks she waits around for Prince Charming. Her only job is to be beautiful. As a matter of fact, many fathers will also throw that adjective in too: "My beautiful little princess," they might say.

Girls have been systematically and culturally discriminated against – to the point that they often don't pursue careers that they would be well-suited for. We need more female engineers! We're missing out on a great pool of talent, much like Major League Baseball was missing out on talent before Jackie Robinson broke the color barrier.

And then there's the issue of pay. Women do receive less pay than men for the same work, although how much less is a matter of contention. The reasons they receive less are also a bit misunderstood. The main reason, actually, is that women are often forced to choose between having a family and having a career. Part of this has to do with government policy: we need family-leave with pay and we need it to last at least twelve weeks. A woman should not have to give up all she's worked for career-wise when she decides to have a child.

Yet another reason for the pay gap is how we as a society characterize women who promote their own interests. When a man is demanding, we say he's a "go-getter" or "tough." When a woman is demanding, she's "a bitch." It's a terrible double-standard that discourages women from pursuing their true monetary value.

Finally, there's the "All Boys Club." Like it or not, people tend to hire others whom they share traits with, even if they're not doing so consciously. Men who are entrenched in the business world tend to hire other men. A study out of Harvard and Stanford found that when women are doing the hiring, they split things evenly, hiring 50% women and 50% men. But when men are doing the hiring, it's 60/40 in favor of hiring other men. That's probably one of the reasons why less than 5% of Fortune 500 companies are headed by women and they make up less than 20% of the board members for those companies.

It's good to see that the #MeToo movement is bringing attention to sexual harassment, aggression against women, and other misconduct by men. But we need to do a great deal more. We need to teach girls that they can be just as good at math and science as boys. We need to work toward pay equity. We need laws to prevent women from having to sacrifice their careers in order to have a family. And we need to change our culture to ensure that female voices are being heard and that women are not being discriminated against.

26. Bigotry

On Friday, May 26th, 2017, two teenagers, one black, the other a Muslim girl wearing a hijab, boarded a train in Portland, Oregon. Immediately, a white man named Jeremy Christian began verbally abusing them, shouting anti-Muslim slurs and telling them that they should get out of the country. Three good Samaritans: Rick Best, 53, Taliesin Myrddin Namkai Meche, 23, and Micah David-Cole Fletcher, 21, tried to intervene and calm Christian down. Best and Meche paid for their efforts with their lives after Christian pulled a knife and slit both of their throats. Fletcher was injured as well, but survived, as did the two girls. Later, in the courtroom after his arrest, Christian continued his anti-Muslim tirade, telling the judge and all present, “You call it terrorism, I call it patriotism!”

It’s easy to dismiss Christian’s crimes and his rantings as an isolated incident – a one-off perpetrated by a single loon. But, sadly, that’s not the case. As the Council on American-Islamic Relations has reported, both hate crimes and incidents of bigotry against Muslims have been steadily rising with the rise of Donald Trump. In 2015, there were 180 anti-Muslim hate crimes; by 2016, it had risen to 260; in 2017, it was 300. “Anti-Muslim Bias Incidents,” meanwhile, went from 1,409 in 2015 to 2,213 in 2016, then rose again to 2,599 in 2017. This data aligns with FBI statistics tracking hate crimes through 2016.

In 2017, Pew took a poll to judge how Americans feel about different groups. While Jews topped the list with 67% of people having “warm” feelings toward them, Muslims registered a mere 48%. The widespread bigotry against Muslims is surely part of the reason Trump was able to receive the support of some 63 million Americans, despite having called for the “total and complete shutdown of Muslims entering the United States.” And despite what the Trump campaign would later claim, the proposed ban was in no way temporary, but “until our country’s representatives can figure out what the hell is going on.”

Much like Muslims, Atheists tend to incur people’s prejudices: the same Pew poll found that only 50% of Americans had warm feelings toward them. Likewise, a 2016 survey from Pew that found that 51% of Americans said they would be less likely to vote for an Atheist for president (though it should be noted that the number had fallen from 63% in 2007).

Perhaps that’s why no one in Congress is an avowed Atheist. Pew reports on that as well. They found that the 115th Congress is over 90% Christian and has exactly three Buddhists, two Muslims, and one person, Kyrsten Sinema of Arizona, who considers herself "unaffiliated." Ten members of Congress didn't respond to the survey. Not one was willing to admit to being an Atheist, although it's probable that some are – they just know that declaring yourself an Atheist in this country is a quick way to lose your position. Ironically enough, Sinema serves openly as a bisexual (which is great), but keeps her atheism in the closet for fear of the political reverberations.

Not that being part of the LGBTQ community is any bargain either. According to the Southern Poverty Law Center, anti-LGBTQ groups rose from just 6 in 2006 to 51 by 2017. FBI data shows that in 2016 there were over a thousand hate crimes committed against individuals in the US due to their sexual orientation, and another 124 perpetrated against transgender people. Transgender people can't even use the bathroom without it becoming a national issue. Conservatives use a "religious freedom" argument to deny LGBTQ citizens their rights, when in reality their only crime is being different.

Trump's ascendancy has made it ever clearer that we are not quite living in the post-racial, post-bigotry, gender-equal society that many had hoped we were. Racism, bigotry, and sexism are alive and well. Yet the problem isn't simply manifested in KKK rallies or Trump's questioning of Obama's citizenship or his calls to ban all Muslims or his numerous sexist comments and acts. The problem goes much deeper than that: it is institutionalized. There are those in this country, including our president, our vice president, and several cabinet heads, who feel that we should be a nation dominated by Christianity. When Fox "News" talks about the so-called "War on Christmas," the true message is clear: they want to scare their viewers into thinking that the Muslims, Atheists, Hindus, and others are taking over.

And Trump has gotten that message loud and clear. It's why he held a rally in Missouri not long before Christmas in 2017 with Christmas trees interspersed with American flags in the background and made sure to point out a sign adorning the platform that read "Merry Christmas." He told the crowd, "I told you we would be saying 'Merry Christmas' again." The next day, at the White House Christmas tree dedication on the Ellipse, he said it was his "tremendous honor to finally wish America and the world a very MERRY CHRISTMAS," emphasizing the last two words and capitalizing them in his tweet about the event. The key word, of course, was "finally," which implied that Christians had somehow been suffering discrimination in recent years, and that his predecessor, Barack Obama, was not Christian enough, and therefore not 100% American.

They want us to know: this nation is for Christians; all others are simply guests.

27. Rule by Church

Kenneth Copeland (seen here in 2011), the head of Copeland Ministries, is estimated to be worth $760 million. For him, Christianity really day pay off. Big time. Credit: Kenneth Copeland Ministries

You may not have heard of Paul Weyrich, but, trust me, he's had a tremendous impact on your life. Weyrich is often considered the founder of the "Christian right" movement, which exercises dominating control over much of our politics today.

Following the 1963 Supreme Court decision outlawing mandated prayer in public schools, Weyrich, a University of Wisconsin student at the time, decided to devote his life to bringing the forces of Christianity to bear on politics. At the time, the conventional wisdom was that churchgoers did not want their politics and their religion mixing. But Weyrich challenged that notion. In 1973, with financial support from beer magnate Joseph Coors (think about this the next time you pop open a "Silver Bullet"), Weyrich co-founded two organizations dedicated to promoting conservative, Christian causes: the Heritage Foundation and the American Legislative Exchange Council (ALEC), both of which we'll get into more in chapter 40. The next year, to combat union power, he started the Committee for the Survival of a Free Congress (now known as the Free Congress Foundation). His right-hand man for CSFC was Laszlo Pasztor, in his youth a member of the fascist Arrow Cross Party in Hungary, which collaborated with the Nazis during World War II.

After the 1973 *Roe v. Wade* ruling, numerous Christian organizations began springing up, and Weyrich was right in the center of it all. In the late 1970s, Weyrich helped co-found two major Christian-political networks: the Christian Voice and the Moral Majority. In an attempt to prove his overall point that politics and religion could be combined, Weyrich had gathered funding to conduct a poll of Christians to see if they would tolerate political preaching from their pastors. The results not only showed that they would, but that they were eager to embrace the idea. Weyrich, seeking a preacher who could provide such political proselytizing, decided on Jerry Falwell, who operated a small Christian TV program out of Virginia at the time. Weyrich successfully recruited Falwell, who was eager to spread his message to "the moral majority" – a term Weyrich is credited with coining.

Both Christian Voice and the Moral Majority dedicated themselves to attacking what they saw as the sins of pornography and homosexuality. If you've seen *The People vs. Larry Flynt*, you may be familiar with Falwell's crusade. The Moral Majority disbanded in 1989, but by that point numerous other Christian-political organizations had formed, and many more would come.

Some of these organizations have tremendous endowments and exert enormous influence. In 2015, James Dobson's Focus on the Family reported about $75 million in revenue, plus over $64 million in assets. Liberty University, which was founded by Falwell in 1971 and is now operated by his son, Jerry Falwell Jr., has an endowment worth over $1 billion. Falwell Jr. is paid $900,000 a year.

Many of these Christian groups have reduced their political donations – not because they don't want to be involved, but because they no longer need to lobby: they're already in. The Christian right has an inordinate say in our political process because they have an entire party – the Republicans – dedicated to making them happy. In fact, out of 286 Republican members of Congress, all but two (Jewish) are Christian. The vice president of the United States has even been accused (with good reason) of being a "Christian Supremacist." And Trump makes certain to kowtow to the Christian right as much as possible. After all, they make up a great deal of his base.

* * *

Throughout its history, the US has had several periods of religiosity. As David Sehat has pointed out, the Second Great Awakening in the early 1800s led to an explosion in church membership, and religious immigrants entering from 1890 on caused more than half the country to be church members by 1906. Sehat also notes that, even early on, states made religious "blue laws," many of which still affect us today.

Yet more and more Americans are now becoming less and less religious. According to Pew, the percentage of Americans who were religiously unaffiliated grew from 16% to 23% from 2007 to 2014. That's tremendous; and yet Americans are still subjected to a woefully inadequate separation of church and state.

There are movements afoot to bring school prayer back.

Secretary of Education Betsy DeVos is part of an effort to divert more and more public funding to private, religious institutions.

Our Pledge of Allegiance, said every day in schools across the nation, also promotes religious views. It includes the words "Under God," added in 1954 to separate us from those "godless communists." Kids who refuse to say the pledge risk being ostracized by peers and teachers alike.

But that's not all: Our money says "In God We Trust." That same statement appears in all of our courtrooms. And every congressional session, both in the House and the Senate, begins with a prayer from each respective body's anointed chaplain. Taxpayers pay for that, whether they're religious or not. They also often pay for religious displays and demonstrations during the holidays. Even more egregious, though, is the fact that religious institutions do not pay federal or property taxes, which means that other taxpayers are subsidizing them. Add to that that donations to churches, synagogues, et al are tax-deductible, and we're talking around over $80 billion a year that taxpayers are forced to come up with in order to subsidize religion. And now Donald Trump is considering getting rid of the Johnson Amendment prohibiting religious institutions (who, again, receive tax subsidies) from endorsing political candidates.

But Trump is merely riding a wave that existed before he arrived on the scene. The movement springs from a fundamental misinterpretation of the First Amendment. While the amendment guarantees that government will not target any particular religion, it does not state that religious people can carve out legal exceptions for themselves purely on religious grounds. It's a good thing it doesn't too: Otherwise, hypothetically speaking, a person who believed in human sacrifice could murder someone, then claim that they had a First Amendment right to do it.

The amendment states, "Congress shall make no law respecting an establishment of religion, or prohibiting the free exercise thereof...." What it does not state is that Congress has to make exceptions for religious people. Making laws that apply to the population as a whole does not prohibit anyone from practicing their religion. While the US government cannot *target* a religion, it does not have to bend to one either.

Or at least it shouldn't have to.

When it comes to Christianity, however, more and more bending seems to be taking place. Politicians and jurists have bought into dubious religious freedom arguments that allow individuals to disobey laws which apply to others and to discriminate at will – all claiming that it's their First Amendment right to do so.

In *Burwell v. Hobby Lobby* (2014) the Supreme Court, in yet another 5-4 decision along partisan lines, found that the Green family, owners of some 500 Hobby Lobby stores, did not have to follow parts of the Affordable Care Act which they disagreed with on religious grounds, including the requirement to provide contraceptives to employees. It's, of course, a ridiculous premise. One has to wonder if they would accept a religious argument stating that I don't believe in paying taxes or driving the speed limit or having to buy car insurance. The answer is: Of course not.

But the Supreme Court did it again when it came to gay rights. In *Masterpiece Cakeshop, Ltd. v. Colorado Civil Rights Commission*, the court said that a baker who refused to make a cake for a gay couple was within his rights. I guess his rights trumped the rights of the couple who wanted the cake. The petitioner, Jack Phillips, had argued that designing cakes is an art form and his way of expressing his love for his god. And since he does not believe in gay marriage, he shouldn't be forced to make a cake for a gay couple, he said. And the court said OK!

Maybe next some people will be able to say they object to Jewish weddings or Muslim weddings and that they shouldn't have to make those cakes either. Or take their pictures. Or allow them to use a catering hall. Maybe we'll just get rid of the Civil Rights Act and replace it with "do whatever suits you."

The Supreme Court seems to think that personal belief somehow is more valuable than the rule of law and standards we have set up as a society. The cake-maker still maintained his freedom of speech; he could still speak out against gay marriage, submit editorials about it, or even protest outside of a gay wedding. But we've decided as a society that, once you decide to be a restaurant owner, you have to allow all races and religions to eat at your restaurant. Once you've decided to be a mechanic, you can't turn certain ethnicities away from receiving car service simply because you've deemed them inferior.

There are some reasonable exceptions, of course. If you're casting someone to play Malcolm X, you can indeed limit auditions to black actors. If you're looking for someone to teach a class on evolution, you don't have to allow in religious types who reject the science. If a club can only afford to hire two bouncers, it makes sense for them to choose two strong men instead of two tiny women.

But the exceptions should be based on logic and logistics, not on religion. We should be doing our utmost to preserve basic rights and dignity.

I wonder what would happen if a Muslim came before the Supreme Court saying that Sharia law should trump federal law…? Hmmm.

Somehow I think the five conservative justices wouldn't find the argument so plausible then.

28. The Destruction of Unions

Quick history lesson: Prior to the Civil War, there were no nationwide unions in the US. In 1866, the National Labor Union appeared. It did not last long. But in 1869, the Knights of Labor was formed, and by 1886, under the leadership of Terence Powderly, it had grown to over 700,000 members. Yet the small but burgeoning labor movement was already internally divided: some believed in only including skilled workers, others believed in admitting unskilled workers as well; some were fighting for better wages and a shorter workday, while a minority contingent were fighting against capitalism itself.

In May of 1886, violence erupted (literally, in this case) during a labor rally at Haymarket Square in Chicago. Seven police officers were killed when a bomb was tossed in their path as they tried to approach the speaker's platform. Eight labor organizers were arrested, despite the existence of little or no evidence as to their guilt. Seven of the organizers were sentenced to death and one to fifteen years in prison (two of those sentenced to death would have their sentences commuted and one would commit suicide before his scheduled execution). Some saw the trials as completely unfair and elevated the convicted to martyrs, but others saw in unions a dangerous (and foreign) element.

Divisions within the Knights of Labor helped bring about the American Federation of Labor by the end of 1886. The suspicions against unions and the internal strife, however, caused union membership to drop to around 6% of the workforce. Then came the Sherman Antitrust Act. The Act, of course, was intended to eliminate unfair business practices. But anti-labor forces used the courts to fight against unions on the notion that they violated the collusion prohibitions of the act, even though the crafters of the law had clearly not intended it to be used in such a fashion. Theodore Roosevelt's administration was more tolerant of unions, negotiating the end of the 1902 coal strike – the first time a president ever got so involved in a labor dispute. One could also argue that Roosevelt's regulatory efforts ensured greater competition and therefore a fairer labor market. Then, during the Wilson administration, Congress passed the Clayton Anti-Trust Act of 1914, which targeted trusts and monopolies while recognizing the right of workers to organize.

Membership in unions increased until the 1920s, when court rulings against unions, fear of anarchists, and a general malaise caused membership to drop steeply. However, the onset of the Great Depression and FDR's New Deal brought unions back to the fore. After the Supreme

Court struck down the National Industrial Recovery Act in 1935, the Wagner Act was created to fill the void, providing worker protections and creating the National Labor Relations Board. Union membership skyrocketed, growing to over 35% of the workforce during World War II.

Unfortunately, since then, unions have been in steady decline. Some of that decline was probably due to the Taft-Hartley Act, which shifted power back toward management. For one, the act forbid union members from engaging in secondary strikes in support of other workers. It said that workers could not picket or boycott a business that was working with another business experiencing a strike. For example: If you and I are part of a tire union, and that union is doing business with GM, and there's a strike at the GM plant and we decide we want to go on strike too unless our employer agrees to seek doing business with GM until the other strikers' demands are met, we can't do it. We are prohibited by law. And we can't boycott over that strike – at least not as a union – something that you would figure is a fundamental right.

Taft-Hartley also required unions to give notice before a strike, made it legal for employers to fire supervisors who participate in union activity, and outlawed "closed shops" (contracts with employers which force them to hire union labor – "union shops," which require new workers to join the union within a short time frame were still legal).

Other factors have also contributed to the downward trend in union membership, including subsequent acts of Congress, a management-friendly environment, and covenants not to compete (as Paul Krugman brilliantly outlined).

According to the Bureau of Labor Statistics, union membership today is 10.7%, about half of what it was in 1983. Even that, though, is in danger after two recent Supreme Court decisions: *Epic Systems v. Lewis* and *Janus v. American Federation of State, County, and Municipal Employees*, both 5-4 rulings decided by the stolen seat of Neil Gorsuch.

In *Epic*, the court declared that the Wagner Act (also known as the National Labor Relations Act) did not protect workers from arbitration clauses in contracts. Yet Wagner guaranteed workers the right to join unions and to "engage in other concerted activities" for "mutual aid or protection." Arbitration clauses that explicitly prohibit workers from joining together in class action suits and require them to act individually – which would be financially prohibitive, of course, since court cases are extremely expensive – would seem to fly in the face of that. Yet that's not how the court saw it, ruling for the employers and dealing a blow to unions across the country.

As the *New York Times* Editorial Board noted, the court, in the majority opinion authored by Gorsuch, essentially treats workers and employers as if they're somehow operating on the same even playing field. Harvard law professor Noah Feldman put it this way: "Gorsuch's opinion is neatly argued and clearly written. If you lived on the moon, with no knowledge of the realities of labor relations or the politics of class actions, you'd think it was obviously correct." He added, "The whole point of the NLRA, [Justice] Ginsburg convincingly argued, was to reject the idea that employers could use their structural power in forming employment contracts to make employees give up their rights."

Back in the 1920s, something known as "yellow-dog contracts" were popular amongst employers. Essentially, they contractually prohibited employees from unionizing as a condition of their employment. In 1932, Congress made such contracts illegal with the Norris-LaGuardia Act, recognizing that employers and employees did not have equal bargaining power. Yet, with *Epic*, the Supreme Court appears to have endorsed yellow-dog-type contracts once again, forcing employees to give up their rights in order to secure a job.

But the conservative justices weren't done: just a few weeks later, in *Janus*, they hit unions again, declaring that they could not collect fees from any non-union members who were enjoying certain benefits from the union. The decision overturned a 1977 case, *Abood v. Detroit Board of Education*, which declared that non-union members could be forced to pay some union fees because they were sharing in union benefits. It addressed the "free rider" problem that plagues unions: If someone can receive union benefits without having to pay union fees, why join the union? So *Abood* said that these non-union members could be forced to pay *certain* fees, though those fees could not be used for political activities. But Mark Janus, a public service employee in Illinois, claimed that any support of unions was inherently political, and that forcing him to pay any fees at all was an infringement upon his free speech because it was essentially forcing him (through the fees) to support unions. And the court agreed.

Justice Kagan, in an extremely critical dissent, didn't buy the First Amendment argument, noting that the decision did a great deal more to quash the First Amendment than to protect it, since it made it difficult for unions to bring cases, act as a voice for workers, or even exist. Surely, all unions are now in an existential crisis. Kagan wrote: "The First Amendment was meant for better things. It was meant not to undermine but to protect democratic governance – including over the role of public-sector unions."

(If you're interested, here's a pretty good five-minute explanation of the case done by a layperson that was made before the ruling came out.)

Unions, meanwhile, are a key part of shielding us from income inequality. As this chart from the Economic Policy Institute indicates, as union membership has gone down, income distribution to the wealthy has skyrocketed.

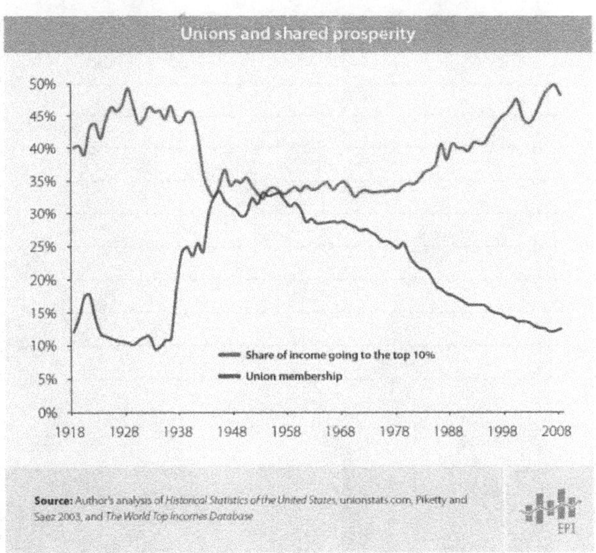

And that's how you get the richest 10% controlling 76% of the wealth. And with Donald Trump and the Republicans seeking to give even more money to the wealthiest among us, this issue isn't likely to get any better any time soon. The union voice is being replaced by the corporate voice. And they're not speaking for most of us.

29. Excessive Corporate Power and Moneyed Interests

"We know now that government by organized money is just as dangerous as government by organized mob. Never before in all our history have these forces been so united against one candidate as they stand today. They are *unanimous* in their hate for me and I *welcome* their hatred!"

–Franklin Roosevelt, 1936

FDR said that when union membership was around 35% of the workforce. Even in the deepest, darkest days of the Depression, the corporate class was fearful of losing its grip on power. Yet in the aftermath of World War II, when union membership was still strong, we saw tremendous economic growth. Union membership is not a hindrance to prosperity, it is a pillar of it; unions ensure economic stability and act as a check against excessively concentrated wealth. It's no coincidence that, as union membership has gone down, the wealth gap has gone up.

As unions have deteriorated, we've witnessed a massive shift in power, with management and moneyed interests coming to dominate the economic sphere and workers' rights on the decline. Rather than corporations and workers having a symbiotic relationship in which both depend on the other to produce viable products that can be brought to market, a system of subjugation has taken hold in which many workers find themselves with few options and even fewer avenues of redress should they have grievances. Arbitration clauses and non-compete contracts have rendered workers virtually powerless, and the Supreme Court has condoned such behavior with its partisan conservative majority (which, I'll remind you, includes a completely stolen seat and another filled by a president who was not the choice of the people), refusing to recognize the imbalance of power and the damage being done to the First Amendment's right to organize.

The moneyed interests received a "yuge" boost from the Trump tax bill. They'll be able to repatriate some $2.6 trillion they've stashed overseas at greatly reduced rates: rather than pay the 35% they would've paid when they hid the money in the first place, they'll be able to bring cash home at a rate of 15.5% and money tied up in real estate or machinery at an 8% tax rate. We were told that the windfall corporate America received would trickle down to the rest of us and that wages would increase. But – surprise, surprise – that hasn't happened so far, with corporations instead buying back stock and increasing their own bottom lines.

I know it must come as an enormous shock that, without unions to protect them, and without governmental support, workers – forced to rely on the kindness of their corporate overlords – haven't seen much benefit. But that is in fact the reality.

Both Apple and Amazon just passed the $1 trillion mark in terms of market value. But if you work as one of Apple's geniuses at its "Genius Bar," you'll pull in somewhere between $15 and $23 an hour, depending on what city or state you're in. I suppose Apple doesn't value "genius" as much as they make out.

But it's better than Amazon, I'd say. The median salary at Amazon is $28,446 (brought down somewhat by seasonal workers). If you just considered Jeff Bezos's salary as CEO – a mere $1.7 million – you'd calculate that he only made about 59 times what the typical employee makes. Of course, it would be a nonsense calculation. In reality, Bezos, who is now considered the world's richest human with a value of $131 billion, has averaged about $6.5 billion a year since Amazon went public twenty years ago. Figuring it that way, his average annual income is 230,000 times that of his workers. Perhaps headed in the right direction, though, the company did just announce a wage increase for its workers.

Yet Amazon is also dangerously close to becoming a monopoly. While the company will tell you that it makes up for less than 1% of retail sales throughout the world (a ridiculous metric, of course), it largely controls the book industry and its dominance of the delivery market in the United States often effectively quashes competition.

For consumers, of course, Amazon has been terrific. Full disclosure – I use it myself. And, obviously, I made this book available on Amazon. I don't think Jeff Bezos is evil. I also recognize that many good products and ideas come out of Amazon, and that it provides employment for about half a million people.

But Amazon's practices have brought to the fore a new argument about trusts and monopolies, notably posed by Lina Khan: In the past, consumer pricing was the main consideration when it came to determining whether or not an entity was a trust or monopoly. But Khan has argued that other factors must be given more weight, such as the effect a dominant business has had on competitors. Does Amazon allow for any competition in its fields? And even if it's not quite a monopoly now, can we stop it from becoming one?

We're living in an era of deregulation. Dodd-Frank did some good things, but didn't go far enough, and now we're seeing efforts to dismantle it. There are few cops on the economic highway, and businesses are driving as fast as they like, confident that there will be no speeding tickets and no consequences.

Let's look at one company from the financial crisis of 2008 as a microcosm. The company is known as Magnetar Capital, and it currently oversees some $13.5 billion – pretty good considering it was only founded in 2005.

Prior to the crisis and near global economic collapse, Magnetar was busy sponsoring Collateralized Debt Obligations (CDOs), buying up some of the riskiest equity (the lowest "traunch," as it's known) so that the CDOs could be created. According to *This American Life*, Magnetar would pay for 5% or 6% of the CDO, so that they could then bet against 100% of it once it was created. Magnetar claims it was simply hedging against its investments, but that seems to fly in the face of the facts. The company was pushing investment banks to include riskier and riskier assets in these CDOs. That would indicate that the company preferred that the CDOs failed. They took advantage of the system, knowing that banks would put these awful billion-dollar deals together because, every time a bank did, bankers could charge fees and make millions. It didn't matter to the bankers if the deal collapsed; they still made out.

When these investment banks sold other traunches of the CDOs to investors, they didn't share all of the details about Magnetar. They didn't tell investors that Magnetar was both a sponsor of the CDOs and a major bettor against them. When the CDOs collapsed, Magnetar made a fortune. Twenty-three of the twenty-four CDOs they saw to the creation of became completely worthless, but Magnetar made out like a bandit. The head of Magnetar, Alec Litowitz, took in $280 million in 2007 alone.

And, of course, no one went to prison. The same can be said for the Goldman Sachs executives who defrauded investors: a fine, but no jail time. As tends to be the case in America, a guy who steals $20 from a cash register can expect to see cinderblock walls if he's caught, but if you steal $20 million or $20 billion, you'll probably be just fine.

We should be going after these big-time crooks, and yet we have a Congress largely influenced by money that makes laws in favor of the moneyed interests. The World Justice Project gives the US a score of .55 in terms of absence of corruption in the legislature. Australia gets a .65;

England a .67; Norway garners a .89; Canada a .72.

Politicians can be influenced by unlimited donations from corporate donors, then rule on legislation that affects those corporations, then go work for one of those corporations as soon as they leave office and lobby their old colleagues on the corporation's behalf. There are no efforts to even the playing field because the refs have largely been bought off. Rather than looking to protect the people, these politicians – especially Republicans – look to protect Big Business at all costs. The more money you have, the more responsive you can expect our government to be. It's government of Big Business, by Big Business, for Big Business.

We need a government that fights back. We need sensible campaign finance regulations. We need a Supreme Court that will hold up such regulations. We need to regulate banks like they're utilities and we need to stop allowing them to oppress the poor with usurious fees and unfair practices.

And we need to overhaul (for real this time) our ridiculously convoluted and incredibly biased tax system. Let's talk about that next.

30. A Ridiculously Skewed Tax Code

The US has one of the most complicated, one of the stupidest, and one of the worst skewed tax codes in the world.

As T.R. Reid points out in his book, *A Fine Mess*, the US tax code is rife with special exceptions, inefficiency, and policies that favor the wealthy. Reid argues that we could lower rates across the board and greatly simplify the tax code if we got rid of all of the special exceptions, most of which are extraordinarily biased in favor of the well-off. Keep in mind that tax write-offs only work for Americans who do itemized deductions. Most Americans don't do itemized deductions: two-thirds of us use the standard deduction that the IRS offers, since it's usually larger and saves time. But itemized deductions, which are both more

complicated and more comprehensive, allow those who use them the ability to take advantage of government giveaways.

The government doesn't count these giveaways as spending, but it is indeed a way of spending, at least relatively speaking, because the result is the same. Whether the government spends $100 million more or gives $100 million in tax breaks, revenue-wise it winds up in the same place (putting aside arguments about which would stimulate the economy more). In the 1960s, a Harvard economist by the name of Stanley Surrey came up with a name for this type of "spending": he called it tax expenditures. The US keeps track of all such expenditures – basically, a tally of all of the special tax breaks offered. Reid went through and added them up; they exceeded $1.1 trillion in 2014 – and yes, that's trillion with a T. To compare, that year the US spent $845 billion on Social Security, $807 billion on Medicare and Medicaid, and $696 billion on defense.

The US pays oil companies to drill for oil, pays for real estate depreciation, and pays companies for having old machinery. Of course, there are also tax credits and deductions offered for people who adopt children, people with disabilities, and numerous other noble-minded exemptions. But the overall effect is tremendously negative and strongly favors those with more income.

One of the stupidest tax expenditures is the mortgage interest rate deduction. As Brandeis professor and author of *Toxic Inequality*, Tom Shapiro told Mike Pesca on *The Gist*, all rent support systems total about $35-40 billion, while approximately $86 billion is given to the top 10% through the mortgage interest rate deduction. In his book, Reid called the mortgage interest rate deduction a "reverse Robin Hood" plan, by which those already in the best position receive the greatest benefit.

"Is there any chance that these ancient printers could provide $46,000,000 in depreciation deductions?"

It's essentially a gift to those who are already better off: the more money you make, the more the government gives you. Those in the highest bracket (now 37%) can deduct 37% of their mortgage interest payments. That means that if they're paying $1,000 a month for interest on their mortgage, the government is actually paying $370 of that. The higher tax bracket you're in, the more the government pays for you. Worse still, it does nothing to stimulate home-buying: Reid points out that homeownership rates are roughly the same in countries with the mortgage interest rate deduction and those without it. Yet we're wasting tens of billions of dollars every year on it – money that could be used for much better causes.

Reid notes other ridiculous breaks as well. If you can afford a Tesla, you can get a tax break for buying one. And although many people appreciate the fact that the US government doesn't tax insurance payments employers make for employees, that exemption will cost the government over $235 billion in 2018, according to Brookings. Think of what all that money could do if it went toward a public option or single-payer/Medicare-for-All plan.

Over $108 billion was lost to reduced capital gains taxes on investments – a huge giveaway to the rich that Trump promised to end, then did nothing about.

Then there are charitable deductions. Nothing against charity, of course – it's great to give. But the US exemption for charity is really just another free giveaway to the rich. First off, it's been shown that deductions don't have much of an effect on charitable giving: historically, when people have received fewer deductions, they've been pretty much just as generous as before. So why is the US government costing itself $50 billion a year with this giveaway? Also: as Reid notes, there's something distasteful about rewarding charity. Shouldn't charity be done just for its own sake?

But the problem's worse than that. Charitable-giving deductions are ripe for exploitation. Reid uses the example of art work: Wealthy people can hire private evaluators to give high appraisals to works of art, then donate that art and count it as a tax deduction. The best part is that they often don't really have to even part with the work of art! One scheme Reid describes is the "private museum" scam: A wealthy person puts their private art collection in a "museum" by their house. Basically, the museum is just for them, since there are no main roads leading to it, no signs, etc. They then take a tax break for "donating" this art to themselves. Can *you* do that? Well, do you happen to have a $60 million Picasso?

The wealthy can also start their own "charitable foundations," which they can use for all sorts of chicanery. As comedian John Oliver has famously pointed out, it's ridiculously easy to be classified as a charity in the US. Reid says that the IRS "grants 'exempt' status to 95% of all the groups that apply for it." A charitable trust set up by a wealthy parent can provide one of their heirs with a nice, salaried job, or even a mansion to use for free. Maybe the charity requires a private jet….

The rich have other methods as well. That $150,000 car you saw one of them driving? That's not theirs – it belongs to the company. It's a business expense, they'll say, and no taxes will be paid for the use of it. Corporations pay for things all the time. The CEO likes the Knicks? Season tickets – paid for by the company. It's not part of his pay – it's a *business expense*. After all, he has to entertain! He had to order those expensive bottles of wine, too!

And let's take a look at some of that compensation they receive while we're at it. That rich CEO – most of his compensation was given in stock or stock options. Even if it's millions and millions of dollars worth, he'll pay nothing (and, as we noted in chapter 25, it's a *he* 95% of the time). Remember: no taxes are paid for wealth appreciation – meaning that a person doesn't pay taxes on a stock until they sell it. The stock can rise in value from $10 to a $100 and they'll pay nothing. If they hold it for at least a year before selling it, by the way, they'll be taxed at the much-lower capital gains rate of 20% (for those making $500,000 or more a year – the rate is lower for those making less). But they don't have to sell it at all – that's the best part! Since the US doesn't tax wealth accumulation, they can simply use the value to borrow against it and live like a king.

Here's what I mean: Let's say, hypothetically, that you start a tech company in mom's garage that grows to be worth $15 billion. You manage to retain $10 billion worth of the stock. Instead of selling it, you get loans to do everything you want to do in life – own a mansion, a boat – you name it. You pay very low interest on these loans because you're a very, very low risk borrower (being a billionaire and all). You can also write the interest off on your tax returns. When you die, all of your stock can be passed on to your spouse and he or she will pay nothing. That's right: no income tax and no capital gains. Billions earned, zero taxes paid. What a country!

Much of this comes down to who's crafting the rules. Thousands upon thousands of tax lobbyists are angling for every advantage for their clients, be they private citizens or corporations. Politicians, meanwhile, count on those same corporations and wealthy donors to provide campaign funds. That's how it's possible that a yacht can be written off as a "vacation property."

Even before the Trump tax cut, reducing corporate taxes to 21%, corporations were already paying a fairly low rate. Before the cut passed, Republicans frequently pointed out that the US corporate rate was among the highest in the world, at 35%. What they failed to mention was that the *effective* rate – the rate once you factor in all of the loopholes – was actually much lower. An analysis by the Institute of Taxation and

Economic Policy of 258 Fortune 500 companies found the effective rate to be 21.2%. Some billion-dollar corporations manage to pay nothing in taxes at all, or even get back money from the government.

How is this possible?, you might wonder. It's called inversion, and it involves setting up offices in foreign countries for the sole purpose of avoiding US taxes. Corporations use involved tax schemes with names like "the Double Dutch Sandwich" to park money overseas at greatly reduced rates. Since they're not taxed on these funds in the US until they bring the money home – what's known as repatriation – they simply wait till a low repatriation rate is offered (as it was in 2004), then do so. The Trump plan was exactly that: it allowed companies to repatriate money they had stashed overseas for the bargain rate of 8% for hard assets, including real estate, and 15.5% for cash, stock, and other types of liquid assets. They can then deduct any taxes they may have paid to other governments.

Even better, these inversion schemes often allow companies to transfer money to themselves through loans from themselves. That's right: they can get a loan from the designated parent company, use it to pay down debts, then write off the interest payments. You read that right: they write off interest payments on loans they make to themselves! As Reid puts it in *A Fine Mess*, "Why should a company be allowed to lend itself money, pay itself interest, and then take a tax deduction for that interest it paid to itself? No individual taxpayer could get away with that scam."

Apple, one of the worst culprits when it comes to tax avoidance, will be repatriating some $285 billion now, yet have to pay taxes on less than $40 billion worth.

The EU has cracked down on inversion somewhat with its new "state aid" approach that forbids companies from receiving special privileges. They ordered Apple to pay €13 billion (over $15 billion) for its tax avoidance scheme in Ireland. But the EU can only intervene in specific cases; it cannot prevent the race to the bottom that's occurring. And even once a loophole is closed, tax lawyers are quick to find others to exploit and to construct brand new tax avoidance schemes. The accounting firm PricewaterhouseCoopers is particularly expert at this.

Companies like GE, meanwhile, can take huge write-offs for what they classify as machinery depreciation, essentially charging the wear and tear on their machines to us, the US taxpayer. GE had a tax rate of -4.5% – again, not a typo: GE had a negative tax rate and got paid $400 million by the government.

Other companies use stock options to reduce their tax burdens. A stock option is essentially the right to purchase stock later at a certain price. For instance, if I become VP at a new internet startup, part of my package deal may be the option to purchase 100,000 shares at $2 a pop. Now let's say I work for the company for ten years and it does great – the stock is listed at $80 by the time I'm ready to cash in. My 100,000 shares, which was originally worth $200,000, is now worth $8 million. The company only had to pay me $200,000 worth of stock when we made the deal, yet they can now write off $8 million from their taxes. Facebook managed to reduce its tax burden by $5.78 billion between 2010 and 2015 by doing this.

Companies also get discounts (free money, really) for doing research, for gas drilling, and even for building racetracks. Yes – for racetracks. These are just some of the special exemptions that are built into the tax code. And the more complicated the tax code is, the worse it is for poor and middle class people who can't afford top-notch accountants and tax attorneys.

The problem is that there is an absolutely enormous tax preparations lobby that fights vigorously against any attempt to simplify the tax code. And one thing that these companies, like H&R Block, do not want to see, is a government service that does people's taxes for them – what's known as "pre-filled forms." Yet such a thing would potentially save US taxpayers both billions of dollars and billions of hours (according to Reid, in 2015 alone, Americans spent over 6 billion hours and over $12 billion on tax preparation).

In the Netherlands, the average time it takes for a citizen to pay his or her taxes is fifteen minutes. In Estonia, it's seven minutes. In Japan, the government simply sends out a postcard with the figures that have already been deducted, meaning that 80% of Japanese people have to do nothing at all.

California has given pre-filled forms a try with its CalFile system. Unfortunately, most Californians don't know about it. But of the 90,000 who have used it so far, they've loved it, reporting a 98% satisfaction rate.

To be fair, a pre-filled system would probably work better if the tax code was simpler and if the IRS was better staffed (as it should be). But that doesn't mean it can't work for many Americans. Ideally, if we could institute both a simpler code – what's known as BBLR (broad base, lower rates) and a pre-filled form system at the same time, that would constitute legitimate tax reform, as opposed to the giveaway to the wealthy we just saw under Trump's "plan."

Sadly, one of the reasons a lot of people feel uncomfortable with the idea of the government doing your taxes for you (no matter how sensible an idea it might be), is that people simply don't trust government much anymore. We'll get to that next.

31. Lack of Confidence in Our Institutions

"We're leaving out the brain and running him for Congress."

Pick a governmental institution in the US that hasn't been severely tainted. Congress? It's gerrymandered and its members are largely bought and paid for. The Supreme Court? We all know Neil Gorsuch's seat was stolen and we just witnessed the fiasco that was Brett Kavanaugh's confirmation. The court's also as political now as ever it's been. The FBI? Please. – Were you around for the 2016 election? The NSA? We found out they were regularly spying on us. The Environmental Protection Agency? Well, it no longer protects the environment, its sole purpose for existing. How 'bout the presidency? –

I'm kidding, of course.

Really, the number of governmental agencies that can still be counted on is shrinking. They're not gone, of course: we still trust in the military to defend us, even if we don't trust in how Trump might use that military. We still trust in police to protect us, even if we're fed up with the lack of accountability. And the post-office still manages to get mail where it's supposed to go – most of the time, at least.

But there is a serious lack of confidence occurring right now when it comes to institutions that many of us trusted in for our entire lives.

Since 1958, the National Election Study has asked people about their trust in the government. When it started, 73% could affirm that they indeed trusted the government. The Vietnam War, the Pentagon Papers, Watergate, Iran-Contra, Newt Gingrich, and more did a great deal to deteriorate that trust. But, believe it or not, it is now lower than it's ever been: the December, 2017 survey found that only 18% of people expressed trust in the government. 18%! If you surveyed how many people would like to get stuck with a pin you might get a higher percentage!

Gallup, meanwhile, conducts its own confidence polls each year, asking people about governmental and other institutions. They offer four choices: people can have a "Great deal" of confidence, "Quite a lot," "Some," or "Very little." Gallup combines the "great deal" and "quite a lot" figures into one high confidence number. That number for the Supreme Court in 2018 was 37%. For Congress it was 11%. The public schools got a 29%. The presidency received a 37% (no surprise there). The police did a bit better: 54%; yet the criminal justice system as a whole only managed a score of 22%.

Non-governmental institutions didn't fare much better. Only 26% of people said they had high confidence in organized labor. (Does that speak for a distrust that's arisen against unions, a recognition that unions have become impotent, or both?) Just 25% had a high degree of trust for "Big Business," which is sad because Big Business is largely running the show now. Just 36% put a lot of trust in the medical system, which is only important if you want to live. Still, the medical system did better than HMOs, which registered a mere 19%. That put HMOs just behind television news, which received a score of 20%. *But what about newspapers?* you say. Don't worry: they did better than TV news: newspapers got a high confidence score of 23%, with 38% saying they trust newspapers "very little" – although I suppose it depends on which newspaper you're talking about – I wouldn't trust the *New York Post* if it told me my own name. Still, the overall lack of confidence in newspapers can't bode well for the country. Even banks beat out newspapers, with 30% of people giving them a high confidence score. Banks nearly sunk the global economy with unrestrained greed in the early 2000s, yet are somehow still trusted more than newspapers. It works in a certain way, though: a lot of people don't want to read newspapers and don't want to read bank contracts.

These numbers have definitely trended lower. Back in 1973, when they first asked, 42% of people gave Congress a high confidence score. That same year, public schools got a 58%. Even in the 1980s, when there was a great deal of debate about the effectiveness of education, confidence scores for education ranged from 39% to 50% – ten or more points higher than today. Back in 1993, TV news got a score of 46%. Newspapers hit 51% in 1979 and have been mostly in decline since, being now at their near nadir.

Now, there can be many reasons why people lack confidence in institutions – some become disillusioned after rational analysis, while others are convinced that the Freemasons or Illuminati are secretly controlling things.

But one thing can't be denied: our institutions are legitimately deteriorating.

32. Deterioration of Our Institutions

Credit: Mike Licht

So we know from previous chapters that the House is gerrymandered and not very representative; in the Senate about eighteen senators represent half the country, while the other half of the country gets 82 senators; and the president was not the choice of the people, but of the antiquated Electoral College. We've also discussed the problems with our news media, our educational system, and our correctional system. We'll talk about the Supreme Court more later, but suffice it to say that it's become ridiculously partisan and not a deliberative body that most of us can have much confidence in.

Let's spend this chapter taking a brief look at other institutions.

The FBI

The FBI is in turmoil right now. First James Comey made the utterly stupid decision to reopen the Hillary Clinton email probe some eleven days before the election and throw our electoral process into chaos and (it seems) the election to Donald Trump (current incompetent president). Then Trump fired Comey for looking into Russian election meddling. Then Trump fired Comey's replacement, McCabe. FBI agents Lisa Page and Peter Strzok, meanwhile, were made examples of by the Trump administration to try to make the FBI's efforts look tainted. At this point, I have to wonder if the FBI is happy they chose Trump to be president.

The Justice Department

Under Trump's instruction, Attorney General Jeff Sessions (operator of what Trump calls "the Jeff Sessions Justice Department") has given orders to separate families at the border and has failed to properly defend the integrity of the FBI. Voter suppression has continued, and Sessions has done nothing to end mass incarceration or prosecutorial zeal.

The Environmental Protection Agency

This might come as a surprise, but the Environmental Protection Agency is supposed to protect the environment (shocking, I know). Yet it's been doing the exact opposite, making deals with mining and energy companies and advocating policies of deregulation.

The Department of Education

Betsy DeVos's goal is to bring religion back into education, and divert public education funds to private, religious institutions. She's also overseen the deregulation of the for-profit college industry, which preys on vulnerable students. Also: she's about as qualified to run the Department of Education as Donald Duck is to be Secretary-General of the UN.

The NSA

Does this one even need to be discussed?

OK. Well, in case you missed it, the NSA spied on ordinary Americans for years.

The CIA

People have been legitimately weary of the CIA since they did that small thing and cherry-picked evidence to help lie us into a disastrous war in Iraq, resulting in hundreds of thousands of deaths. There was also the water-boarding and Abu Ghraib.

The Federal Election Commission

Talk about a completely ineffective body! The FEC has been rendered largely impotent by the Supreme Court, of course, but it's also failed to prevent large-scale voter suppression and the closing of polling stations. For an agency dedicated to protecting Americans' right to vote, it's doing a fairly terrible job.

The Department of Veterans Affairs

As the AP has pointed out, Donald Trump has fallen far short on his promises to properly staff our veterans' hospitals. Although there are indeed many caring professionals at the VA, the lack of resources and poor record-keeping continue.

The Police

We've discussed police brutality and the lack of accountability. But it should also be kept in mind that the nation's largest police union, the Fraternal Order of Police, with more than 300,000 members, endorsed Donald Trump for president – a person who has shown little respect for the rights of the accused and for the rights of minorities.

Libraries

Libraries are still great places with fantastic resources. I love 'em, and many Americans do too, with 76% saying that libraries serve their communities well. The only problem is that Americans often don't show up there. It's true! – Most Americans do not go to the library in a given year – not even once. Pew reported that only 46% of Americans visited a library or book mobile in 2016, down from 53% in 2012. Remarkably, 22% of Americans have never been to a library. Never. Ever. That's pretty scary.

Now, we could go on. I'm sure many of you don't have much confidence in the Department of Energy under Rick Perry or Housing and Urban Development with Ben Carson at the helm, but I think you get the point: Our institutions aren't what they used to be, and it's part of the reason for our next topic: the deterioration of checks and balances.

33. Deterioration of Checks and Balances

"We believe we have checks and balances, but have rarely faced a situation like the present: when the less popular of the two parties controls every lever of power at the federal level, as well as the majority of statehouses."

-Timothy Snyder, *On Tyranny*

As kids we all learn about the "three branches of government." Those branches are supposedly separate, but equal. But what if the tree itself has been poisoned? What if the rains that feed it are acidic? The tree begins to rot away, and soon all that's left is one solid stump with no discernible branches whatsoever.

We're seeing that now in a way: rather than Congress acting as a check on the power of the presidency, the extremist Republican Party which controls both houses indulges the president's excesses and looks to cover up his wrongdoings. They're about as interested in investigating Russian collusion with the Trump campaign, for one, as OJ is in finding the "real killer."

And if you're counting on the Supreme Court to step in, you're also going to be sorely disappointed. The court has already allowed a version of Trump's bigoted travel ban to go into effect, despite abundant evidence that the purpose is to deprive people entry on religious grounds, in direct violation of the First Amendment. Two of those justices were Trump appointees who have already proved they have little or no honor: Gorsuch, who accepted a stolen seat and who's unlikely to rule against Trump (or any conservative cause, for that matter); and Kavanaugh, who disgraced himself with his mad and maudlin performance during his confirmation hearings, during which he not only spouted ridiculous conspiracy theories directed at the Clintons, but also showed he doesn't have the temperament to referee a children's soccer match, much less sit on the highest court in the land. It's also interesting (to say the least) that, in Kavanaugh, Trump chose a justice who has come out against special prosecutors (having managed to have his anti-prosecutorial epiphany sometime after he participated in the Whitewater investigation).

Despite the political posturing of the Republicans on the Senate Judiciary Committee, the end result was never in doubt – the entire thing, sadly, was little more than a charade. They were going to vote for Kavanaugh's nomination and send it on to the full Senate no matter what, where Mitch McConnell and his majority of senators representing a minority of the country were sure to approve of it. In fact, McConnell gave his hand away during the hearings when he promised to "plow right through" the accusations of Christine Blasey Ford.

To be fair, the process of approving Supreme Court justices has been little more than a farce ever since Robert Bork was "borked" and denied a Supreme Court seat. Since then, potential justices have done their best to answer nothing and give no indication of how their ideology might affect their future decisions on the court.

If the Senate was truly doing its job, though, this would not be permitted. Why shouldn't justices – be they liberal or conservative – be made to answer questions and give an indication on how they would rule? In Kavanaugh's case, the Senate didn't even demand that all of his papers be given over. Republicans rushed the vote through, desiring that people know as little about Kavanaugh as possible.

So where did Kavanaugh come from in the first place? Was his nomination the result of intense research and great reflection on the part of Donald Trump? Of course not. Thinking, after all, is not Donald Trump's strong-suit.

It was known around Hollywood back in the day that Jack Warner never wanted to read a script. The synopsis was all he ever asked for. If anyone ever questioned him, he'd point to the water tower bearing the Warner name and ask, "Who's name's on that tower?"

Well, Trump's like that as well. Books are his kryptonite. The most you can expect him to read is a double-spaced one-page outline. The good news for Trump, though, was that he didn't have to do any research to land on Kavanaugh, Gorsuch, or any of the other justices he was considering. All of them came via the recommendations of the Heritage Foundation and the Federalist Society, both ultra-orthodox conservative organizations with extremist views. Later, we'll get into how shadow organizations like these have inordinate influence over government. For now, though, what you must understand is that all of these rotten apples – all of the conservatives who want to disregard the First Amendment, stretch the Second, and put unions out of business – all of them come from the same demented cesspool that has linked ideology with identity and has placed party over country. These people identify more as conservatives than they do as senators, members of the House, Supreme Court justices, or administrators. They operate like one mass unit, and because of that, we can no more expect a conservative justice on the Supreme Court to check the president than we can expect the chancellor of Germany to. Their first allegiance is to one another, and not the duties of their office.

Republicans have come to believe that their ideological goals – anti-tax, anti-abortion, anti-big government – justify the abdication of their responsibilities. Law and order has taken a backseat to tax cuts for the wealthy, the appointment of conservative judges, and industry-friendly, anti-environmental policies.

The president of the United States admitted on national television that he fired the FBI director because of the Russia investigation. His son, son-in-law, and campaign chair took a meeting with a Russian agent who promised secret information about Hillary Clinton; DNC and campaign emails were later leaked, causing tremendous damage. That same campaign chair, Paul Manafort, with deep ties to Russia, has now been convicted of multiple financial crimes. Several other indictments and convictions have come out of the Mueller investigation, including a guilty plea by Trump's personal attorney and "fixer," Michael Cohen. We know that Cohen arranged illegal campaign payments to a porn star and a Playboy model, and Trump is on tape conspiring with him to do it. Trump violates the emoluments clause of the Constitution on a daily basis, and refuses to disclose tax information that could tell us where he's gotten his money from (Congress could force him to do so, but, unsurprising, has declined).

Our election was hacked, the president is clearly corrupt, and we're watching our republic rot away. Meanwhile, Republicans in Congress are sitting idly by, essentially saying, "Nothing to see here." Democrats, while a vastly superior choice, are too often afraid of speaking up.

As a country, we would certainly be better off if we had other viable options.

34. Retention of Power Amongst Parties (and Neither One is Liberal)

Bernie is indeed a lone wolf. Credit: DonkeyHotey

Right now we have two political parties in America: Brainless and Spineless. Or, just as accurately, you might say, Ruthless and Spineless.

The Republicans are the pro-Christian domination, anti-Muslim, anti-science, anti-tolerance, anti-immigration party; while the Democrats are the party that either can't decide or (in many cases) is simply afraid to say what they stand for. As Will Rogers memorably quipped, "I am not a member of any organized party. I am a Democrat."

Now, some of you out there right now may be saying, "But wait! What about the Green Party? What about the Libertarians?"

I have bad news for you: If you voted for either Jill Stein or Gary Johnson in the 2016 election, you didn't do much other than help put Donald Trump in office.

That's not to say that third parties can't be valuable – they can. But the Green Party isn't a realistic option, in part because its very name makes it into a one-issue party (albeit a very important issue). Sure, the Greens have other stances (some good, some bad), but those go largely unnoticed. The Libertarians, meanwhile, while maintaining some reasonable ideas, such as being against the death penalty and in favor of legalized prostitution, have some really, really bad ideas as well, including opposing Social Security, government-sponsored health care, and gun control.

More to the point, though, is the fact that neither one of these parties really has had a seat at the table (unless, of course, that table belongs to Vladimir Putin, in which case Jill Stein did in fact have a seat there, right across from Michael Flynn). Neither Stein nor Johnson polled high enough to participate in the presidential debates and, in the end, together they won less than 5% the vote. There isn't a single member of Congress from either party. Nor has anyone in either party ever won an office higher than small-town mayor (and even that has been extraordinarily rare).

Basically, there is no serious third party in America.

Other countries, meanwhile, have multiple parties and often coalition governments. Why, then, don't we?

Well, one reason, of course, is money: the big money is behind the Republicans and, to a lesser extent, the Democrats.

Another reason is time: the Democrats have been around since 1828 and the Republicans since 1854. And both derived from previous parties: the Dems from Thomas Jefferson's Democratic-Republican Party (founded in 1792) and the Republicans from the Whigs (officially founded in 1834). By comparison, the Libertarians started in 1971 and the Green Party in 2001. The head-start of the two major parties has given each time to develop high levels of support.

There's also the "wasted vote" paradox: many people would rather not waste their vote by casting it for a party they know can't win. In order for third-parties to *be* viable, they first have to *seem* viable. And they probably won't seem viable until they start attracting more votes.

How can they do that?

The answer is: star political power. The Democrats were able to form in the aftermath of the 1824 election, in which no one had received a majority of the Electoral College, though Andrew Jackson had won a plurality in both the College and the popular vote (despite J.Q. Adams clearly being a far superior person). As noted in chapter 1, Jackson accused Adams and Henry Clay of forming a "corrupt bargain": Clay (who had himself been a candidate for president) would throw his support to Adams and Adams would make Clay secretary of State, considered a stepping-stone to the presidency at the time. Whether such a bargain was actually struck or not, we don't know for sure; but Adams did become president and Clay assumed the helm at the State Department. Jackson and his supporters used the next four years to form a new political party –

the Democrats – to challenge Adams in 1828, this time soundly defeating him.

In the case of the Republicans, it was the Kansas-Nebraska Act of 1854 that motivated many former Whigs to get together to form a new party opposed to the spread of slavery. And so the GOP started with a great deal of political clout. They also got a boost from their 1856 candidate, John C. Frémont, a military hero, gold prospector, and all around badass.

I'm sorry, Green Party fans – Ralph Nader just isn't quite the same as ole John C.

In 1860, of course, the Republicans would nominate a homespun, story-telling mid-Westerner with his own type of appeal: Abraham Lincoln.

So we don't have legitimate third-parties in the US. Why is that so bad?

Well, first off, third-parties may have legitimately good ideas. As noted earlier, the Libertarians want to legalize prostitution. And we should. By legalizing it, we would be able to tax it, to protect those involved in it, and to limit the spread of venereal diseases. Perhaps George Carlin put it best when he said, "I do not understand why prostitution is illegal. Why should prostitution be illegal? Selling is legal. Fucking is legal. Why isn't selling fucking legal? Why should it be illegal to sell something that's perfectly legal to give away?"

The Green Party platform, meanwhile, includes calls for universal health care and universal childcare. While universal health care has been taken up by Bernie Sanders and some Democrats, nobody talks about universal child care, despite clear evidence that it would provide tremendous benefits to society.

Third parties have also made some significant contributions throughout history. The Progressives, for instance, gave us the direct election of senators and promoted women's suffrage.

When you shut out third parties (or fourth or fifth parties, for that matter), you shut out a lot of new ideas. Democrats are often afraid to venture out of the Overton window, while Republicans frequently won't support anything nowadays that isn't ultra-conservative, since they're reluctant to alienate their Fox "News"-informed base.

Neither party is truly liberal. The Democrats, sadly, are moderates. If they were liberal, they would be pushing for major electoral reform, Medicare-for-All, the end to prohibitions on gambling and prostitution, the inclusion of Puerto Rico as a state, and strict gun control (rather than the we-don't-want-to-take-away-your-guns approach). While it's good that the Democrats are the party of reason, they should also be the party of liberal ideals. Instead, they've let the Republicans frame the debate and determine what stances they can take. Just once it would be nice to hear a Democrat say that the Constitution isn't perfect and that the US isn't the best at everything.

OK. So third parties can be a very healthy thing for a democracy. How can we get them?

Eventually, we'll see a new party in the United States. I'm not sure if it'll happen in my lifetime, but perhaps in yours. It may occur like it's happened in the past: evolving from one of the already-existing parties. And, for a while, three parties may exist until one of the weaker ones folds.

But then, of course, we'll be back to square-one.

If we really want more than two parties to choose from, we have to be willing to change the Constitution. Unlike most industrialized countries, the US suffers from a winner-take-all system. In Germany, Finland, Denmark, Belgium, Israel, the Netherlands, Italy, Greece, and many other nations, proportional systems are in place in which a party that receives less votes can still gain seats (see a map here).

Of course, there can be drawbacks as well: coalition governments aren't always successful, with extremist parties sometimes making unreasonable demands.

But it should also be kept in mind that the US already has an extremist party. They're called the Republicans, and they've kept power by suppressing votes, closing polling stations, gerrymandering districts, and receiving outlandish sums from the corporate class.

35. And One of Those Parties is Corrupt and Dysfunctional…

With the dumpster fire that is Donald Trump, many may have forgotten what a disaster the Republican Party was even before he arrived. Trump didn't come from nowhere: the stage was set for him: for a long time before he came on the political scene, Republicans had been playing to the lowest common denominator, using dog whistles with racial undertones to stoke the anger of their base while encouraging the anti-intellectual streak that was growing within the party. Like an accountant who gets tied up with the mob, they tried to use the misinformed and misanthropic to their advantage, and pretty soon the mob was taking over. It became a race to the bottom, with politicians trying to "out-conservative" or out-extreme one another, no matter how ludicrous their ideological positions. Lower taxes weren't good enough! Taxes could never be raised, ever! Supporting guns wasn't good enough! You had to be against any gun control whatsoever, no matter how reasonable.

The distrust of reliable news media sources, meanwhile, which Trump has used to his advantage, didn't start with him, but with Republican politicians, with GOP political consultants who disguised dissembling by using the word "spin," and, of course, with Fox "News" and other propaganda outfits that profited by stirring up false controversies.

The Republicans haven't had much in the way of an honorable president since Eisenhower (and even he could've done more for civil rights). Nixon was not only a disgrace, but his "Southern Strategy" perhaps set the Republican Party on its current win-at-all-costs course. Ford, of course, was fairly incompetent (LBJ once said that he had "played too much football without a helmet"), and made the mistake of pardoning Nixon, who should certainly have wound up in prison. Reagan, while competently handling the Soviet Union, tripled the debt, increased income inequality, and promoted stereotypes with his "welfare queen" talk. George Bush was a mediocre president who got there by scaring people with Willie Horton and promises of tax cuts. His campaign manager, Lee Atwater, was also largely responsible for the tone and tactics that have damaged our politics ever since. George W. Bush, meanwhile, was pretty much a walking disaster. He lied us into a senseless war in Iraq, allowed over 1,800 to die unnecessarily from Katrina, continued the deregulation that helped bring about the financial crisis, etc., etc., etc.

And now we've got Trump.

Interestingly enough, since Nixon, we've had over 90 convictions from people serving under Republican administrations, while Democratic administrations have given us just one. That's right: 90+ vs. 1 (and you can expect more coming down the pipeline). Keep in mind that these are just the ones who got caught committing *illegal* acts of corruption. It doesn't take into account all of the ways that Congress has found to take kickbacks *legally*, such as through "consultant" positions or questionable donations.

But it's beyond mere corruption. Republicans appear willing to do just about anything to retain power. They'll gerrymander districts, close polling stations, disenfranchise millions, and, as we saw during the Obama years, completely obstruct government for political gain.

Do you remember the self-imposed "Debt Crisis?" Self-imposed, that is, by Republicans refusing to raise the debt ceiling, taking the entire country (and the world) hostage in order to get spending concessions

The "debt ceiling," as it's known, first came about in 1917. It's truly a very stupid thing to have, and here's why: Not raising the debt ceiling doesn't affect spending. Spending is decided on when Congress votes on a budget and appropriations. Raising the debt ceiling simply allows the US to meet the expenditures it's already laid out. If the US doesn't meet its expenses by, say, not paying its bonds off on time, it could damage our credit tremendous and potentially cause massive instability in the markets. It's why practically every economist is against the debt ceiling's very existence: it can only cause damage.

Before 2011, raising the debt ceiling was pretty much a formality: it had been raised at least 75 times before Obama came into office. But the Republicans – acting on the principle of obstruct, obstruct, obstruct at all costs – decided to make the debt ceiling a sticking point. While, in the past, some members of Congress had used the debt ceiling to perform show votes and make certain points, no party had seriously considered defaulting on the United States' obligations before.

But that's exactly what the extremist Republican Party threatened to do. In the end, President Obama and the GOP agreed to a massive $1.1 trillion in cuts, known as "sequestration." Many of these cuts were anti-productive. They cut over $120 billion from Medicare, another $450 billion from defense, and almost $300 billion from important welfare programs. Nobody was particularly happy about the final result, and it's likely that the cuts slowed the economic recovery.

But the Republicans weren't done: they tried the same tactic again in 2013. This time Obama did the smart thing and called their bluff. The public, tired of GOP threats to sink the economy, sided with Obama, and the Republicans were left with egg on their face and not much else. It was one of Obama's best moments. You can be sure that, had he lost that battle, the country would've been paying the price of conceding to the GOP's bully tactics for years to come.

Throughout the Obama years, Republicans constantly preached about the debt and about spending. They did all they could to slow the economy and cast blame on the president. Yet the moment Trump came into office, most of that rhetoric vanished in an instant. And they saw no issue with the Trump tax cuts that largely favored corporations and the wealthy and will, over the next decade, add no less than $2.3 trillion to the national debt they were supposedly so worried about. It's hypocrisy at its highest levels.

The extremist Republican Party never met a tax cut for the privileged class it didn't like, nor an environmental or gun safety regulation that it did. It will stop at practically nothing to preserve its grip on power and answers only to moneyed interests. These irresponsible "leaders" are a major part of what makes the United States so irresponsive to the needs of its people.

36. An Irresponsive Government

The World Bank measures government expenditures in terms of GDP. Its data shows that the US not only spends less in that regard than the world average, but significantly less than industrialized nations. In 2016, the US spent a figure equal to just under 14.3% of GDP on government expenditures, while around the world the average was over 17%; for OECD nations, it was approximately 17.8%. The United Kingdom and Australia both spent about 18.5% in 2016; Japan around 19.8%; Belgium around 23.5%; and France just over 23.75%.

Of course, these nations tend to pay higher taxes as well. But they're spending it on their people – they're spending it on education and health care and support services. The comparison, meanwhile, is likely to get worse for the US: the passage of the egregious Trump tax cuts will cause our government to collect less in taxes to begin with, and future

Congresses will most likely look to cut federal programs in order to pay for them.

Simply put, the US is not responsive to the needs of its citizenry.

Hearkening back to the study from Gilens and Page that reviewed how responsive US politicians are to non-wealthy Americans (first mentioned in chapter 16), the authors wrote, "When the preferences of economic elites and the stands of organized interest groups are controlled for, the preferences of the average American appear to have only a minuscule, near-zero, statistically non-significant impact upon public policy."

It's why even policies with overwhelming support receive no real consideration.

Some examples:

- 0% of Americans (including 51% of Republicans) support a Medicare-for-All plan
- 2% say the government is doing too little about the environment, with 76% believing the government should spend more on research into wind and solar technologies
- 9% favor stricter gun control
- 5% would like to see the Electoral College abolished (including 75% of Democrats)
- 3% think felons should have their rights restored once their time has been served

So…

Think Medicare-for-All is happening anytime soon? You see Congress rushing to pass reasonable gun laws? You expecting the Republicans to come around to embracing the science of climate change? Think Trump's EPA will stop making deals with the mining industry? Holding your breath for stricter gun laws, the end of the Electoral College, and the reinstatement of felons' rights?

Somehow I don't think you are. And you're right not to be expecting much: the politicians who are supposed to work for you are all too often working in their own interest instead. They've learned through experience that you don't matter a whole lot. Right before Trump's tax "plan," a poll came out indicating that 76% of Americans felt taxes should be raised on the wealthy. Guess what? Didn't happen. In fact, the opposite happened, with the wealthy receiving an enormous windfall.

"Maybe not lead off with, 'I don't give a damn what you think'."

Most of this can be blamed on the Republicans, for sure. But there are certainly a fair share of Democrats who deserve blame for the tainted relationships they've formed as well. Chuck Schumer, for one, is pretty much Wall Street's boy: he's taken $13 million in donations from securities and investment firms. His biggest donor over the years has been Goldman Sachs, with contributions totaling nearly $600,000. His cozy relationship with The Street goes back many years: after taking over a million buckaroos from private equity and hedge fund managers, he worked diligently in 2007 to prevent their taxes from going up.

Nancy Pelosi, meanwhile, who may be worth as much as $100 million (estimates vary greatly), still felt the need to violate basic ethics and commit what truly amounts to insider trading in 2011. Try to talk with her about it and you won't get very far.

In fact, part of the problem may be that Congress as a whole, Republicans and Democrats, is an inordinately wealthy institution. The median net worth for a member of the House is (conservatively) $900,000; the typical senator is worth some $3.2 million.

That's not to present a false equivalency: let's face it, there is a vast difference between the two parties, and you're certainly much better off with the Democrats than with the Republicans: at least the Dems still maintain certain ideals and believe in things like campaign finance regulations, the expansion of voting rights, and the protection of unions.

But you cannot expect government to adequately protect the people when its leaders answer only to the privileged class and corporations. When that happens, the goal becomes not to make progress, but to maintain the status quo. It's why we see so little getting done.

37. Government Inefficiency

"Oh ... you want me to work."

"The federal government faces a long-term, unsustainable fiscal path based on an imbalance between federal revenues and spending."
–highlight from the Government Accountability Office report, 2018

The GAO notes the rising costs of health care and the interest on US debt as major drivers of deficit spending. But, of course, tax expenditures – giving away money in the form of tax breaks – doesn't help, especially when those tax breaks (like the ones in the Trump "plan") are targeted toward the rich.

We are indeed wasteful at times. While the GAO pats itself on the back by pointing out that its work has saved the US government some $178 billion, its most recent report noted that a great deal of money continues to be wasted due to agency overlap, poor accounting methods, and just plain stupid policies.

Some examples:

- he GAO says that eliminating duplication and overlap at distribution centers that provide troop support could save the Department of Defense $500 million over five years
- Medicare could save over a billion dollars a year by paying out the same amount for the same service, regardless of location
- undreds of millions could be saved by the IRS just by improving online experiences and anti-identity-theft efforts
- ens of billions could be saved by taking proper safety measures at the Hanford nuclear site in Washington state

Of course, whenever you have a large government there's always going to be some degree of waste. Republicans love to point to such waste and use it as an indictment against all government efforts. Reagan said that "the nine most terrifying words in the English language are, 'I'm from the government and I'm here to help.'" But Reagan didn't seem to have a problem with our military, which is, of course, a government agency. Social Security and Medicare are, likewise, both extremely popular and enormously beneficial. And I'm pretty sure you're happy that the EPA inspects our water and the FDA makes sure our food is safe to eat.

It's not government *action* that's the problem, it's government *inaction*. Wasteful spending most often occurs when there's not proper oversight, or when government leaves its role to private industry, as it's done at the Hanford site, where many workers have experienced severe health issues.

Some of it is just pure foolishness. For instance, there have been massive cuts at the IRS – over $500 million worth since 2012, with a 14% reduction in IRS staff. It's completely counterproductive, of course: less staff not only mean longer wait times to get an agent on the phone, but also less audits. When it comes to individuals, that won't make so much of a difference, since only about 1% of people ever got audited anyhow. But when it comes to corporations, the difference has been enormous: in 2012, 18.9% of corporations were audited; by 2017, it had fallen to just 8.6%. Total enforcement actions fell from nearly 2 million to just 360,000 – in five years! Fewer audits and weaker enforcement mean less money. $40 billion were collected through enforcement actions in 2017, yet it's estimated that unpaid taxes amount to over $400 billion a year, meaning that the IRS is only getting about 10% of what it should get through enforcement actions. By demanding cuts to the IRS, Republicans have found another way to make corporations pay less. It would be like reducing the size of a police force to guarantee that criminals get away with more. See no evil, hear no evil.

A similar statement could be made when it comes to climate change. Between 2007 and 2017, the government spent some $350 billion on disaster relief and insurance payments for flooding and crops. And the GAO estimates that such spending will continue and possibly expand.

Yet Republicans refuse to make efforts to address the causes of climate change.

To their credit, Republicans did work with Democrats to increase the budget for NASA (which had been suffering in the wake of the financial crisis) in their latest fiscal plan. Congress also approved additional financing for the National Institutes of Health, despite Trump threatening to cut funding by 22%. And they went against Betsy DeVos's wishes and increased the budget for the Department of Education, essentially allowing it to keep pace with inflation.

Unfortunately, though, Congress didn't do much to pay for these expenditures, having its cake and eating it too. With the massive tax cuts that went predominantly to the rich and large corporations, all spending had to essentially go on the nation's credit card, which (as the GAO has pointed out) is an unsustainable way to operate.

So why is change so difficult? Why is it so incredibly hard for the US to make progress on so many important fronts, like climate change, educational reform, and health care?

The answer is that we have an unusually laborious system. The World Bank ranks us 72nd in terms of government efficiency, not just behind countries like Canada (#20), Sweden (#3), and the UK (#5), but also behind Mali (#40), Indonesia (#35), and Turkey (#71). Of course extreme efficiency might also mean that you have a dictatorship: Syria ranks 38th, China 26th, and Russia 4th. But the myth that our extraordinarily slow system is somehow necessary is belied by the fact that so many free nations outdo us in terms of legislative expediency.

The reason is that the not-so-divine Constitution actually created a pretty ineffective system, and one that's certainly outdated. An arduous amendment process, disproportionate representation, Senate filibusters, obstructive procedural practices and more do us in.

It got worse when Obama came into office and the Republicans decided to oppose everything he wanted to do. Poor Barack couldn't so much as put lettuce on his sandwich with Mitch McConnell raising an objection. If you compare major legislation through the years, the decline in Congressional productivity becomes tremendously apparent. According to GovTrack, the 93rd Congress (1973-1974) passed 772 laws; the 94th (1975-1976) passed 729; the 95th (1977-1978) passed 804. 529 was the lowest number throughout the 1980s. Bill Clinton's administration saw a low of 337 (1995-1996) and a high of 604 (1999-2000). The high during the Obama years was his first Congress, the 111th (2009-2010), when the Dems controlled both houses and got 385 bills passed. The current Congress, meanwhile, has passed 239 acts as of this writing. You can take that as a sign that the Republicans who control both houses are either too incompetent to mass major legislation or just unwilling to do so.

We're taught that our system is brilliant because it goes so incredibly slowly. I for one could use a little less brilliance. There's a difference between contemplation and obstruction. We don't have a thoughtful system; we have one that allows malevolent operators to interfere with progress. And that's why we've become the Land of Procrastination, as we'll get to next.

38. Passing the Buck

"Today we are going to decide who to blame."

In 1948, Harry Truman campaigned against the "Do-Nothing" Congress for its failure to pass legislation to address inflation, housing issues, and health care. Yet the 388 laws that the 80th Congress passed would seem like an accomplishment today.

At times in our history, Congress has actually worked to solve problems. In its earliest days, it passed legislation to stabilize the monetary system, award land grants, provide for a patent and copyright system, and establish our military forces. In the early 1800s, it created a national bank. The Civil Rights Act of 1866 sought to protect freed slaves. The Pendleton Act of 1883 brought about civil service reform.

When Congress saw a danger in monopolistic business practices, it passed the Sherman Anti-Trust Act of 1890. When it saw that act being misused to battle against unions, it passed the Clayton Anti-Trust Act of 1914. When the Depression hit, Congress actively supported New Deal proposals and progressive legislation, creating the FDIC, the TVA, Social Security, and the WPA. In the 1960s, we got more civil rights legislation to solve the most pressing issues of the times: voter disenfranchisement and human rights violations. Even in the 1980s, there was a major tax overhaul that was the work of bipartisanship which proved to be something all sides could be happy with. We've built canals, reduced trade barriers, won the Space Race, and created the national park system – all through effective Congressional legislation.

But the mentality of Congress today isn't the same as it once was. We simply don't try to solve major problems any longer. For the most part, Congress is happy to kick the can down the road when it can, then declare victory. It's why we haven't done nearly enough to address climate change, gun deaths, the Opioid Crisis, health care, poverty, mass incarceration, and the numerous other problems that afflict us. We have one party in the Republicans who are simply anti-progress, and another in the Democrats who are unwilling to admit that the system is broken and call for massive change.

The national debt currently stands at almost $22 trillion, which is well over 100% of GDP. When we should have been borrowing to fend off the effects of the Great Recession, Republicans balked, refusing to spend on infrastructure and other projects that would've helped the economy out of its hole. Now that things are better and we should be thinking about the debt more, they've gone on a drunken spending spree with mom's credit card. Republicans simply don't worry about the future because it might require them to be responsible. Instead, they'd rather give tax breaks to corporations, then blame the Democrats when things go wrong.

Recently, the amount of carbon in the atmosphere passed 411 parts per million – higher than it's been in 800,000 years. We could take measures to combat climate change, such as considering a carbon tax, increasing government fuel efficiency standards, or refusing to subsidize gas prices. Instead Congress says, "Why worry about it?" and goes on like the Once-ler on drugs.

And speaking of drugs, let's talk about the Opioid Crisis. More than 72,000 Americans died from drug overdoses in 2017. That's up from about 18,000 in 2000. More than 49,000 of the deaths came from opioids alone. Trump talked a big game when it came to addressing the crisis and even put together a panel of experts which came up with 56 recommendations to do so. But the administration ultimately wound up refusing most of their proposals. One of their main recommendations was to declare the crisis a national emergency, but Trump opted instead to simply call it a "national health emergency," which did nothing to provide the major funding that's needed to meet the challenge.

Congress, for its part, has managed to pass the overwhelmingly bipartisan SUPPORT for Patients and Communities Act, which does indeed do some good things, such as lifting restrictions on medications that combat opioid addiction, making changes to Medicare and Medicaid to limit over-prescriptions of opioids, and increasing penalties for manufacturers and distributors who contribute to over-prescribing by not taking proper precautions.

Yet the bill only provides a measly $8 billion over five years for a problem that experts say will require tens of billions of dollars each year to properly address. Elijah Cummings in the House (D-MD) and Elizabeth Warren in the Senate (D-MA) have proposed much larger spending packages, but, of course, these bills have gone nowhere, as Republicans, who had no issue giving away a trillion dollars in tax expenditures – mainly to the wealthy and corporations – suddenly became penny-pinchers when it came to addressing the needs of the poor and suffering. They'll let tens of thousands of people needlessly die rather than provide proper funding to help them, but will never support raising taxes even a dime on the inordinately wealthy class.

The predominant action of Congress is inaction. It can't manage to address the threats against our election systems, pass sensible gun legislation to stop the gun violence epidemic, can't work out a decent plan to provide health care to all Americans, and can't put together a major infrastructure bill, which we also desperately need.

It's not an accident, of course: the extremist Republican party wants to see taxes lowered for the wealthy, see conservative justices appointed, have religion play a prominent role in government, and pretty much get nothing else done. Their inaction isn't a bug, it's by design. And, of course, when you don't address problems – when you allow fires to burn, they only burn stronger, until at last they're out of control.

The question then becomes: How do we get Congress (and the Republican Party in particular) to actually do its job? How can we end Republican obstruction, Democratic timidity, and Congressional stagnation, and motivate our politicians to hear the voice of the People?

Well, one thing we don't have to do is be polite. Just like Trump has been willing to break many norms in politics, if liberal, civic-minded individuals want to see progress, we have to be willing to embrace new tactics. Once again, it comes down to being willing to take that extra step – to not simply to protest in front of the Capitol, but to call for protests in front of representatives' and senators' homes, and even at the homes of the Supreme Court justices who enable them. We need, as MLK said, to create tension and make them uncomfortable, because it's the only thing that will make them do the right thing. We need to take to the streets and stay there, boycott those companies that advertise on Fox "News" and give to Republican candidates, call out lies when we hear them, and refuse to play by rules outlined by conservatives. We need to disrupt – peacefully, but massively. If Democratic politicians are wise, they'll realize that and begin calling for such efforts.

And we need electoral reform. Liberals have to realize that every other issue – guns, climate change, health care – all of it rests on electoral reform, because you can't do anything if you can't seize power. We are currently suffering under a tremendously disproportionate and inadequate system. We have to work on that before we can get Congress to address the major issues of today that need addressing.

We'll have to keep in mind, though, that we're not just up against the politicians: we're also up against corrupt lobbyists and shadow organizations, both backed by a shitload of money.

A shitload of money.

39. Corrupt Lobbying

"The Bosses of the Senate" –Joseph Keppler, *Puck* magazine, 1889

Let's be clear about this: not all lobbyists are bad: there are some out there lobbying for great causes – environmentalists, advocates for the poor, the ACLU, the Brady Campaign to Prevent Gun Violence, veterans groups, etc. And there are lobbyists whom you and I may disagree with, but who do their jobs with integrity and honestly believe in their causes.

But let's face it: the "good" kind of lobbyists are becoming rarer and rarer, and they certainly can't compete with the big money "lobbyists" (or, more accurately, corruption specialists) funded by corporations. These gun-for-hire types aren't schmoozing on Capitol Hill to advocate for causes they believe in; they operate out of greed, bribing members of

Congress with timely donations and lucrative job offers and trying to frustrate efforts at reasonable regulation. They're funded by industries that poison our air, our water, our economic well-being, and our people. And they themselves have poisoned our political system, placing avarice over ideals. Let's call some of these bums out and talk about what we can do about them.

A very helpful list put together by Open Secrets lays out the top twenty lobbying groups in terms of spending over the past twenty years. Not surprisingly, all but one (AARP) are large business groups. You'll find some of your old favorites there, I'm sure – like Comcast, which has spent some $190 million since 1998. Or AT&T and Verizon, which have each spent around $240 million. There's Big Tobacco, Northrop Grumman, General Electric, and of course several groups from the medical, pharmaceutical, or insure fields. Number 2 on the list (at nearly $500 million) is the National Association of Realtors, which explains, in part, why the mortgage interest rate deduction is so hard to get rid of.

Number 1, though, might surprise you: it's the Chamber of Commerce.

Perhaps you're saying, "Wait. The Chamber of Commerce is the Number 1 lobbying organization in America? The organization with all those local chapters representing small businesses?"

Yes and no.

Yes, the Chamber of Commerce is the Number 1 spender on lobbying efforts in the US. No, it isn't doing it for small businesses. In fact, many small business owners do not support the Chamber's lobbying efforts, which tend to align with Big Business. As David Brodwin pointed out in a 2015 article for *US News*, the Chamber of Commerce acts as a sort of front for industries looking to lobby the federal government. Amazingly enough, the organization is listed as a tax-exempt charity. Yet Open Secrets says it's spent around $1.5 billion in the past twenty years in its efforts to defend tobacco, banking, and fossil fuel companies. In 2012, the Chamber collected some $164 million in donations, more than half of which emanated from just 64 donors. Its leader, Tom Donahue, has been paid millions upon millions of dollars – $6.6 million in 2015 alone. He's a good example of someone working for a "non-profit" who himself is making plenty of profit. (He's not alone in this regard: a list put together by *The Chronicle of Philanthropy* reveals that over a hundred heads of "non-profits" have been earning over a million dollars a year. And an analysis by the *Wall Street Journal* found that 2,700 employees at non-profits collected over a million buckaroos each in salary. One of the few good things you can say about the Republican tax bill is that it sought to put an end to this scam, hitting non-profits that with a 21% tax for every dollar over a million that they pay to employees.)

And so we see a ton of corporate money flooding into politicians' coffers, some of it disguised through tax-exempt charity organizations that advocate on behalf of Big Business, some directly from corporate industries. The good guys wind up getting drowned out. According to Open Secrets, the National Wildlife Federation – which, whatever your views on animal rights and protections, I think we can all agree is a morally-motivated group with sincere beliefs – spent just over $500,000 on lobbying in 2017. That's no small amount, you would think. But let's compare that to Apple. They put over $3.7 million into lobbying in 2017. Microsoft went in for over $8.6 million. And AT&T? Its lobbying efforts approached $20 million that year.

The Brady Campaign to Prevent Gun Violence spent less than $80,000 lobbying in 2017. Compare that with Big Sugar, which pumped over $11 million into its lobbying efforts, and Big Tobacco, which spent nearly $22 million (that we know of) in 2017.

Starting to get the picture? It's like playing Monopoly, except you're playing with gangsters and they start off with all the money.

Can anything be done to stop the bastardization of the system? Is corruption simply an unfortunate byproduct of free speech?

I would contend that it is not. Those (like the Supreme Court) who try to argue for unlimited campaign spending and unrestrained lobbying act as if free speech operates in a vacuum, when in truth it sits on a balance. While one can agree that we should attempt to ensure as much free speech as possible, we have to recognize that certain behaviors have the effect of reducing free speech overall and drowning out the majority of voices. And so it is reasonable to place restrictions on those behaviors. They include excessive campaign donations and corporate lobbying. In both cases, the potential for corruption is so abundantly evident, and the strangulation of the voices of the masses so incredibly clear, that no reasonably-minded person can pretend that free speech is aided by their remaining unchecked.

Worse still, many of these groups and the billionaire donor class that supports them have figured out that the best way to get the legislation they want is to simply write it themselves and put it directly into legislators' hands. And one of the best ways to do that is by using shadow organizations to "assist" our politicians.

40. Shadow Organizations

Charles (left) and David Koch. Credit: DonkeyHotey

As we saw in the last chapter, Big Business lobbyists have largely drowned out the voices of ethically motivated groups advocating for progressive causes. We've also seen how organizations like the NRA have filled the ranks of the Republican Party with more and more extremist politicians. If the NRA doesn't give a Republican candidate a high grade, it could be their political death knell. Others, like the Americans for Tax Reform, which forces members of the GOP to sign a ridiculous pledge guaranteeing that they will never raise taxes under any circumstance, threaten to unleash torrents of bad publicity if their wishes aren't met, or to "primary" any candidate who's not extreme enough.

Yet the conservative American Legislative Exchange Council (ALEC) takes things even further. ALEC, which is also classified as a non-profit, crafts legislation, which it then presents to state governments throughout the country. It essentially governs by proxy. Through this method, ALEC has been effective in weakening the EPA, creating "Stand Your Ground" laws, and in promoting voter ID restrictions. In fact, according to the *New York Times*, ALEC presents over a thousand bills a year to legislatures, about 17% of which see passage. The group includes over 2,000 state legislators who pay a $50 fee for membership, as well as corporate members who pay anywhere from $7,000 to $25,000. The bulk of the funding comes from corporations and wealthy donors, such as the Koch brothers, and corporate members can collectively veto legislation proposals before they ever make it out of ALEC. But that's not all! They can also pay for trips for legislators in order to "educate them" – all expenses paid! And the best part is, it's all tax deductible, since the organization is listed as a 501(c)(3) charity. Somehow, even though ALEC consistently emails "talking points" to members and pushes for legislation, it insists that it's not a lobbying group.

The Heritage Foundation, meanwhile, has been largely responsible for much of the Trump administration's staffing. The *New York Times* reported that at least 66 Trump officials came by way of the Heritage Foundation, including Jeff Sessions, Mick Mulvaney, Betsy DeVos, and Scott Pruitt. Heritage has many donors, but one of the biggest is the Mercer family, which worked with Steve Bannon to get Trump into office. Robert Mercer and his daughter Rebekah have exercised unusual control over the administration and its policy goals, and they do it with the help of Heritage.

The Heritage Foundation also makes recommendations in regards to federal judgeships, as does the Federalist Society. If you're not familiar with the Federalist Society, it was founded by conservative law students at Harvard, Yale, and the University of Chicago back in 1982. The faculty advisor in Chicago was none other than Antonin Scalia, strict constructionist and foe to practically every major progressive cause of the last fifty years. By the late 1980s, the Federalist Society had already become a potent force. As Jeffrey Toobin wrote for the *New Yorker*:

> Within just a few years, the group was embraced and funded by a number of powerful, wealthy conservative organizations, which eventually included foundations associated with John Olin, Lynde and Harry Bradley, Richard Scaife, and the Koch brothers. "The funders all got the idea right away—that you can win elections, you can have mass mobilizations, but unless you can change élites and the institutions that are by and large controlled by the élites, like the courts, there are limits to what you can do," Amanda Hollis-Brusky, a professor of politics at Pomona College and the author of "Ideas with Consequences," a study of the Federalist Society, said. "The idea was to train, credential, and socialize a generation of alternative élites."

The current head of the Federalist Society, Leonard Leo, would handpick Scalia's replacement, Neil Gorsuch, after Republicans under Mitch McConnell succeeded in stealing that Supreme Court seat. Leo was also instrumental in choosing John Roberts and Samuel Alito under Bush. And, of course, it was Leo and the Federalist Society that picked Brett Kavanaugh, who has also been a long time member of the group.

The Society has a big bash in DC every year at the Mayflower Hotel, where libertarians and conservatives hobnob and strategize. It was at one of these galas that some of them began to put together two court cases to challenge Obamacare, both of which were fortunately defeated.

With Kavanaugh's approval, there are now five Federalist Society members on the court (Thomas is also a member). But that's not all: the Federalist Society also lists numerous other federal judges as members, and plenty of politicians as well. To give you an idea, here are just a handful of names from its members list:

- Senate Majority Leader Mitch McConnell
- Justice John K. Bush of the US Court of Appeals, 6th Circuit
- White House Counsel Don McGahn
- Senator Tom Cotton of Arkansas
- Representative Barbara Comstock of Virginia
- Attorney General Jeff Sessions
- Justice Amy Coney Barrett of the US Court of Appeals, 7th Circuit
- Senator Ted Cruz of Texas
- Conservative pundit and professional racist, Ann Coulter
- Senator Mike Lee of Utah
- Justice Timothy M. Tymkovich of the US Court of Appeals, 10th Circuit
- FBI Director Christopher Wray

That's right: the Attorney General, FBI Director, and five Supreme Court justices – all of whom could have an effect on Trump's culpability in the Russia probe – are all part of the same conservative cult. And the list goes on and on. Federalist Society members include numerous local, state, and federal judges, tons of attorneys, and plenty of political players.

Democrats should be calling these people out for the extremists they are. If it was up to the members of the Federalist Society, no abortions would ever be permitted, voter-ID laws and other voter suppression tactics would be perfectly OK, convicts would never have their rights restored, unions would cease to exist, and Muslim bans would be approved rather quickly. Yet where is the condemnation for these people? They have a worldview set in 1795, yet no one takes them to task for it.

So, to sum up, here's how it often works: A group like ALEC, funded by people like the Koch brothers, writes up legislation that gets passed on to state legislators, 2,000 of whom also belong to ALEC. In addition, those state legislators are usually subjected to intense lobbying efforts by Big Business groups, including the Chamber of Commerce, a phony charity that represents billionaires and corporations. The legislators pass the legislation ALEC has given them. If the legitimacy or constitutionality of that legislation is questioned, it may be ruled on by judges from the Federalist Society, who may also be members of the Heritage Foundation.

Liberals, of course, often belong to liberal groups as well. But there are some key differences: One: the adherence to single-minded ideology does not exist, as liberals tend to have more nuanced and diversified views. Two: the influence of these groups is negligible, with there being nothing to compare to the Federalist Society, Heritage Foundation, or

Americans for Tax Reform. Three: moneyed interests are not behind these groups, whereas as organizations like ALEC and the Chamber of Commerce act on behalf of wealthy industrialists. The Democrats also don't have anything even resembling ALEC in scope or scale.

These groups have an inordinate amount of influence over our government and laws, and that influence has to cease. It is oligarchy by proxy, and we need to take efforts to put an end to it. These groups should be treated as what they are: lobbyists for industry, not charities. And we ought to insist that the authors of bills presented to Congress or state legislatures be printed right on the front of the bill, so that we know where these laws are coming from and what money is behind them.

That leads us to our next problem with American democracy: a lack of transparency.

41. Lack of Transparency

UNITED STATES DEPARTMENT OF JUSTICE
FEDERAL BUREAU OF INVESTIGATION
WASHINGTON, D.C. 20535

SECRET

February 22, 1972

JOHN WINSTON LENNON

ALL INFORMATION CONTAINED HEREIN IS UNCLASSIFIED EXCEPT WHERE SHOWN OTHERWISE.

SECRET

1972 FBI file on John Lennon released in 1997

The Freedom of Information Act was the brainchild of John Moss, a Democrat from California first elected to Congress in 1952. During the Second Red Scare, led by the notorious Joe McCarthy, the Eisenhower administration had fired thousands of federal employees it deemed potential communists. Moss requested records to account for the firings and was stonewalled. He spent a decade building up support for a bill that would force the federal government to be more transparent. The progressive spirit of the 1960s saw the bill's passage in the wake of the Civil Rights Act and the Voting Rights Act.

President Lyndon Johnson decided not to hold a public ceremony when he placed his signature on the Freedom of Information Act on July 4th, 1966. In the midst of the Cold War, Johnson had reservations about the act, but acknowledged that government transparency was key to maintaining democratic institutions. The last line of the signing statement issued by the president and authored by Press Secretary Bill Moyers read, "I signed this measure with a deep sense of pride that America is an open society."

It was a worthy goal. Still, the bill lacked teeth, not specifying timeframes for meeting requests or penalties for noncompliance. Also, there was nothing to stop government agencies from charging fees to journalists and public advocacy groups. Not surprisingly, the Nixon administration – conspiracy-minded and unusually secretive – didn't do much to adhere to the spirit of the law.

Following Watergate, Congress was determined to give FOIA more force, and so they amended it (over Gerald Ford's veto), adding in numerous compliance measures and tossing out the fees for journalists and non-profits.

The Reagan administration fought back against these measures by widening the definition of what was considered classified information. Other administrations have utilized this loophole as well: if you don't want something to get out, just label it a national secret.

The Clinton administration did take two major steps in terms of transparency: the first was the Government Performance and Results Act of 1993, which stipulated that government agencies had to evaluate themselves for efficiency and report on the results. The second was the Electronic Freedom of Information Act Amendments of 1996, which, recognizing the Digital Age, said that all government agencies had to digitize their documents so that they would be easily downloadable, speeding up access to government info.

Things tightened up again after 9/11, with George W. Bush issuing Executive Order 13233, which limited access to presidential records (Obama would later reverse the order). W redeemed himself somewhat, though, when he signed the OPEN Government law in 2007, extending info to bloggers and creating the Office of Government Information Services to oversee FOIA compliance.

Obama, meanwhile, ran for office with promises of transparency, announcing in a 2007 press release:

More and more, the real business of our democracy isn't done in town halls or public meetings or even in the open halls of Congress....Decisions are made in closed-door meetings, or with the silent stroke of the President's pen, or because some lobbyist got some Congressman to slip his pet project into a bill during the dead of night. We have to take the blinders off the White House. The more people [who] know about what's going on in Washington, and how their tax dollars are being spent, and who's raising money for who, the less likely it is that major decisions will be hijacked by lobbyists and special interests."

So did Obama deliver on his promise? Well, not really. In fairness, he did do some good things, like creating Ethics.gov so that citizens could gain easy access to ethics reports and lobbying activities. He also created a "declassification center" to make more documents available, and singed the DATA Act in 2014 in order to clarify US expenditures.

But he failed to live up to his promise to establish a database for contractors bidding on US contracts and failed to end closed-door meetings. More importantly, Obama's administration went after journalists for protecting confidential sources and was terrible when it came to FOIA compliance. And there was the little matter of the NSA spying on all of us…

How about Trump? Has his administration been any better?

Of course not. In fact, it's been one of the least transparent administrations in history. While the Obama administration had 448 FOIA lawsuits in its last year, the Trump administration had 671 in its first. Trump's kept the White House visiting log a secret, refused to disclose information about the US service members killed in Niger, and has forced members of his administration to sign non-disclosure agreements in an attempt to keep them from talking about the president or his administration. Trump hasn't even bothered to pick a Chief Technology Officer, who could help oversee transparency efforts.

And let's not forget: Trump entered the presidency refusing to release his tax returns, which would've gone a long way toward revealing any potential conflicts of interest. We know he regularly violates the Emolument's Clause of the Constitution, we're just not sure how often and by how much.

As you can see, there are two issues when it comes to government transparency: the laws that are passed and compliance with those laws. Some of the things Trump is refusing to do are not required by law, but should be, such as presidents (and presidential candidates) releasing their tax returns and the White House logging visitors into an official record. And, of course, non-disclosure agreements signed by government agents, while possibly unenforceable, should clearly also be illegal. The goal of Trump's NDAs is to intimidate government employees into maintaining their silence out of fear that they could be sued if they speak out. That's ridiculous. Those employees have a responsibility to the American people that takes precedent over Trump's personal issues about loyalty.

But we also need to tighten up standards for compliance. A president shouldn't simply be allowed to reclassify historic documents as "confidential" in order to protect his own reputation. The US has too much of a shifting standard in this regard. After all, what good is FOIA if FOIA requests can simply be ignored with a little bit of red tape? Keep in mind, FOIA compliance standards only state that someone making a request has to receive an answer within twenty days; they don't say that the answer has to be Yes or even that a reason for a No must be provided.

We also need to do a better job of maintaining vital data. Currently, for instance, there is no federal database that tallies the amount of people killed by police officers. Clearly such information would be extraordinarily useful and go a long way toward determining whether or not cops are being overly aggressive. Yet the federal government refuses to keep such statistics. And while recent language in the spending bill indicates a possible willingness to allow the CDC to conduct research into gun violence, no funding was provided for the CDC to actually do so.

Have we lived up to the ideal of transparency envisioned by Moss that began with the Freedom of Information Act? Certainly not. Have we made strides? Some. But we still have a long, long way to go. And if we want to avoid corruption, the "open society" that Moyers wrote about in Johnson's press release is a good place to begin.

42. Legalized Corruption

"Can the Law Reach Him?" - Thomas Nast, *Harper's Weekly*, 1872

One of the reasons we're seeing such blatantly unethical actions by politicians is because we've essentially legalized it.

Schoolhouse Rock taught us that a bill first gets proposed because people demand it. Yet the study from Princeton and Northwestern first cited in chapter 16 shows us that that's not the case:

our politicians only respond to the wealthy corporate class. And there's good reason for it: their jobs depend on it and often so do their (very lucrative) future careers. It's known as the revolving door: they help Big Business and Big Business helps them, with campaign donations, fundraisers, and well-paid jobs after they leave office.

And don't worry about the companies doing it all – they do just fine. An analysis by the Sunlight Foundation, for one, found that the top 200 politically engaged companies spent about $5.8 billion in lobbying efforts from 2007 to 2012 and were well rewarded, reaping some $4.4 trillion in government support – and yes, that's trillion with a T. They grease the pols, the pols pass laws that favor Big Business, Big Business reaps big profits, and the cycle starts all over again. In fact, oftentimes there really is no distinction between the two: laws that we think of as written by our representatives are actually written by the industries they're supposed to be regulating.

For instance, a 2013 bill that passed the House permitted banks to once again gamble in the derivatives market. *Coincidentally*, seventy of the 85 lines in that bill were exact replicas of what Citigroup had recommended (sarcasm intended). Basically, Citigroup wrote their own banking bill, an altered version of which later passed both houses of Congress as part of an omnibus package. An omnibus bill, if you're unfamiliar, is a large spending bill that incorporates many things. It's often approved without much debate and with little scrutiny. This makes it easy for companies to slip laws in without a great deal of fanfare. In the latest omnibus spending bill, for instance, agricultural lobbyists succeeded in obtaining several giveaways, including the scrapping of air quality regulations.

Big Ag knows how to get a big bang for its buck. Between 2012 and 2014, 600 companies spent around $500 million to ensure giveaways in the Farm Bill, which is renewed every five years. It's estimated that such companies made around $13 billion from redundancies in the bill. Remarkably, these companies receive crop insurance from the government, no matter how profitable they are.

It shouldn't surprise you that the agricultural industry knows how to navigate the system so that they can get what they want. According to Taxpayers for Common Sense:

> Agribusiness and crop insurance interests...fielded 764 lobbyists, more than one for each member of Congress. More than half of these lobbyists were revolving door personnel, meaning they know the ins and outs of Washington, having previously worked or interned on Capitol Hill, at the White House or presidential campaign, or for a federal agency. Of these lobbyists, about two-thirds (510)...worked or interned on Capitol Hill and one of every four worked or interned for a House or Senate Committee. More specifically, at least 33 lobbyists formerly worked at the U.S. Department of Agriculture (USDA) and 38 worked or interned on the House or Senate Agriculture Committee.

But it gets even better:

In many cases, it's not just that industries are crafting the laws from the outside; at times they're doing it from the inside.

The Department of Education under Betsy DeVos is one of the worst offenders. It's been so friendly to the for-profit college industry, that many for-profits have cut their lobbying efforts, figuring such efforts are unnecessary. After all, DeVos has been using for-profit college execs to "regulate" these scam-riddled enterprises, which are notorious for ripping off students who often find themselves in massive debt and with little to show for it in terms of a career. DeVos's special assistant, Robert S. Eitel, a Department of Education lawyer during the Bush administration, worked for two different for-profits: Career Education Corporation and Bridgepoint Education Inc. At Bridgepoint, he oversaw a settlement of $31.5 million for deceptive student loan practices. Another Department of Ed hire (since resigned), Taylor Hansen, who served as an advisor to DeVos, had worked as an attorney for a for-profit college lobbying association.

And then there's Julian Schmoke Jr., a former dean at DeVry (now Adtalem Global Education), which had to pay $100 million to settle claims that it had misled students with false promises. DeVos chose Schmoke to head the department's Student-Aid Enforcement division, which is tasked with cracking down on fraud in higher ed. After the appointment was announced in August of 2017, Senator Chris Murphy of Connecticut asked if it was a joke, tweeting that it was "akin to nominating influenza to be the Surgeon General."

"There's no question that there's a fast-moving revolving door between the Education Department and the industries that it regulates," Rohit Chopra, who worked in both the Consumer Financial Protection Bureau and as a special adviser in the Education Department, told the *New York Times*.

A revolving door indeed. And, boy, has that proved profitable for the for-profit college rip-off industry! Not only have they saved on lobbying costs, but their stock prices have sky-rocketed. Bridgepoint, for one, Eitel's former employer, has seen its stock price grow 40% since Trump won his Electoral College victory and promised to deregulate these charlatans. Adtalem's stock price has doubled since Election Day, 2016, going from $23.50 to almost $46 as of this writing. And Apollo Education, which operated the notorious University of Phoenix, was sold outright to a group of investors for over $1.1 billion.

So much for regulation at the Department of Ed. Now how about those lucrative defense contracts given out by the DOD and other departments? Who's in charge of those? This might come as a shock, but it's largely former defense industry execs. So many, in fact, that as chairman of the Senate Armed Services Committee, John McCain publicly requested that the Trump administration stop nominating them for key Pentagon positions.

Here's just a brief list to give you an idea of how major defense industry contractors have penetrated US government ranks:

- Secretary of the Army Mark Esper was vice president of Government Relations at Raytheon for seven years
- Esper's undersecretary, Ryan McCarthy, was a VP at Lockheed Martin
- Benjamin Cassidy, Assistant Secretary for Legislative Affairs at the Department of Homeland Security, was a senior executive at Boeing
- Ellen Lord, a former CEO at Textron Systems Corporation, is now Undersecretary of Defense for Acquisition, Technology, and Logistics – meaning that she's in charge of Department of Defense

purchases from companies like, say, Textron Systems Corporation

- The assistant secretary for public affairs at Homeland Security, Jonathan Rath Hoffman, previously worked for the Chertoff Group, founded by former Secretary of Homeland Security Michal Chertoff; the group advises defense contractors seeking government contracts
- Deputy Secretary of Defense Pat Shanahan worked for Boeing for over three decades
- Meanwhile, the secretary of defense himself, James "Mad Dog" Mattis, has been made quite wealthy serving the defense industry, raking in $242,000 in pay from the defense contractor General Dynamics, plus between $600,000 and $1.25 million in stock options from the company; he's also received $20,000 as a paid consultant to Northrop Grumman and $150,000 from the now-disgraced phony biotech company, Theranos
- And Chief of Staff John Kelly was paid $166,000 a year from defense contractor DynCorp before taking up his current position

I suppose Ike was right to warn us of the "military-industrial complex." Perhaps it's not so much a "revolving door" as a door that's been removed altogether, so that anyone who wants can pass in and out, going from the Pentagon, Homeland Security, or the White House directly to their office at the highest-bidding defense contractor.

Indeed, we are suffering from an epidemic of corruption.

The courts, meanwhile, have not done much to help, giving politicians incredible leeway when it comes to taking kickbacks. As Professor Zephyr Teachout of Fordham, who has written extensively about the subject, has said, "For years, the [Supreme Court] has been hacking away at the prosecutorial tools for combating bribery and corruption. Increasingly, the court has made it really hard to bring cases against anyone but the most inept criminals."

Actually, even some really inept ones have managed to get away with things. William Jefferson, a Democratic representative from Louisiana, was caught on tape receiving a bribe of $100,000. $90,000 of that was found in his freezer – literally, cold hard cash. Yet a federal judge ordered most of the charges vacated. Why? Well, because of a decision the Supreme Court made in 2016 regarding the former Republican governor of Virginia, Bob McDonnell.

McDonnell had been convicted of bribery after receiving expensive gifts and promises of personal financial assistance from Jonnie Williams, the founder of a company known as Star Scientific. Williams wanted the FDA to label the company's product, Anatabloc, which they said could treat chronic inflammation, as a pharmaceutical rather than a nutraceutical (a medicinal food containing additives). In order for that to happen, costly studies would need to be performed. And so McDonnell and his wife introduced Williams to the appropriate people at the University of Virginia and Virginia Commonwealth University who could fund such studies. They also hosted a launch party for Williams at the governor's mansion.

Federal law makes it illegal for a politician to take "official action" in exchange for anything of value. McDonnell was convicted on 11 counts, but appealed the conviction on the notion that "official action" was never properly defined at trial. An appeals court upheld his conviction, but the Supremes voted 9-0 to overturn it, their logic being that McDonnell's behavior did not constitute "official action." The court expressed a fear that criminalizing such acts would lead to politicians avoiding meeting with constituents.

While the court's concern may be legitimate, no one can seriously believe that Williams was giving McDonnell all of those gifts and financial assurances out of the kindness of his heart. He wanted something in return, and it's fairly obvious that that was understood by McDonnell. The court held to a narrow definition of what an "official action" is, not giving consideration to whether or not McDonnell was using his office for personal profit, which he clearly was. How taking a bribe and, in return, using the governor's mansion to help sell a product made by the person who bribed you is not an "official action," is beyond me. But Congress can clarify the matter rather easily simply by passing another statute – one that prohibits representatives of the people from receiving anything of value – money, gifts, services, loan guarantees, etc. – from companies or individuals with business before the government they serve. Better yet, Congress and the states could both pass laws simply making it illegal for politicians to accept anything worth more than $50 from anyone outside of their families. If you can't deal with that, don't become a public servant.

The McDonnell case echoed another unanimous Supreme Court decision, *United States v. Sun-Diamond Growers of California* (1999), which declared that a direct quid pro quo must be established to prove bribery, and that the reception of gifts by a public official alone was not enough. In that case, Secretary of Agriculture Michael Espy had received some $6,000 in gifts from a company with business before his department. Yet the court said "No crime!" Apparently, to the Supreme Court, bribery done with a wink and a nod is just fine, so long as politicians aren't too blatant about it.

In the wake of *McDonnell v. United States*, cases against convicted dirtbags like Sheldon Silver and Dean Skelos, both powerful New York pols, had to be retried. Fortunately, each was found guilty again (Silver is currently out on appeal). Yet others, like Senator Bob Menendez of New Jersey, who was accused of using his office to help a donor with official business, have so far evaded conviction.

As Jessica Tillipman of George Washington University Law School told the *New York Times*, "The McDonnell case opened the door to the point where selling access is now essentially legal."

And so we live in a country wherein politicians can sell their influence and government officials can slide back and forth between administrative positions and jobs working for the very industries they're supposed to be regulating. It's no wonder that three-quarters of Americans believe that there's widespread government corruption in the US.

The question is: Is this an inherent flaw in democracy or is it something we're doing? Surely, there will always be some overlap between government and industry. But we've failed to put in place even the bare minimum of standards that would safeguard against corruption.

If businesses can have non-compete contracts, government should be able to do so as well: former government employees, depending on the position they've held, should be banned from working for any industry that they've had to regulate for 2 to 5 years. (Congress has a rule like this, but it's gotten around easily enough, with lobbyists instead listing themselves as "consultants.") They should also be prohibited from owning any stock in a company with business before their agency or legislative body and from accepting any gifts from companies or individuals affected by their decisions. The selling of influence, even if indirect, should, likewise, be prohibited. If we don't hold our politicians and our government workers to high standards, we're not going to have much of a government.

We also need to make more of a concerted effort to find more people from academia and the non-profit sector to serve in government. Even honest individuals from the business sector tend to have a business mentality. And despite what some Republicans would have you believe, the government should not operate like a business: businesses are designed to turn a profit; the government is there to provide services. We need people who take a macro view and don't think that the best answer to everything is always to buy more missiles or put more people in prison.

And liberals need to do a better job of calling out wrong-doings. When three-quarters of Americans think that corruption is widespread, that's a problem – it leads to many losing confidence in government and embracing a they're-all-crooks mentality. That makes it hard for them to distinguish who the real crooks are – the ones selling them out to Big Business.

And then, of course, there's Public Crook #1: the president of the United States.

43. Lack of Presidential Accountability

Trump and his enablers. Credit: DonkeyHotey

We've had two presidents impeached. Neither one was thrown out of office.

In the first case, Andrew Johnson, it was a set-up job: the Radical Republicans purposely passed the Tenure of Office Act just so Johnson would violate it. And he did. And they impeached him. Johnson survived his trial in the Senate after Edmund G. Ross, senator from Kansas, essentially sacrificed his political career to vote his conscience and keep Johnson in office. The Tenure of Office Act, meanwhile, was repealed in 1887 after Grover Cleveland disputed its constitutionality.

Of course, the real reason the Republicans impeached Johnson was because he was an incompetent idiot who was not only difficult to work with, but was also impeding their plans to punish the South and ease the burden of former slaves. Johnson would've been missed by no one. Still, they could not get rid of him.

This exposes the first flaw of presidential accountability: there's no method for removing a Chief Executive simply with a "no confidence" vote. If there had been back then, Johnson would've been packing for Tennessee a heck of a lot earlier.

Other nations do have "no confidence" mechanisms built into their constitutions. Australia, Canada, the UK, India, and Israel all have "no confidence" provisions that allow them to remove ineffective administrations. The UK used it back in 1979 to remove James Callaghan (via a new election). India used it to remove V.P. Singh in 1990. And Canada used it to bring about an election in 2011 (its prime minister survived).

The very threat of a "no confidence" vote forces governmental leaders to seek comity and compromise and not attempt to run roughshod over political opponents. It ensures that they cannot act with impunity or irrationality and expect to remain in office.

True, if we were to make it too easy to remove a president in this way, the process could become overtly political and result in excessive attempts to replace opponents without just cause.

But there's no reason that would have to be the case. The standards for removing a president from office for lack of confidence could be similar or the same as those required for impeachment, and certainly those standards are not lax.

But if such a method were available, it would rid us of the need of finding a "crime" in order to dispose of an amoral or ineffective president; odious behavior or incompetence would be enough.

Imagine, if you will, that, say, President Crude calls the French ambassador a "dumbass," starts inviting KKK Grand Wizards to the White House, and says that Jews are involved in a worldwide banking conspiracy. Should we have to wait, or should we be able to kick him out on his ear before he does more damage to the country and our reputation?

Bill Clinton, of course, was the other president who was impeached. A "no confidence" vote may have made no difference in his case. But maybe it would've changed some votes. Who knows? And one can certainly see how it could make a difference with the current occupant of the White House.

But what about Nixon? some of you may be asking. *He was forced to resign! So the system works!*

Not really. Nixon was done in by a remarkable series of events and could've easily avoided being booted from office if not for his own arrogance and utter stupidity (despite his obvious intelligence). Had the Watergate burglars not been caught; had one of them, a former CIA agent named James McCord, not written a rather extraordinary letter to a judge overseeing the case; had Nixon not recorded his own White House meetings; had an aide not accidentally let the fact that Nixon made such recordings slip out; had the deputy director of the FBI not started leaking info; had we not had a dogged and determined news media; had John Dean not turned against the administration; had the Supreme Court failed to order the tapes released – had any of those things gone down differently, Nixon most likely would have remained. Leon Neyfakh of *Slate* did an excellent job of detailing all of the possible ways Nixon's downfall could've been avoided in his podcast, *Slow Burn*. Listening to it, it becomes very clear that Nixon wasn't forced to resign because of our system, but in spite of it. We were, frankly, fortunate to have caught him. And even then he escaped prosecution when Ford pardoned him.

Many liberals are hoping that the Mueller investigation will produce evidence that leads to Trump's impeachment and removal from office. Sadly, I wouldn't bank on it. That's not to say that it's impossible; but it is extremely unlikely, and here's why: Unless Mueller's group produces some overwhelming evidence that Donald Trump did something that's both criminal and highly unpopular (and yes, it would have to be both), Republicans in the House would be extremely unlikely to impeach him and put him on trial in front of the Senate.

But what if, you say, *the Democrats take control of the House?*

Well, first off, we don't know if that'll happen. As detailed earlier, gerrymandering has made that considerably more difficult.

But, for the sake of argument, let's say that the Dems do recapture the House. And let's say that, after Mueller produces his results, they succeed in impeaching Trump. Well that just means that Trump's fate would be left to the Senate. Except unlike the House, where just more than half have to vote to impeach, in the Senate a two-thirds majority is required to oust the president. That means 67 senators would have to vote for removal. Right now the Republicans have 51 seats in the Senate. And the 2018 Election favors the GOP there, so they may even expand that lead. But even if the Dems managed to pick up the majority, they're not going to control anywhere near 67 seats, and you can be fairly sure that, barring some remarkable revelations, not a single Republican will vote against the president. After all, they're the party of see no evil, hear no evil, remember?

We already have emails from Donald Trump Jr. accepting Russian assistance; we already know that Trump Jr., Trump's campaign manager Paul Manafort, and Trump's son-in-law Jared Kushner met with Russians in an effort to receive stolen information; and we know that Trump himself lied about it and tried to cover it up and even fired the FBI Director in order to obstruct the investigation, as the president admitted (on video) to Lester Holt. Yet there was no effort to impeach him. That tells us that it would take a heck of a lot for Republicans to move against Trump.

Don't count on it.

And let's not forget the Supreme Court either. The court has become highly politicized, with conservative justices voting as a bloc. That's how George W. Bush was able to steal the presidency. And it could become how Trump manages to remain in it. His latest appointment – the second from a president who didn't win the popular vote – has been clear in his views that the special counsel position shouldn't even exist.

Trump violates the Emoluments Clause on a daily basis; admitted to obstructing justice when he told Lester Holt that he fired Comey because of the Russia investigation; obstructed justice again when he orchestrated a cover-up for his son, Dumbass Junior; and clearly violated election laws with his payments to Katie McDougal and Stormy Daniels. So if just being an incompetent idiot isn't enough, can we possibly get him on any one of those things? Or do we have to wait till he embarrasses himself in front of Vladimir Putin again?

44. Restrictions on Running for President

Harry Truman as a boy. If this kid from Missouri can grow up to be president of the United States, why not a kid from Pakistan or Guatemala?

Perhaps if we didn't have some pretty ridiculous limitations on running for president, we might've been able to avoid Donald Trump altogether. If, for instance, Barack Obama could've run again, you would've voted for him in a heartbeat, no? Obama may have his faults, but surely you'd be happy to have good ole Barry back in office, wouldn't you?

In his book *Where the Buck Stops*, Harry Truman, the last president unaffected by the 22nd Amendment limiting presidents to two terms, called it "the worst thing that's ever been attached to the Constitution," save for Prohibition (perhaps he forgot about the three-fifths compromise). He noted that it was done simply as an angry reaction to FDR, and pointed out that "there are clearly times when more than two terms are necessary and wise."

Of course he's right. If ever we're in another world war situation, do we really want to be unable to reelect a strong leader because of this ridiculous ban?

But that's not the only silly limitation we place on the presidency. Immigrants, for one, are banned from running for president. Again, the question must be asked: Why? If we're the "Land of Opportunity," why not let immigrants run for the highest office in that land?

To make matters worse, the Constitution doesn't do a very good job of clarifying who is a "naturalized citizen" and can be president and who can't. The Senate has tried to correct this over the years, but still people aren't certain. Was Ted Cruz eligible to run for president even though he was born in Canada and didn't come here till he was one? I'd say yes, others might say no.

And although it's unlikely that you're pining about the loss of a Cruz administration, it's still a ridiculously arbitrary requirement. If a kid comes to the US at four-years-old, say, from Brazil, and rises up to become governor of a state, why not allow her to run for president? Do we honestly believe that she was somehow tainted at age four and can't be trusted? And shouldn't the people be the ones to decide anyhow? Fourteen percent of our population is immigrants. Why shouldn't they be afforded the same consideration as the rest of us?

The bad news, of course, is that since these restrictions are in our antiquated Constitution, the only way to change them is through the Constitutional amendment process, which (as outlined in chapter 8) is nearly impossible to overcome. But that doesn't mean that we shouldn't try. And it doesn't mean that Democrats can't make the immigration restriction on running for president an election issue, especially at a time when immigrants are being discriminated against by the Republican Party.

The presidency should reflect the will of the people. And while that certainly means there should be no silly Electoral College mechanism, it also means that we shouldn't have unnecessary barriers that stop people from choosing the candidate they'd like.

One thing you can be happy about, though, is that the president doesn't get to be appointed for life. That's something we sadly can't say about our corrupted Supreme Court.

45. A Partisan Supreme Court

If Brett Kavanaugh manages to serve on the Supreme Court as long as his predecessor, Anthony Kennedy, he'll be there till at least 2048. That means that a kid born this year will have to contend with Kavanaugh's decisions all through her schooling, well past the time she reaches the age of legal maturity, and perhaps even after she gets married and has kids of her own.

The US is the only country on Earth that appoints justices to its highest court for life. And here's the funny thing: the Constitution doesn't even say anything about lifetime appointments. The rather poorly phrased applicable passage, Article III, Section I, simply states: "The judges, both of the supreme and inferior courts, shall hold their offices during good behavior, and shall, at stated times, receive for their services a compensation which shall not be diminished during their continuance in office." And that's it! Not a word about being appointed for life or even anything about what constitutes "good behavior." Theoretically, one could argue that if Clarence Thomas gets caught stealing Sonia Sotomayor's yogurt out of the office fridge, we can ax him.

It's also accurate to say that, historically speaking, the Supreme Court hasn't been very diverse: Justice Thomas is only the second African American on the court. Justice Sotomayor is either the first or second Hispanic justice, depending on how you count Benjamin Cardozo (who was of Portuguese ancestry). Only four women have ever served on the court, and three of them are serving now. There's never been an Asian American; no Muslims, Buddhists, or avowed Atheists; no Native Americans. Kavanaugh is the 114th Supreme Court justice, and all but six of them have been white men.

The Supreme Court also isn't quite the "wise body" we make it out to be. Despite its undeservedly esteemed reputation, it's been evident for much of our history that the court is just as likely to make the wrong decision as the right one. *Citizens United* (2010) allowed for the unrestricted flow of money into politics. *Bush v. Gore* (2000) handed a tainted victory to a presidential candidate who had really lost by some 500,000 votes. *Bowers v. Hardwick* (1986) permitted states and localities to outlaw homosexuality. *Plessy v. Ferguson* (1896) established the doctrine of "separate but equal." *Korematsu v. United States* (1944) said that the Japanese internment camps were A-OK. And, of course, the *Dred Scot* decision of 1857 said that a black man isn't really a man, but property. There are many, many more that we could name, all awful in their own way: some illogical, some immoral, many both.

Recently, the court permitted states to make voting more difficult for millions of voters in *Shelby v. Holder* (2013), allowed for discrimination against women in *Burwell v. Hobby Lobby* (2014), permitted discrimination against gay couples in *Masterpiece Cakeshop, Ltd v. Colorado Civil Rights Commission* (2018), allowed unions to be crushed through arbitration clauses in *Epic Systems v. Lewis* (2018), stopped unions from being able to collect fees for services rendered to non-union members in *Janus v. American Federation of State, County, and Municipal Employees* (2018), and upheld Trump's Muslim ban in *Trump v. Hawaii* (2018). All but *Masterpiece Cakeshop* were 5-4 decisions completely along partisan lines.

During the nomination process, Supreme Court nominees try their best to answer nothing at all, often relying on the trope that they'll simply act as umpires calling balls and strikes. Of course, we all know that's complete and utter nonsense, but they look to pass it off anyhow. The process, which should be about making determinations regarding a nominee's fitness, instead is nothing but a performance – a waste of time and money.

After all, Republican votes are a foregone conclusion. As outlined in chapter 40, the five conservative justices now on the court were all the choices of the Federalist Society or the Heritage Foundation. They were not chosen because they are excellent judges, but because they could be counted on to exercise the will of the conservative movement.

All of it filters down from a faulty system that's been further corrupted to ensure that conservatives remain in power. Big Business gives big money to Republican politicians and those Republican politicians look to appoint judges who will side with Big Business – on the Supreme Court and on the lower courts.

With a ridiculously disproportionate Senate, Senate Majority Leader Mitch McConnell was able to deny Merrick Garland, Barack Obama's nominee, a proper hearing. The Electoral College (with an assist from Russia and FBI Director James Comey) gave Trump the presidency, despite his actually having lost by 2.9 million votes. The disproportionate Senate, funded by Big Business, then approved a Supreme Court seat for Neil Gorsuch, and another for Brett Kavanaugh, darling of the Federalist Society (which Mitch McConnell also belongs to). The Supreme Court is then sure to continue to rule in favor of Big Business and Big Religion and against the rights of women, unions, voters, and minorities.

The court's also been moving at a snail's pace lately, granting fewer hearings and deciding fewer cases. In 2016, only 61 majority opinions were given – the lowest amount since 1946. In 2017, it was just a bit higher – 68 cases. To compare, in the 1980s the average amount of cases decided was approximately 140 a year. Congress is frequently criticized for its inactivity, but many don't realize that the Supreme Court isn't much better.

So what can we do to check the regressive Supreme Court?

Three things, but all three require liberals to take back the White House and both houses of Congress.

The first is that a bill should be passed placing term limits on Supreme Court justices. While the appropriate length of a justice's term can be debated, no reasonable person can argue that a set term limit of seven, ten, or twelve years, say, would make it impossible for justices to be impartial. Instead, it would allow new ideas to permeate the court and ensure more reasonable decisions, since we wouldn't have to worry that a group of five could lock up the court for fifteen or twenty years. Justices could be guaranteed a pension, but would have to agree to never get paid anything for any other job – literally – we wouldn't want to take the chance that justices could be influenced in the way that our Congress has been influenced.

The next step would be to pressure Neil Gorsuch to resign. While it would be difficult to impeach Gorsuch for "high crimes or misdemeanors" (the standard dictated by the Constitution), his seat was undoubtedly stolen and he should not be there. In fact, anyone appointed by an unpopularly "elected" president like *President Trump shouldn't be there, and should also be pressured to resign. That pressure should include massive demonstrations. And, yes, we should go to their houses and camp out – make their lives hellish (in a peaceful manner) until they do the right thing and leave office. Any Supreme Court justice appointed by Trump – and especially Gorsuch – should have to worry every time he goes out to a restaurant that he could meet with peaceful protestors who are going to make sure he doesn't quite enjoy his meal. And when the right complains that such a tactic is uncivilized, our answer has to be that stealing a Supreme Court seat is considerably worse, and that preserving democracy doesn't always mean being polite. Of course, this can't happen until we can get a Democratic president who will appoint a liberal justice in Gorsuch's place. And, yes, it should be a *liberal* justice – not a moderate one. Nominating Merrick Garland, after all, didn't get Barack Obama very far; we might as well look to appoint a real liberal who can ensure real change.

Finally, the third thing we should do if we have the chance is pack the court. That's right: pack it. Court-packing has gotten a bad rep since FDR tried to do it during the Depression. FDR was rightfully criticized for overstepping his bounds. But now times are different, and packing the Supreme Court would be a completely appropriate thing to do.

The number of Supreme Court justices is not set by the Constitution and has indeed changed before. At times in our history it's been six, seven, even ten justices. The last time it was changed was in 1869 – nearly 150 years ago. And now it should be changed again. To do so, all that's required is an act of Congress. If the extremist Republican Party is willing to steal a Supreme Court seat, reasonably-minded progressives have to be willing to change the number of seats on the court – especially if we can't apply term limits.

Ironically, of course, any attempt at term limits could be constitutionally challenged. And if that were the case, the matter would probably work its way up to the Supreme Court. A Constitutional crisis could arise. Ideally, the best way to avoid this would be to pass an amendment to the Constitution clarifying the matter. But, as noted earlier, this would be nearly impossible to do, given our current amendment process.

* * *

The conservative majority that comes with the Kavanaugh appointment puts us all in danger of being placed, in the words of Justice Kagan, under the thumb of "black-robed rulers." The Roberts court has consistently been on the side of Big Business and has repeatedly undermined the rights of unions and common citizens. It refuses to recognize the vast power differential between corporations and individuals, helping to create a civil justice system in which those with the money and the lawyers get to set the rules. The court has done nothing to advance the rights of the oppressed or to combat mass incarceration, and it's contributed to the systematic disenfranchisement of poor and minority voters.

What's not a viable option is to sit back and accept the conservative majority in the court that's been imposed upon us.

46. Failure of the Patent and Copyright System

Thomas Edison with his phonograph, circa 1878

We've now seen how the corporate class can buy off politicians, write their own laws, influence the courts, and abuse workers through restrictive, yellow dog contracts, wage depression, and union-busting. But there's also another way that corporations have managed to seize inordinate power: by manipulating our copyright and patent system.

You may be familiar with some of the more ridiculous examples. In 2013, a company known as Personal Audio, LLC began going after podcasters, saying that it owned a 2012 patent that covered podcasting, believe it or not. Fortunately, the Electronic Frontier Foundation (which bills itself as "the leading nonprofit defending civil liberties in the digital world") successfully petitioned the US Patent and Trademark Office to invalidate the ridiculously broad patent.

It also took a legal battle for the lyrics to "Happy Birthday to You" to finally become part of the public domain in 2016.

While those may have ultimately been success stories, they also illustrate how our patent and copyright system is – forgive the pun – patently ridiculous and can be flagrantly abused.

In terms of copyrights, we grant excessively long protective terms to authored works. Mickey Mouse, for instance, debuted in the 1928 cartoon *Steamboat Willie*. At the time, copyrights lasted 56 years, meaning that Mickey should've gone into the public domain in 1984. But he didn't, as you've probably noticed. Why? Because Congress extended the copyright for anything made after 1923 till 1998 or later. Then, when 1998 rolled around, Congress extended it again – till at least 2018. In Mickey's case, that meant that the copyright was good till 2024. When 2024 rolls around, it's likely that you'll see Disney make a trademark argument for Mickey and keep him out of the public domain that way, even though that little rodent should definitely be a public domain character by now.

International standards for copyrights are determined by the terms of the Berne Convention for the Protection of Literary and Artistic Works, which was last amended in 1979. The US officially became a signatory in 1989. One hundred and seventy-five countries have signed the governing document, which stipulates that copyrights must last for at least fifty years after an author's death.

In the US, copyrights last even longer: the author's lifetime, plus seventy years. Such a long copyright prevents works from being more widely distributed and prevents fictional characters from being used in new and interesting ways. If, for instance, J.K. Rowling lives till 90 (and I hope she lives even longer), the copyright for her works won't expire until 2125. Keep in mind that *Harry Potter and the Sorcerer's Stone* was first published in the US in 1998. That means that the copyright would last 123 years!

The patent system is even worse.

A bit of history:

Back in 2006, Apple was sued by a Singapore-based company called Creative Technology, which had received a patent for a "portable music playback device," which it claimed Apple had infringed on with its iPod. The patent was, of course, overly broad, but Apple agreed to pay Creative $100 million to settle the suit. Afterwards, Apple co-founder and CEO Steve Jobs changed the company's strategy, announcing to his managers that they were going to "patent it all." By all he meant every single aspect of Apple's technologies.

"His attitude was that if someone at Apple can dream it up, then we should apply for a patent, because even if we never build it, it's a defensive tool," former Apple general counsel Nancy R. Heinen told the *New York Times*.

Engineers began meeting with patent attorneys for "invention disclosure sessions." The goal was to register as many patents as possible. It didn't matter if all that was suggested was something obvious or a minor modification to an already-existing technology – things that shouldn't have been patentable – they'd seek out a patent anyhow.

"Even if we knew it wouldn't get approved, we would file the application anyway," a former Apple attorney recalled. "If nothing else, it prevents another company from trying to patent the idea."

In 2007, in the case of *KSR International Co. v. Teleflex Inc.*, the Supreme Court unanimously ruled that a more liberal standard should be applied for dismissing patents that were obvious and therefore lacked the necessary inventiveness requirement to receive a patent. Still, it did not stem the tide of software applications that tech companies like Apple, IBM, and Intel were flooding the US Patent and Trademark Office with. Grants for software patents, which had already been steadily increasing since 1984, shot up from around 25,000 in 2006 to nearly 70,000 in 2012. Total applications would increase six-fold from around 100,000 in 1980 to about 600,000 by 2015.

Apple and others began using the patent system for leverage. For seven years beginning in 2011, Apple and Samsung were locked in a tremendous legal battle over patented design elements of the iPhone that Apple said Samsung had copied. (The case was recently settled for an undisclosed sum.) Ridiculously enough, Apple even applied for (and was eventually granted) a patent for a rectangle with rounded corners, saying that it had created the shape for its phones. (Perhaps next they'll convince the USPTO that Steve Jobs invented triangles.)

The problem has gotten steadily worse. In 2017, Apple was granted no less than 2,229 patents. That might seem remarkable, but it only warranted eleventh place for that year. Google, with 2,457 patents granted, ranked 7th. Intel's 3,000+ patents gave it 4th place. Samsung, with 5,837 patents, took the number 2 spot. The number 1 spot, with over 9,000 patents granted, went to the same company that's held it for the past 25 years: IBM. Facebook, meanwhile, made it to the top 50 for the very first time. (See the top 20 here).

This might lead one to believe that we're in an unparalleled age of invention, and that all of these patents are being granted because we're seeing an unusual amount of innovation. But, alas, that is not the case.

The truth is that tech companies are using their armies of lawyers to seek out patents on practically anything they possibly can, no matter how ludicrous, obvious, or useless. The idea is not to innovate, but to litigate: the companies use these patents as cudgels to go after one another. Some businesses, in fact, are built on using the system in this way.

"Non-practicing entities" are companies that are in the patent business. They often don't have any intention whatsoever of actually developing products; their business model is to get as many patents as possible and to have those patents be as broad as possible. This allows them to use litigation to extort money from companies, artists, and inventors. You might know them as "patent trolls."

Some of these patent trolls are legendary. By 2012, Round Rock Research was estimated to hold over 3,600 patents – none of which it sought to develop or use beyond licensing and litigation. But Round Rock didn't even come close to Intellectual Ventures. Founded in 2000 by former Microsoft execs Nathan Myhrvold and Edward Jung, former Intel VP Peter Detkin, and a prominent attorney named Greg Gorder, by 2012 Intellectual Ventures had grown into a monstrous holder of tens of thousands of patents. As of now, the company claims to have over 95,000 patents to its name, over 30,000 of which it says are involved in "active monetization programs." Such "monetization programs" – or, perhaps more accurately, extortion methods – can be very costly for businesses. According to the Rational Patent Exchange, $7.4 billion was spent on such litigation in 2015 alone.

For a while, Apple, Microsoft, Research in Motion, Sony, and Ericsson teamed up to form their own patent troll company, Rockstar Consortium. The company's sole purpose was to find ways to sue emerging companies and budding inventors. The effort started in 2012 and lasted till 2014. By that time, the America Invents Act had changed the playing field and the tech giants had changed their game plans.

The America Invents Act was signed into law by President Obama in September of 2011 and began to take effect in September of 2012. The idea was to speed up the process of invalidating bogus patents and therefore help rid the system of some of the more egregious patent trolls. Rather than having to take patent challenges to federal court, patents could be challenged through an administrative process within the US Patent and Trademark Office. The Patent Trial and Appeal Board (PTAB) was established to oversee this process, essentially conducting relatively quick trials that would rule on the legitimacy of patents.

The good news is that the AIA did speed up the process for invalidating nonsensical patents and eased some of the pressure on the federal court system. The bad news is that many of the changes favored companies with entrenched power and teams of lawyers. It's why companies like Google supported passage of the AIA. Google spent nearly $10 million on lobbying efforts the year the AIA was passed and over $18 million on lobbyists the year it took effect. Microsoft spent $7 million in 2011 on lobbying and another $8 million in 2012. It spent another nearly $5 million in political contributions in 2012. There was additional spending by groups set up by Google, Microsoft, and others, such as the "Software Alliance," which spent some $4 million between 2010 and 2011 and the "Internet Association," which spent $1.6 million in 2013.

Three methods of challenging a patent were established after the passage of the AIA: Post-Grant Reviews have to take place within the first nine months after a patent is granted and can challenge a patent based on obviousness, lack of novelty, insufficient methodology, or what's known as "unpatentable subject matter" (natural phenomenon, atomic weaponry, etc.). Covered Business Methods challenges are based on the notion that a patent involves practices already in use and known to people in the industry. Neither one of these first two types of challenges is used very much. The big one – the one employed 92% of the time – is what's known as an Inter Partes Review, or IPR. To issue an IPR challenge, petitioners have to wait nine months till the Post-Grant Review period ends. Once that period is over, though, an IPR proceeding can be used against newer patents at any time, meaning that someone with an older patent can claim infringement and have the newer patent invalidated. Worse still, there's no limit to the amount of IPRs that can be filed, meaning that companies like Apple, Amazon, Microsoft, and Google can simply keep filing claims again and again and again, forcing younger companies or individual inventors to go bankrupt trying to defend their patents.

Many of the smaller fish are forced into selling or settling to avoid such a fate. They know that about half of all challenges submitted to the PTAB will be accepted for review, and that even if the challenge isn't accepted, they'll be other challenges to come. Fighting them off would be akin to fighting off a swarm of bees and hoping to never get stung. One analysis found that "only 4 percent of all PTAB petitions for review proceedings end with a final written decision in which all claims are upheld as patentable." While federal courts only invalidated around 29% of patents brought before them, IPR hearings invalidate over three-quarters of patents put up for review.

The effects were felt right away. If patents were indeed stronger, as the AIA intended them to be, you'd expect that the price of a sold patent would have gone up. But the opposite happened: between 2012 and 2014, the average selling price for a patent went from $422,286 to $164,232 – a 61% drop. Patents were under attack, and were therefore less safe. Even the Chamber of Commerce has recognized this, lowering the US's rank in terms of patent rights and protections from 1st to 12th, taking note of the "uncertainty over patentability standards."

Medical companies, meanwhile, have found their own unique way of extending the lives of patents. Patents for medicines are supposed to last twenty years, after which generics can come in and lower the costs by as much as 90%. To prevent this from happening, drug makers have hit upon the strategy of "evergreening": applying for new patents for old medicines by making incremental changes.

An analysis out of the University of California's Institute for Innovation Law found that between 2005 and 2015, 74% of medical patents granted were for medicines already available on the market. When the researchers looked at just the top-selling drugs, the number rose to 80%. Half of them were granted patent extensions at least twice. Predictably, this has resulted in unnecessarily high costs for consumers.

One example of such greed in action is the cancer drug Revlimid, made by Celgene. A year's treatment on Revlimid costs $125,000. The patent should've expired in 2016, but Celgene has managed to extend it till at least 2036 by taking out no less than 105 patents on the same drug. It's estimated that consumers will have to cough up an additional $45 billion – and, yes, that's billion with a B – because of Celgene's monopoly.

So what can be done to fix our messy and monopolistically-oriented patent and copyright system?

First, the US should reduce the length of time granted to copyright holders to the minimum required by the Berne Convention: fifty years after the life of the author – no extensions. Ideally, it would be better if a copyright lasted twenty or twenty-five years and no more. But we can't ignore the standards set by the rest of the world and put ourselves at a disadvantage, so a lifetime plus fifty years will have to do.

In terms of patents, we can't continue to allow large tech and pharmaceutical companies to abuse the system. While the America Invents Act may have been crafted with good intentions, it clearly helped solve one problem while creating another that's at least as massive. Patents should not be used to stifle invention; yet that is exactly how they're being used. The AIA should be amended in a way that limits the amount of Inter Partes Reviews a company can file against a particular patent. Right now, these hearings are like coin flips wherein, if the inventor loses, he or she is done for; but if the company trying to stop them loses, they get to flip again and again still. Inventors shouldn't have to worry that Big Business is going to prevent them from reaping the rewards of their inventions.

Of course, as is often the case, a lot of it comes down to money. So long as Big Tech and Big Pharma can give unrestricted campaign contributions and spend millions upon millions of dollars lobbying our politicians and offering them lucrative positions after they leave office, they're going to continue to get what they want.

We now have a patent and copyright system that allows companies to become monopolies. We're not going to change that unless we first change our corrupted government.

47. Immigration

Shepherd Fairey, We the People campaign, Amplifier.org

We often brag about being a nation of immigrants, and certainly we are one: over 46 million people who currently live in the US are foreign-born, and all of us, save for Native Americans and most black Americans (whose ancestors were dragged here in chains), descend from those who came here seeking opportunity. In terms of sheer volume, the US brings in the most immigrants: about a million each year.

But it must be remembered that the US is the world's third most populated country, behind only China and India, and fair comparisons should go by percentage. When compared on a per capita basis, the US moves to the middle of the pack, coming in at 65th. That's right: the country known as the "Land of Opportunity" is not so welcoming as people think. In fact, if Donald Trump has his way, we'll become even less so, since he's endorsed an immigration bill sponsored by senators Tom Cotton of Arkansas and David Perdue of Georgia that would essentially cut immigration in half and make it more difficult for non-English speakers to enter. In the meantime, the Trump administration has limited the amount of asylum seekers the US is willing to take in, has sent hundreds of thousands of immigrants home by canceling their Temporary Protected Status, has fought against DACA, and has proposed kicking out immigrants who use too many government services. The administration's also issued fewer green cards: approvals for residency fell 9% in 2017 and another 6% so far in 2018. And, of course, there was the completely racist travel ban that managed to get past our Supreme Court.

Curbing immigration, though, is nothing new. The US has a history of alternately welcoming immigrants and turning our backs on them, as I've written about before. After the Chinese helped build the railroads, we banned them with the Chinese Exclusion Act of 1882. After World War I and the Bolshevik Revolution, we severely clamped down on immigration in the 1920s.

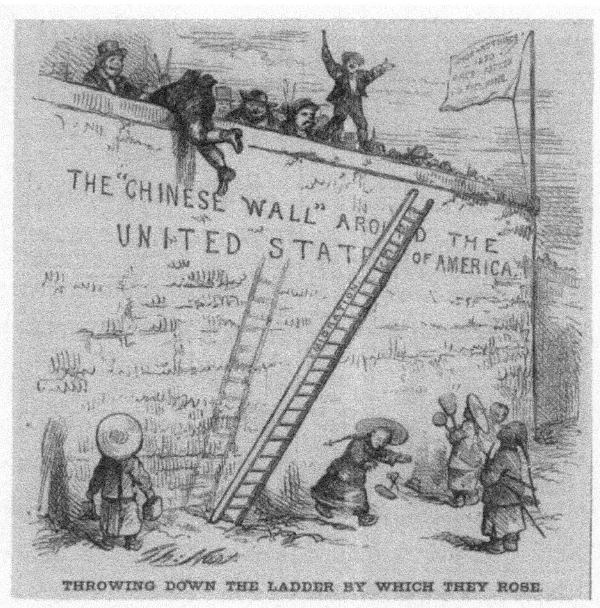

Above, Thomas Nast's "Throwing Down the Ladder by Which They Rose" (1870) demonstrated American hypocrisy when it came to immigration, as did "Looking Backward" (1893), by Joseph Keppler.

Likewise, at certain times we've been more accepting of refugees and other times less so. Before the Holocaust, we refused to open our doors to Jewish refugees, and it's estimated that we could've saved between a million and two million lives if we had simply let them in. After Vietnam, despite concerns from the public, we did allow in tens of thousands of Vietnamese refugees, and they proved to be a boon to our economy and our country as a whole. Cuban Americans have consistently been allowed in since Castro declared himself a communist. But we refused to take in more than 10,000 Syrian refugees, even while other nations such as Germany and Jordan were stepping up to take in many more. The Trump administration, meanwhile, has cut the number of refugees overall that we'll allow into the country, from 110,000 under Obama to just 45,000. That's 65,000 people who will most likely die because we didn't let them in. Many of them are children.

When it comes to being granted visas outside of refugee status, the major, glaring problem with our system is that it has quotas that don't seem to take into account population. Currently, no country of origin is allowed to make up more than 7% of immigrants. What that means in practical terms is that if you were, say, looking to come here from Ireland, you won't have a problem. But if you're poor and coming from Mexico, you might have to wait twenty years. For many, this amounts to them having truly little or no chance of ever getting in. It's not about "waiting their turn," as the saying goes; it's that they'll never get a turn. This is especially true if we limit family reunification, as the Trump administration has proposed.

Have no doubt about it: immigration is under attack right now, from *President Trump and from the extremist Republican Party. It's not just illegal immigration – they are trying to cut down on immigration as a whole in order to keep this country white and Christian. They're also exercising a sort of classism: they've abandoned "Give me your tired, your poor, your huddled masses yearning to breathe free" for "Give me your rich, your comfortable, and only those who can provide an immediate benefit to us."

The GOP ignores the fact that, while immigrants may present an initial financial cost, subsequent generations derived from those immigrants represent an enormous financial benefit to the country. In fact, a 2016 report from the National Academy of Sciences, Engineering and Medicine said that they are "among the strongest economic and fiscal contributors in the U.S. population, contributing more in taxes than either their parents or the rest of the native-born population."

Of course, not everything can be measured in terms of finance alone anyhow. Immigrants mow our lawns, clean our clothes, care for our children, act as our doctors and nurses, and become valuable members of our communities. They are our police officers, firefighters, teachers, and engineers. Heck, a Kenyan immigrant even became president of the United States (this is a joke – don't get your liberal dander up). In all seriousness, though: while Barack Obama was born in Hawaii, his father came from Kenya and was able to come here on a student visa. And that's how he met Ann Dunham, Obama's mother. But that's not all: James Buchanan's father was from Ireland. Woodrow Wilson's mother was an immigrant as well, as was Herbert Hoover's. And so was Donald Trump's, as were both his paternal grandparents.

According to Neil deGrasse Tyson's count, one-third of America's Nobel Prize winners in the sciences (95 out of 289) have been immigrants. In fact, since 2000, 39% of American winners in Chemistry, Medicine, and Physics were immigrants. Albert Einstein was an immigrant to this country, as was Nikola Tesla, Andrew Carnegie, Joseph Pulitzer, Irving Berlin, Enrico Fermi, Thomas Nast, and Levi Strauss – to name a few. As *are* former secretary of State Madeleine Albright, Google co-founder Sergey Brin, YouTube founders Steve Chen and Jawed Karim, baseball star Albert Pujols, actor/politician Arnold Schwarzenegger, singer Gloria Estefan, and architect I.M. Pei. And, of course, we could go on…for a long, long time.

Immigrants are not a drag on the US – immigrants are the US. Immigration is what has made us strong; it's what made us who we are. And not every immigrant who came here seemed to offer an immediate financial benefit. *President Trump's "pay at the door" mentality would've kept Carnegie, Tesla, and Irving Berlin out, which would mean that Trump supporters would've had no "God Bless America" song to play when they dream about "making America great again."

We need to fight back against the nativist spirit that has gripped much of our country. We cannot allow the bad ideas of the Steve Bannons and Stephen Millers of the world to dominate the conversation. We should be expanding and reforming immigration, not cutting it off. Dreamers should be able to become citizens, the refugee and asylum programs should be extended, as should TPS, and we need serious immigration reform that makes adjustments to our outdated quota system.

We also need to stop subjugating people and ensure that all Americans can participate in their own governance.

48. Subjugation

"Coasting" - Victor Gillam

2,975 people. That's how many deaths are estimated to have occurred in Puerto Rico in the aftermath of Hurricane Maria. Now ask yourself this: If Puerto Rico was a state – with senators and representatives and the power to vote in presidential elections – do you really think nearly so many people would've died, or do you think our government would've done a better job of getting those people the help that they needed? You think the power grid would've taken a year to repair or that people – American citizens, mind you – would've been scrounging for food and water like they were? Do you think, even, that Puerto Rico would've been suffering from the poverty that plagued it before the hurricane struck? Granted, the Puerto Rican government has made some poor decisions, but would they have made those same decisions if it wasn't for the fact that the islands are subjugated?

As the Special Rapporteur, Philip Alston, put it in his report to the UN:

> The link between poverty and the absence of political rights is perfectly illustrated by Puerto Rico. If it were a state, it would be the poorest in the Union. But it is not a state, it is a mere "territory". Puerto Ricans who live on the island have no representative with full voting rights in Congress and cannot vote in presidential elections, although they can vote in Presidential primaries. In a country that likes to see itself as the oldest democracy in the world and a staunch defender of political rights on the international stage, more than 3 million people who live on the island have no real power in their own capital.

Quick hypothetical: How do you think Republicans would react if they were told that all of the people in Montana, Alaska, and both Dakotas would no longer have their votes counted? Something tells me that they wouldn't go for it. Yet those four states combined have a smaller population than Puerto Rico. Puerto Ricans have no say in their government, yet Montana, Alaska, and the Dakotas not only get to vote for the president, but also get a combined four representatives and eight senators. Puerto Rico gets one non-voting representative in the House.

The Northern Mariana Islands, the US Virgin Islands, and Guam, with a combined population around 350,000 people, also receive no representation. The same holds true for Washington, D.C., whose sole representative cannot participate in floor votes. D.C. has a population of some 700,000 people – more than Wyoming and about the same as Alaska – yet no power in Congress. Ted Kennedy once said that, when it comes to potential statehood, DC suffers from the "four toos": it's "too urban, too liberal, too Democratic, and too black." Almost half the district is made up of African Americans. Kennedy knew what still holds true today: if it was made up predominantly of white Republicans, it would most likely be a state already.

American Samoa (population just over 50,000) is in even worse shape. Despite its name, people born in American Samoa are not considered American citizens. Some old (racist) court rulings and a lack of legislative action have made American Samoa the only US territory wherein those born there are not automatically granted citizenship. Instead, they're referred to as "American nationals," which means that they have no right to vote, but do have to pay certain taxes (though not income tax). Ironically enough, the army recruitment center in American Samoa has been ranked #1 out of 885 recruiting centers worldwide.

The US, of course, was largely built on the subjugation of others: we murdered and abused Native Americans, kicking them off their lands and breaking treaties at will; we brought black slaves over in chains; we took advantage of Chinese labor, then closed the door on Asian immigration. We also decry undocumented immigrants, yet our businesses use their labor and we often depend on the services undocumented workers provide.

So what can we do to end the subjugation taking place?

Let's start with DC:

Article I, Section 8, Clause 17 of the Constitution spells out Congress's power "to exercise exclusive legislation in all cases whatsoever, over such district (not exceeding ten miles square) as may, by cession of particular states, and the acceptance of Congress, become the seat of the government of the United States, and to exercise like authority over all places purchased by the consent of the legislature of the state in which the same shall be, for the erection of forts, magazines, arsenals, dock-yards and other needful buildings."

Once again, as is often the case, the language is convoluted (perhaps the Founders could've used a better editor). There's been a statehood movement in DC that's argued that statehood would only require the federal government agreeing to limit its territorial claims to areas in which the federal government is operating (the White House, the Capitol, the various department buildings, et cetera). Of course, additional stipulations could always be included to make certain that the federal government would in no way be under DC's jurisdiction.

Others have contended that Section 8 makes it impossible for DC to become a state without a Constitutional amendment, which, of course, would be much harder to come by.

But it should be noted that Congress provided DC with self-governance in 1973 when it passed the Home Rule Act. That would seem to go against the idea that the Constitution prevents DC from becoming a state. Also: since Congress would have the ultimate authority to approve statehood, it's hard to argue that Congress can't find a way to make statehood a possibility.

The effort to make DC a state should therefore be taken seriously. Democrats often make the mistake of failing to push for things because they don't yet see a path for those things to happen. Republicans, on the other hand, will push their agenda regardless of political possibilities: they look to change the conversation and are, sadly, often successful at doing so. Democrats should push for DC and Puerto Rico to become states, and they should push hard. It might not happen tomorrow, but it's not going to happen at all unless liberals make it an issue.

The other territories present some more complications. Their populations make statehood a more difficult argument. We could, of course, consider giving all US territories combined representation in Congress, plus the right to vote in presidential elections. It's definitely a plausible idea and worth investigating. More importantly, though, we must make it clear that the people in US territories ought to be able to determine their own fate. And American Samoans ought to be immediately classified as American citizens – by birth.

And now for the radical, yet simple idea that would work and – as a bonus – really tick off Republicans:

We start moving people.

That's right: we move 'em on in.

We take people from Puerto Rico, Guam, the Northern Marianas, and the Virgin Islands and we begin relocating them to Florida, Pennsylvania, Michigan, Ohio, Wisconsin, and North Carolina. Donald Trump won Florida by 113,000; he won Pennsylvania by 44,000; Michigan he took by just 11,000 votes; in Ohio he won by 450,000, but it's typically a swing state; Wisconsin he won by just 23,000; in North Carolina, he won by 173,000, but it's likely to be even closer in 2020. We may also want to send some to Minnesota, which Clinton won, but only by about 45,000.

Now, it's illegal to give anyone something in exchange for their vote; we won't do that. Instead, the Democratic Party and outside liberal groups should simply pay to relocate people to those states and not ask anything from them. They're already overwhelmingly Democratic voters and they'll be very grateful for the assistance.

But, better yet, just the fact that we're doing it would cause Republicans to shit their pants – and that's a very good thing. We'd be giving people from the territories the power to turn our presidential and Congressional elections, and you can bet your bottom dollar that as soon as that happens, Republicans will be more interested in making Puerto Rico a state and solving our subjugation issues.

Remember, all of the people in these territories – save for American Samoa – are not only free to move around, but are free to vote in our elections and have their votes counted once they reside on the mainland. If we start bringing those who want to come here here, you'll see a fire lit under the GOP.

We could target young people, aged 18 to 27, say, who are looking to make a new life for themselves. Two hundred thousand well-placed voters would probably be all it would take to change the entire election scenario. It might cost a few hundred million dollars to move them, but it would be money better spent than all the money that's wasted on (predominantly) ineffective campaign ads. And, unfortunately, it would be only a fraction of what the 2020 election is going to cost. We'd also be making a tremendous difference in the lives of those young people and their families.

Would Republicans cry foul? Of course. But it's completely legal and it would either help us win or help Puerto Rico, at least, become a state. Maybe even both.

We have to learn to fight with our sleeves rolled up. If the Republicans are willing to suppress votes, purge voting lists, and close polling stations to keep Democrats from winning, Democrats have to be willing to take bold action to advance progressive goals.

And we can't be afraid of new ideas, even if they sound alien to us. That's a problem that the US as a whole often has. We'll get into that next.

49. Jingoism and Idea Intolerance

"We reject the ideology of globalism and we embrace the doctrine of patriotism," Donald Trump told the UN Assembly in September of 2018. It was shortly after he had been laughed at for declaring that his administration "has accomplished more than almost any administration in the history of our country."

Of course Trump got into office by preaching pure, unadulterated jingoism. His campaign was all about keeping others out – not just their persons, but their ideas as well. The wall he proposed building on the southern border wasn't just a physical barrier, but an ideological one. Isolation is what he proposed – an exit from the world stage. He wanted to "Make America Great Again" by putting "America First!"

What that really meant was that we would no longer look to lead the world: we'd take a backseat in terms of global affairs and largely ignore international issues. His ascendency was very much about us keeping our eyes closed, our ears covered, and our minds unreceptive.

Oddly enough, when asked about American Exceptionalism a month before he declared his candidacy in 2015, Trump said, "I don't like the term. I never liked it....I think you're insulting the world." During the same talk, though, he added, "I want to take everything back from the world that we've given them."

Of course, how you view American Exceptionalism has a great deal to do with how you define the term. If you define it as America having a special responsibility and place in the world due to our vast power, then saying that the US is not exceptional gives you an excuse to ignore the Monroe Doctrine, the Roosevelt Corollary, genocide, the refugee crisis, and more. You can abandon the Paris Climate Agreement and hang out a sign saying, "Not our business."

But the idea of "American Exceptionalism" has also been used, essentially, to say, "We can do whatever we want," "We don't need to hear from other countries," and "We're smarter and better than everybody else."

It's this "we're different" mentality that should really be alarming. It says that rules and standards shouldn't apply to us in the same way, and that we are somehow automatically superior. Despite what you may have learned in school, it's truly a dangerous idea. It's what leads us to believe that we're invincible, that we can't be beat – that we'll always be Number 1.

US student performance on standardized tests is a keen example. American students, perhaps egged on by the self-esteem movement, are extraordinarily confident when it comes to taking tests: after participating in the Trends in International Mathematics and Science Study of 2003, 84% of them agreed with the statement "I usually do well in mathematics," including 39% who agreed "a lot." By contrast, only 56% of kids in Singapore agreed with the statement, and only 18% agreed "a lot." Of course, Singapore crushed us on the assessment. In fact, the average for their students who disagreed "a lot" with the idea that they do well in math was a 551 – ten points higher than the average of American kids who agreed "a lot." Yes – their least confident kids did better than our most confident ones.

"I solved my low self esteem by becoming arrogant."

Confidence can be a great thing; but it has to be separated from delusion. A kid who's led to believe he's already the world's greatest chess player, point guard, mathematician, or bobsledder, for that matter, isn't going to practice and work hard. Likewise, a nation which believes that it already has the best ideas isn't going to listen to new ones.

It's why many Americans issue an immediate rejection when they hear that something's being done in France or Belgium or Sweden. We have this tendency to believe that we're smarter or cooler or that those nations just aren't as tough or inventive as us.

That's not to say that overconfidence can't be good at times. Our overconfidence at the start of our nation led us to believe that we could take on the world's greatest power and win. Later it led us to tame the untamable wilderness, to build a canal through Panama, and to put a person on the moon.

But overconfidence also led us to believe that we would be greeted as liberators in Iraq, that the housing market was invulnerable, and that Russia posed no threat to us in 2016. It's what led a narcissist who is perhaps the epitome of our overconfidence – the physical embodiment of it, even – to believe that he could be president of the United States – that somehow, despite having no experience, reading no books, and knowing practically nothing about government, he could be the head of state.

Americans often reject foreign notions out of hand. Bernie Sanders brought the issues of free universities and Medicare-for-All to the fore, and now most Americans support both. But somehow they still can't bring themselves to support socialism, even though both are clearly socialistic ideas, as is Social Security. In Gallup's latest poll, only 37% of Americans had a positive view of socialism, while 56% had a positive view of capitalism. In the same poll, 50% of Americans reported having a positive view of Big Business, meaning that corporations are more popular than socialism, even though every American who cashes a Social Security check, uses Medicare or Medicaid, or sends their kids to public schools is truly enjoying the benefits of socialism.

It's as if a policy being successful in another country is a knock against it to many Americans. In France, new mothers automatically receive paid maternity leave. The French also provide large tax breaks for nanny care and free childcare for kids starting at two and a half. The programs are exceptionally popular. Yet Americans hear this and say, "You want to be like the French?" (The answer is, Yes; in this way, I most certainly do.)

Interestingly enough, other nations don't quite have such a positive view of the US, especially since Donald Trump became our president. Pew asks people around the world how they view the United States. In 2016, 30% of Canadians had an unfavorable view of the US; in 2017, it shot up to 51%. Twenty-six percent of people in the UK had an unfavorable view of the US in 2016; in 2017, it was 40%. Thirty-eight percent of Germans had an unfavorable view of the US in 2016; it rose to 62% in 2017. In fact, the highest "unfavorability" total in 2016 was Greece, where 58% of those polled had an unfavorable view of the US. By 2017, eight nations beat that number, with the highest, Jordan, registering an 82%.

Maybe American Exceptionalism hasn't exactly made us terribly popular. And it's hard to lead the world when the world doesn't respect you.

So what can liberals do to bring about new ideas and help reestablish the US as a world leader?

First, we have to throw the Overton Window *out* the window and be willing to take stands and express ideas that might initially meet with skepticism. Don't forget: we have a binary party system right now. That means when the Republicans fail, independent voters will most likely shift to the Democrats. If we're tepid and offer nothing new, we're less likely to attract them. But if we have ideas and we do this crazy thing known as "convincing people" that our ideas can work, we'll be able to shift the narrative and bring about change. We'll also, of course, attract more new voters. Don't forget, only 56% of eligible voters actually voted in 2016.

Some of it also comes down to branding. "Medicare-for-All" is a great term because it takes something that is already very popular and simply suggests we give it to everyone. Who wouldn't like that?

We should do the same thing with other ideas. People might not like hearing about French crèches, but they can certainly be sold on "Parent Aid" or "universal childcare." Government banking might not be a popular notion, but "Free Banking" definitely could be.

Of course, to convince Americans of these things, it would be helpful if you could convince them that we're not already the best at everything, and when it comes to Republicans (and, like it or not, we will have to contend with them), that may not be so easy. Amazingly enough, the Republican Party largely manages to operate on two completely contradictory ideas: One, that liberals have ruined America; and two, that America is perfect. The very same people who want to "Make America Great Again" also somehow believe that America is already the greatest country on Earth, bar none.

What liberals have to realize is that the Republican Party isn't just a party; it's a political cult. If you're debating a Republican or trying to convince him or her of something, you must keep that in mind. They're often not arguing a viewpoint, but defending what they see as part of their identity. Rather than draw conclusions from facts or observations, they'll tend to draw conclusions first, then seek out details to defend their preconceived notions.

If you were dealing with someone from a religious cult, you wouldn't expect that you could reason with them in the same way as someone who's thinking rationally. And you shouldn't expect that someone in a political cult – like the extremist Republican Party most certainly is – is thinking rationally either. That's why, as you've probably noticed, no matter how much you reason with them or present information disproving their beliefs, they'll still stick to those beliefs.

That's not to say that Republicans are insane – of course not. It's just to say that most are so personally invested in being Republican that their minds are closed to any new ideas or any information that might contradict their worldview. They take pride, even, in being intolerant to new ideas, as if it somehow makes them smarter than the "libtards" who cite "studies" and "facts." If there was a fictional personification of how the Republican Party sees itself, it would be Dirty Harry: tough, able to see through bullshit, nagged by liberals who just don't understand how the world actually works, and able to solve any problem with a really big gun.

And just like an avid sports fan is not going to be receptive to criticism from a fan of his team's arch rival, most Republicans are going to close their minds to anything coming from what they view as "the liberal media" – aka, objective, reliable sources. The same goes for you: no matter how logical your argument is, they're going to dismiss it – not because it's wrong – but because it challenges the nonsensical narrative they'd like to believe.

In that case, you can't simply reason with a Republican: you have to first confront them – not in an aggressive way, but calmly and honestly. When they present bigoted views, you have to tell them that their views are based on prejudice, and although you may like them personally, you wish you could change that about them. You cannot allow them to think that racist, bigoted, and ignorant views are somehow tolerable. You have to be willing to challenge them – to question them and their beliefs – to put them to the test and make them answer for themselves.

Here's a good example for you:

At a bar mitzvah lunch, I was confronted with a religious person of Jewish faith who was a proud Trump supporter. With other Trump supporters, also Jewish, surrounding us, he started telling me the so-called virtues of *President Trump. And so I said, "But doesn't it bother you that Trump called for banning all Jews from entering the country?"

They were astonished. The man said to me, "What? Banning Jews from entering the country! He said that?"

"Yes," I said. "Don't you remember? He said he was going to ban all Jews from entering the country."

There was silence. Finally, I said, "Oh, wait! That's right! It wasn't Jews, it was Muslims! Same thing, though, right?"

The ardent Republican had no answer. I left him in a position of either having to admit that he would've been OK with Trump saying that all Jews should be banned from the US or showing his prejudice by saying that Muslims were somehow different.

Likewise, when people would argue with me about letting in refugees, I'd explain that most of these refugees were children, then ask, "You wouldn't just let these children die, would you?"

That really puts it to them, and there's nothing wrong with that. In fact, that type of questioning gives people the chance to reconsider their views and redeem themselves, even. If someone tells you that we shouldn't let refugees in because they're "dangerous," show them pictures of murdered children in Syria and ask them, "How about that? Does that look dangerous to you?"

This is how you change people's minds – not by pretending that their racist, bigoted, and ignorant views are somehow deserving of respect. If you want to win Republicans over, you have to think about how they think and attack the Dirty Harry mentality. When they tell you some nonsense that they heard from Sean Hannity or Rush the Bloviate Limbaugh, say to them, "You don't really believe that bullshit, do you? Come on, I thought you were smarter than that." That's how you shame a Republican onto your side. When they tell you how tough *President Trump is, say, "You mean Captain Chickenshit who got out of Vietnam five times and has never gotten his hands dirty or been in a fight in his entire life? Please! You think that's tough? My grandmother would've whooped his ass!"

As Sean Connery said in an analogy Republicans will certainly understand, when they pull a knife, you pull a gun (metaphorically speaking – don't shoot anyone). "That's the Chicago way." And that's how you win over Republicans. First humiliate them, then allow them to redeem themselves. And never let them think that their intolerable views are somehow tolerable.

And remember: it's not just about convincing that person; it's about giving the Republican Party the bad reputation it deserves and stopping others from going that way. It's about making people want to avoid the Republican Party like the plague because they'll know that they'll be damaging their own reputation by association.

The mistake many liberals made in 2016 was in pretending that Trump supporters weren't all bigots, racists, and misogynists, but that argument never made any sense: either his supporters agreed with the racist, bigoted, and misogynistic things he said or those things didn't bother them enough to stop them from voting for him. Either way, their decision to support him reflected on them, and they should've been told that. Instead, many liberals grasped on to a nonsensical narrative that allowed them to believe that their mothers, brothers, sisters, cousins, coworkers, and friends who supported Trump were somehow not bigots, even though Trump clearly is. It's time to abandon that narrative. You can't change minds if you're going to be dishonest and allow them to believe that their views are legitimate.

Liberals also have to stop accepting Republican doctrines, such as "American Exceptionalism" or Founding-Father worship or the idea that the president is always entitled to respect because we have to "respect the office." We don't, and we shouldn't – not when Donald Trump sits behind the Resolute Desk.

The same goes for the Constitution. Republicans treat it as if it's some brilliantly crafted document that set us on a path to greatness and has always served us well. It isn't; and it hasn't. And it's frankly time we got rid of it and replaced it with something better.

50. The Constitution

Despite what you may have learned in school, the Constitution is not divine; it did not descend from the heavens blessed by the gods. In other sections of this book, we've discussed problems within the Constitution. Now it's time to consider the possibility that part of the problem is the Constitution itself. And not just the Constitution – but our ridiculous, over-the-top, unwarranted reverence for it. You'll hear many lawyers, politicians, pundits, and others boast about how the Constitution has endured and how that makes it a great document. But why? Have you ever stopped to question that premise? Is the Constitution like wine and somehow gets better with age? Is it really a good thing that we have such an antiquated document as the basis for our government – a document, I'll remind you, that is nearly impossible to change?

Originalists want the Constitution interpreted the way the Framers intended. Putting aside how difficult it is to make such an interpretation (pretty much impossible), why would we want to do such a thing? The Constitution was written in 1787. Times change. Standards change. Needs change. Many of the Framers were slave owners. They did not seek out input from women or minorities. They were aristocrats who often looked down on common people. Must we really treat their words as sacred?

The Constitution is like an old, outdated medical book that's very difficult to change yet must be followed. And just as you wouldn't trust an outdated medical book for your health, we shouldn't trust a document as antiquated as the Constitution to save us. In fact, the Constitution has done at least as much to impede rights as to guarantee them. It ingrained slavery in our system till 1865, requiring a terrible war and a great deal of political shenanigans to finally bring it to an end. Its ridiculously burdensome amendment process also prevented women from gaining the right to vote for over 130 years. In fact, even then – in 1920 – they still almost didn't get it: Extraordinarily enough, it largely came down to one twenty-four-year old legislator in Tennessee named Harry Burn. That's right: because of our stupid Constitution, one twenty-four-year-old man could've stopped women from being able to vote. Fortunately, after receiving a letter from his mother, he switched his vote and made the right decision.

Nowadays, the Constitution continues to burden us with the plainly stupid and undemocratic Electoral College, a Senate that is ridiculously disproportionate, a House of Representatives that can be gerrymandered, lifetime Supreme Court appointments, a Second Amendment that is somewhat ambiguous and tremendously destructive, and a Commerce Clause that is unnecessarily restrictive on the Congress and its ability to pass legislation, to name just a few. Just as important are the things that the Constitution doesn't do: it doesn't address campaign spending, doesn't allow for a reasonable amendment process, doesn't have a reasonable mechanism for removing a president (either for incompetence or malfeasance), doesn't ensure equal educational opportunities for all, doesn't provide adequate protection for unions, and doesn't protect citizens from civil inequality in the courts.

If this is a perfect document, I'd really hate to see what an imperfect one looks like.

So what can we do about our antiquated, anti-productive Constitution?

Well, there are some things that can be done, but none of them are easy.

The first thing, of course, would be to amend it. And the best way to amend it would be to pass an amendment that changes the amendment process. I know this sounds like using a wish from a genie to wish for more wishes, but it's actually perfectly logical. Amendments to the Constitution should only require a two-thirds vote in the House (and not the ridiculously disproportionate Senate) and passage through national referendum – like they do in France. And that's it. That would make amendments reasonably difficult to pass, but not impossible. And amending the Constitution to make it more easily amendable is something a lot of people might actually be in favor of – at least until Fox "News" and the Republicans convince their followers that doing so would somehow destroy America.

If we can't pass an amendment to change the amendment process, we can still propose amendments to get rid of lifetime appointments on the Supreme Court, end gerrymandering, abolish the Electoral College, and more. And we should. Instead of complaining about how difficult it would be to get them passed, liberals should push for these amendments and keep pushing. Alice Paul was told that she was just too militant and that the country wasn't ready for women's suffrage. But she pushed anyway. It didn't happen overnight, but eventually – guess what – she won. And we haven't looked back since. If we don't take up the fight to get rid of the Electoral College, say, then – shocker – we'll never get rid of it.

Also: proposing amendments to the Constitution forces conservatives to come out against them. It will make them have to defend gerrymandering and lifetime Supreme Court appointments and unrestrained money in politics. Proposing an amendment guaranteeing health care for all would not only be popular, but would force the GOP into the position of denying that we all have the right to lead dignified lives.

And if one effort fails, we start another. And another. And then another again. And we don't stop. Ever. Put them on the defensive and keep them there. That's the first tactic.

Another possible method would be to call for a Constitutional Convention to amend the Constitution. The Constitution gives power to the states to do so, so long as two-thirds of state legislatures (which would currently be 34 states) approve of it. After the convention, the amendments proposed would still have to be approved by three-quarters of the states.

Of course, this has never happened before, and with good reason, since it's an even more arduous process than going through Congress first. Also: like with the amendment process itself, this method suffers from the problem of treating all the states as equals, with Wyoming getting just as much say in terms of calling for a Constitutional Convention as California. Moreover, since Democrats only control both the legislature and the governorship of eight states while the Republicans control both the legislature and governorship in twenty-six, using state legislatures to call for a Constitutional Convention would probably be extremely anti-productive to progressive causes at the moment.

Another option, then, would be to simply ignore this stipulation in the Constitution and to call for a Constitutional Convention once states representing at least three-fifths of the population agree to it. That would ensure that it couldn't simply be states that currently lean Democratic, but also states like Florida and Texas. If, on the other hand, Florida, Texas, New York California, Illinois, Pennsylvania, New Jersey, and enough other states approve of a convention, should we really allow states like Wyoming, West Virginia, and North Dakota to stop us from having one just because some slave-owners from the eighteenth century said we can't do it like that?

Each of these methods would surely be difficult, but that doesn't mean they shouldn't be tried.

But there is another method which is much simpler and only requires winning elections: appoint liberal judges who understand that the

Constitution is flawed and will seek to interpret it in the most liberal ways possible. Conservatives have strict constructionist judges like Gorsuch, Thomas, and Alito, who are ideologically bound to the extremist position that we should be beholden to the wishes of eighteenth-century slave-owners. They don't take into consideration that women, blacks, Asians, Atheists, Jews, Muslims, Native Americans, and others had no say in the creation of the Constitution. They treat the Constitution as holy and adhere to it as if it arrived from a burning bush.

Liberals need the opposite of that: we need justices who are sensible enough to know that the Constitution is flawed, and that it should be interpreted in a way that protects people and their rights. We need not just a liberal construction, but an extremely liberal one.

To accomplish this, we need to elect politicians who recognize the Constitution's limits and imperfections. Every politician we elect swears they love the Constitution. Every Democrat will tell you what an amazing, great, brilliant document it is, even though it's not. It would be nice to hear some Democrats say that they don't love the Constitution so much – that they recognize its flaws and think it's outdated and ought to be changed.

It comes down to mindset: if we want to see real change, we have to stop selling ourselves on the American narrative and admit that we're not a perfect country and that our governing document isn't perfect either. America has become like Narcissus, staring at our own reflection and admiring ourselves.

And going nowhere.

Conclusion

March on Washington, August 28th, 1963

There's no doubt that we're in trouble. Our institutions are crumbling; voter suppression is growing; we had a presidency and a Supreme Court seat stolen from us; we have a ridiculously disproportionate Senate, an uneven, gerrymandered House, and a judicial branch that's extremely partisan in favor of Big Business and Big Religion; our educational system is terribly inadequate; racism and bigotry run rampant; mass incarceration continues; unions are in decline; our tax system is skewed toward the wealthy; shadow organizations have inordinate influence over legislation and governmental appointments; and, of course, there's just too much damn money corrupting our politics.

This book has presented a great deal of potential solutions to our problems, but none of those solutions can come about unless we have leaders who are willing to challenge the status quo and a public that demands action.

You now have facts and figures with which to combat the lies and distortions of the extremist Republican Party. And fight back you should: by voting, by protesting, and by getting involved. It's a fight that ought to take place not just in the lobbies of Congress or the streets of New York or Washington, D.C., but in town halls, libraries, and living rooms. We are in a battle of ideas for the future of our country, and if we don't act, we'll be waving goodbye to the nation we know and many of the progressive reforms we've fought so hard to achieve.

Make no mistake: the Rubicon has already been crossed. We're not facing an impending crisis; the crisis is here; the enemy is already inside the gates. The decision we need to make now is about what we're going to do to take our democracy back.

You'll hear the timid and the tepid tell you that we can't protest against officials in restaurants or outside their homes; that we shouldn't call people liars, racists, or bigots; that we shouldn't boycott or shut down cities; that we should engage in "civil discourse" and not "impugn the motives of others." But remember: you can be civil and honest at the same time, and racism and bigotry should always be called out, as should lies and misconceptions. And remember one more thing: everyone who ever made a difference was told that they were doing it wrong; that they shouldn't do it that way; that their protest was uncivil or undignified. That was true for Martin Luther King, for Alice Paul, for Gandhi, for Henry David Thoreau, and it's true for Colin Kaepernick today.

It's time to stop allowing the right to dictate the rules of engagement. Was it "civil" when they stole a Supreme Court seat? Was their "civility" on display when they gerrymandered the House to such an extent that it's no longer a representative body? Are their policies of mass incarceration and mass disenfranchisement "civil?" When they take inordinate sums of money from oligarchs and corporations, is that "civil?"

We should never resort to violence, but we must also never succumb to subjugation. We have to keep our voices up, keep new ideas in the mix, and refuse to accept that change is impossible. One of the biggest arguments from the right or the so-called "moderates" is that we shouldn't "waste time" trying to get rid of the Electoral College or pushing for action on climate change or seeking out legislation to curb gun violence or campaign contributions. "It can't be done" is their favorite mantra because it guarantees that nothing ever *will* be done.

Don't buy it. Better to fight for a lifetime than to live one day accepting that their way is the only way.

You have the tools. Now get out there and fight.

And be sure to do one more thing as well: VOTE. (And don't let them stop you.)

www.ingramcontent.com/pod-product-compliance
Lightning Source LLC
Chambersburg PA
CBHW021614270326
41931CB00008B/691

* 9 7 8 1 7 3 2 9 4 3 8 0 3 *